CLEOPATRA

THE WORKS OF

H. RIDER HAGGARD

CLEOPATRA

Being an Account of
The Fall and Vengeance of
Harmachis, The Royal Egyptian,
As Set Forth by His Own Hand

WILDSIDE PRESS
Berkeley Heights, NJ ▼ 1999

BIBLIOGRAPHICAL NOTE.

First printed June 1889.

Reissued in the 'SILVER LIBRARY,' December 1890.

Reprinted June 1893, February 1894, June 1896, March 1900, August 1902, June 1905, April 1907, October 1910, March 1914.

Colonial Edition, February 1894. Reprinted June 1896, March 1900, June 1905, May 1907, October 1910, March 1914.

WILDSIDE PRESS
P.O. Box 45
Gillette, NJ 07933-0045

Dedication.

MY DEAR MOTHER,

I have for a long while hoped to be allowed
to dedicate some book of mine to you, and now I bring
you this work, because whatever its shortcomings, and
whatever judgment may be passed upon it by yourself
and others, it is yet the one I should wish you to
accept.

I trust that you will receive from my romance of
'Cleopatra' some such pleasure as lightened the labour
of its building up; and that it may convey to your
mind a picture, however imperfect, of the old and
mysterious Egypt in whose lost glories you are so
deeply interested.

Your affectionate and dutiful Son,

H. RIDER HAGGARD.

January 21, 1889.

Author's Note

THE history of the ruin of Antony and Cleopatra must have struck many students of the records of their age as one of the most inexplicable of tragic tales. What malign influence and secret hates were at work, continually sapping their prosperity and blinding their judgment? Why did Cleopatra fly at Actium, and why did Antony follow her, leaving his fleet and army to destruction? An attempt is made in this romance to suggest a possible answer to these and some other questions.

The reader is asked to bear in mind, however, that the story is told, not from a modern point of view, but as from the broken heart and with the lips of an Egyptian patriot of royal blood; no mere beast-worshipper, but a priest instructed in the inmost mysteries, who believed firmly in the personal existence of the gods of Khem, in the possibility of communion with them, and in the certainty of immortal life with its rewards and punishments; to whom also the bewildering and often gross symbolism of the Osirian Faith was nothing but a veil woven to obscure secrets of the Sanctuary. Whatever proportion of truth there may have been in their spiritual claims and imaginings, if indeed there was any, such men as the Prince Harmachis have been told of in the annals of every great religion, and, as is shown by the testimony of monumental and sacred inscriptions, they were not unknown among the worshippers of the Egyptian Gods, and more especially of Isis.

Unfortunately it is scarcely possible to write a book of this nature and period without introducing a certain amount of illustrative matter, for by no other means can the long dead past be made to live again before the reader's eyes with all its accessories of faded pomp and forgotten mystery. To such students as seek a story only, and are not interested in the Faith, ceremonies, or customs of the Mother of Religion and Civilisation, ancient Egypt, it is, however, respectfully suggested that they should exercise the art of skipping, and open this tale at its Second Book.

That version of the death of Cleopatra has been preferred which attributes her end to poison. According to Plutarch its actual manner is very uncertain, though popular rumour ascribed it to the bite of an asp. She seems, however, to have carried out her design under the advice of that shadowy personage, her physician, Olympus, and it is more than doubtful if he would have resorted to such a fantastic and uncertain method of destroying life.

It may be mentioned that so late as the reign of Ptolemy Epiphanes, pretenders of native blood, one of whom was named Harmachis, are known to have advanced their claims to the throne of Egypt. Moreover, there was a book of prophecy current among the priesthood which declared that after the nations of the Greeks the God Harsefi would create the 'chief who is to come.' It will therefore be seen that, although it lacks historical confirmation, the story of the great plot formed to stamp out the dynasty of the Macedonian Lagidae and place Harmachis on the throne is not in itself improbable. Indeed, it is possible that many such plots were entered into by Egyptian patriots during the long ages of their country's bondage. But ancient history tells us little of the abortive struggles of a fallen race.

The Chant of Isis and the Song of Cleopatra, which appear in these pages, are done into verse from the writer's prose by Mr. Andrew Lang, and the dirge sung by Charmion is translated by the same hand from the Greek of the Syrian Meleager.

Contents

BOOK I.

THE PREPARATION OF HARMACHIS.

CHAPTER I.

CHAPTER II.

CHAPTER III.

CHAPTER IV.

CHAPTER V.

CHAPTER IV.

CHAPTER V.

CHAPTER VI.

CHAPTER VII.

CHAPTER VIII.

CHAPTER IX.

CHAPTER X.

Cleopatra

INTRODUCTION

the recesses of the desolate Libyan
mountains that lie behind the temple
and city of Abydus, the supposed burying place of the Holy Osiris, a tomb was
recently discovered, among the contents of
which were the papyrus rolls whereon this
history is written. The tomb itself is
spacious, but otherwise remarkable only
for the depth of the shaft which descends
vertically from the rock-hewn cave, that once served
as the mortuary chapel for the friends and relatives
of the departed, to the coffin-chamber beneath. This
shaft is no less than eighty-nine feet in depth. The chamber
at its foot was found to contain three coffins only, though it
is large enough for many more. Two of these, which in all
probability inclosed the bodies of the High Priest, Amenemhat, and of his wife, father and mother of Harmachis, the
hero of this history, the shameless Arabs who discovered them
there and then broke up.

The Arabs broke the bodies up. With unhallowed hands
they tore the holy Amenemhat and the frame of her who had,
as it is written, been filled with the spirit of the Hathors—

B

tore them limb from limb, searching for treasure amidst their bones—perhaps, as is their custom, selling the very bones for a few piastres to the last ignorant tourist who came their way, seeking what he might destroy. For in Egypt the unhappy, the living find their bread in the tombs of the great men who were before them.

But as it chanced, some little while afterwards, one who is known to this writer, and a doctor by profession, passed up the Nile to Abydus, and became acquainted with the men who had done this thing. They revealed to him the secret of the place, telling him that one coffin yet remained entombed. It seemed to be the coffin of a poor person, they said, and therefore, being pressed for time, they had left it unviolated. Moved by curiosity to explore the recesses of a tomb as yet unprofaned by tourists, my friend bribed the Arabs to show it to him. What ensued I will give in his own words, exactly as he wrote it to me :—

'I slept that night near the Temple of Seti, and started before daybreak on the following morning. With me were a cross-eyed rascal called Ali—Ali Baba I named him—the man from whom I got the ring which I am sending you, and a small but choice assortment of his fellow thieves. Within an hour after sunrise we reached the valley where the tomb is. It is a desolate place, into which the sun pours his scorching heat all the long day through, till the huge brown rocks which are strewn about become so hot that one can scarcely bear to touch them, and the sand scorches the feet. It was already too hot to walk, so we rode on donkeys, some way up the valley—where a vulture floating far in the blue overhead was the only other visitor—till we came to an enormous boulder polished by centuries of the action of sun and sand. Here Ali halted, saying that the tomb was under the stone. Accordingly, we dismounted, and, leaving the donkeys in charge of a fellah boy, went up to the rock. Beneath it was a small hole, barely large enough for a man to creep through. Indeed it had been dug by jackals, for the doorway and some part of the cave were entirely silted up, and it was by means of this jackal hole that the tomb had been discovered. Ali crept in on his hands and knees, and I followed, to find myself in a place cold after the hot outside air, and, in contrast with the light, filled with a dazzling darkness. We lit our candles, and, the select body of thieves having arrived, I made an examination. We were in a cave the size of a large room, and hollowed by hand, the further part of the cave being almost free from drift-dust. On the walls are religious paintings of the usual Ptolemaic character, and among them one of a majestic old man with a long white beard, who is seated in a carved chair holding a wand in his hand.[1] Before him passes a procession of priests bearing sacred images. In the right hand corner of the tomb is the shaft of the mummy-pit, a square-mouthed well cut in the black rock. We had brought a beam of thorn-wood, and this was now laid across the pit and a rope made fast to it. Then Ali—who, to do him justice, is a courageous thief—took hold of the rope, and, putting some candles into the breast of his robe, placed his bare feet against the smooth sides of the well and began to descend with great rapidity. Very soon he had vanished into blackness, and the agitation of the cord alone told us that anything was going on below. At last the rope ceased shaking and a faint shout came rumbling up the well, announcing Ali's safe arrival. Then, far below, a tiny star of light appeared. He had lit the candle, thereby disturbing hundreds of bats that flittered up in an endless stream and as silently as spirits. The rope was hauled up again, and now it was my turn; but, as I declined to trust my neck to

[1] This, I take it, is a portrait of Amenemhat himself.—EDITOR.

the hand-over-hand method of descent, the end of the cord was
made fast round my middle and I was lowered bodily into
those sacred depths.   Nor was it a pleasant journey, for, if the
masters of the situation above had made any mistake I should
have been dashed to pieces.   Also, the bats continually flew
into my face and clung to my hair, and I have a great dislike
of bats.   At last, after some minutes of jerking and dangling,
I found myself standing in a narrow passage by the side of the
worthy Ali, covered with bats and perspiration, and with the
skin rubbed off my knees and knuckles.   Then another man
came down, hand over hand like a sailor, and as the rest were
told to stop above we were ready to go on.   Ali went first
with his candle—of course we each had a candle—leading the
way down a long passage about five feet high.   At length the
passage widened out, and we were in the tomb-chamber: I
think the hottest and most silent place that I ever entered.
It was simply stifling.   This chamber is a square room cut in
the rock and totally devoid of paintings or sculpture.   I held
up the candles and looked round.   About the place were strewn
the coffin lids and the mummied remains of the two bodies
that the Arabs had previously violated.   The paintings on the
former were, I noticed, of great beauty, though, having no
knowledge of hieroglyphics, I could not decipher them.   Beads
and spicy wrappings lay around the remains, which, I saw,
were those of a man and a woman.[*]   The head had been
broken off the body of the man.   I took it up and looked at it.
It had been closely shaved—after death, I should say, from the
general indications—and the features were disfigured with
gold leaf.   But notwithstanding this, and the shrinkage of the
flesh, I think the face was one of the most imposing and
beautiful that I ever saw.   It was that of a very old man, and
his dead countenance still wore so calm and solemn, indeed,

[*] Doubtless Amenemhat and his wife.—Ed.

so awful a look, that I grew quite superstitious (though as you know, I am pretty well accustomed to dead people), and put the head down in a hurry. There were still some wrappings left upon the face of the second body, and I did not remove them; but she must have been a fine large woman in her day.

' " There the other mummy," said Ali, pointing to a large and solid case that seemed to have been carelessly thrown down in a corner, for it was lying on its side.

' I went up to it and examined it. It was well made, but of perfectly plain cedar-wood—not an inscription, not a solitary God on it.

' " Never see one like him before," said Ali. " Bury great hurry, he no ' mafish,' no ' fineesh.' Throw him down there on side."

' I looked at the plain case till at last my interest was thoroughly aroused. I was so shocked by the sight of the scattered dust of the departed that I had made up my mind not to touch the remaining coffin—but now my curiosity overcame me, and we set to work.

' Ali had brought a mallet and a cold chisel with him, and, having set the coffin straight, he began upon it with all the zeal of an experienced tomb-breaker. And then he pointed out another thing. Most mummy-cases are fastened by four little tongues of wood, two on either side, which are fixed in the upper half, and, passing into mortices cut to receive them in the thickness of the lower half, are there held fast by pegs of hard wood. But this mummy-case had eight such tongues. Evidently it had been thought well to secure it firmly. At last, with great difficulty, we raised the massive lid, which was nearly three inches thick, and there, covered over with a deep layer of loose spices (a very unusual thing), was the body.

'Ali looked at it with open eyes—and no wonder. For this mummy was not as other mummies are. Mummies in general lie upon their backs, as stiff and calm as though they were cut from wood; but this mummy lay upon its side, and, the wrappings notwithstanding, its knees were slightly bent. More than that, indeed, the gold mask, which, after the fashion of the Ptolemaic period, had been set upon the face, had worked down, and was literally pounded up beneath the hooded head.

'It was impossible, seeing these things, to avoid the conclusion that the mummy before us had moved with violence *since it was put in the coffin.*

' " Him very funny mummy. Him not ' mafish ' when him go in there," said Ali.

' " Nonsense ! " I said. " Who ever heard of a live mummy ? "

'We lifted the body out of the coffin, nearly choking ourselves with mummy dust in the process, and there beneath it, half hidden among the spices, we made our first find. It was a roll of papyrus, carelessly fastened and wrapped in a piece of mummy cloth, having to all appearance been thrown into the coffin at the moment of closing.[2]

'Ali eyed the papyrus greedily, but I seized it and put it in my pocket, for it was agreed that I was to have all that might be discovered. Then we began to unwrap the body. It was covered with very broad strong bandages, thickly wound and roughly tied, sometimes by means of simple knots, the whole work bearing the appearance of having been executed in great haste and with difficulty. Just over the head was a large lump. Presently, the bandages covering it were off, and there, on the

---

[2] This roll contained the third unfinished book of the history. The other two rolls were neatly fastened in the usual fashion. All three are written by one hand in the Demotic character.—ED.

face, lay a second roll of papyrus. I put down my hand to lift it, but it would not come away. It appeared to be fixed to the stout seamless shroud which was drawn over the whole body, and tied beneath the feet—as a farmer ties sacks. This shroud, which was also thickly waxed, was in one piece, being made to fit the form like a garment. I took a candle and examined the roll and then I saw why it was fast. The spices had congealed and glued it to the sack-like shroud. It was impossible to get it away without tearing the outer sheets of papyrus.[4]

'At last, however, I wrenched it loose and put it with the other in my pocket.

'Then we went on with our dreadful task in silence. With much care we ripped loose the sack-like garment, and at last the body of a man lay before us. Between his knees was a third roll of papyrus. I secured it, then held down the light and looked at him. One glance at his face was enough to tell a doctor how he had died.

'This body was not much dried up. Evidently it had not passed the allotted seventy days in natron, and therefore the expression and likeness were better preserved than is usual. Without entering into particulars, I will only say that I hope I shall never see such another look as that which was frozen on this dead man's face. Even the Arabs recoiled from it in horror and began to mutter prayers.

'For the rest, the usual opening on the left side through which the embalmers did their work was absent; the finely-cut features were those of a person of middle age, although the hair was already grey, and the frame was that of a very powerful man, the shoulders being of an extraordinary width. I had not time to examine very closely, however, for within a few seconds from its uncovering, the unembalmed body began

[4] This accounts for the gaps in the last sheets of the second roll.—ED.

to crumble now that it was exposed to the action of the air.
In five or six minutes there was literally nothing left of it but
a wisp of hair, the skull, and a few of the larger bones. I
noticed that one of the tibiæ—I forget if it was the right or
the left—had been fractured and very badly set. It must
have been quite an inch shorter than the other.

   ' Well, there was nothing more to find, and now that the
excitement was over, what between the heat, the exertion, and
the smell of mummy dust and spices, I felt more dead than
alive.

   ' I am tired of writing, and the ship rolls. This letter, of
course, goes overland, and I am coming by " long sea," but I
hope to be in London within ten days after you get it. Then
I will tell you of my pleasing experiences in the course of the
ascent from the tomb-chamber, and of how that prince of
rascals, Ali Baba, and his thieves tried to frighten me into
handing over the papyri, and how I worsted them. Then,
too, we will get the rolls deciphered. I expect that they only
contain the usual thing, copies of the " Book of the Dead,"
but there *may* be something else in them. Needless to say, I
did not narrate this little adventure in Egypt, or I should
have had the Boulac Museum people on my track. Good-bye,
" Mafish Fineesh," as Ali Baba always said.'

   In due course, my friend, the writer of the letter from
which I have quoted, arrived in London, and on the very next
day we paid a visit to a learned acquaintance well versed in
Hieroglyphics and Demotic writing. The anxiety with which
we watched him skilfully damping and unfolding one of the
rolls and peering through his gold-rimmed glasses at the
mysterious characters may well be imagined.

   ' Hum,' he said, ' whatever it is, this is *not* a copy of the
" Book of the Dead." By George, what's this? Cle—Cleo—

Cleopatra—— Why, my dear Sirs, as I am a living man, this is the history of somebody who lived in the days of Cleopatra, *the* Cleopatra, for here's Antony's name with hers! Well, there's six months' work before me here—six months, at the very least!' And in that joyful prospect he fairly lost control of himself, and skipped about the room, shaking hands with us at intervals, and saying 'I'll translate—I'll translate it if it kills me, and we will publish it; and, by the living Osiris, it shall drive every Egyptologist in Europe mad with envy! Oh, what a find! what a most glorious find!'

And O you whose eyes shall fall upon these pages, see, they have been translated, and they have been printed, and here they lie before you—an undiscovered land wherein you are free to travel!

Harmachis speaks to you from his forgotten tomb. The walls of Time fall down, and, as at the lightning's leap, a picture from the past starts upon your view, framed in the darkness of the ages.

He shows you those two Egypts which the silent pyramids looked down upon long centuries ago—the Egypt of the Greek, the Roman, and the Ptolemy, and that other outworn Egypt of the Hierophant, hoary with years, heavy with the legends of antiquity and the memory of long-lost honours.

He tells you how the smouldering loyalty of the land of Khem blazed up before it died, and how fiercely the old Time-consecrated Faith struggled against the conquering tide of Change that rose, like Nile at flood, and drowned the ancient Gods of Egypt.

Here, in his pages, you shall learn the glory of Isis the Many-shaped, the Executrix of Decrees. Here you shall make acquaintance with the shade of Cleopatra, that 'Thing of Flame,' whose passion-breathing beauty shaped the destiny of Empires.   Here you shall read how the soul of Charmion was slain of the sword her vengeance smithied.

Here Harmachis, the doomed Egyptian, being about to die, salutes you who follow on the path he trod.   In the story of his broken years he shows to you what may in its degree be the story of your own.   Crying aloud from that dim Amenti [5] where to-day he wears out his long atoning time, he tells, in the history of his fall, the fate of him who, however sorely tried, forgets his God, his Honour, and his Country.

* The Egyptian Hades or Purgatory.—Ed.

BOOK I.

The Preparation of Harmachis

CHAPTER I.

OF THE BIRTH OF HARMACHIS; THE PROPHECY OF THE HATHORS; AND THE SLAYING OF THE INNOCENT CHILD.

Y Osiris who sleeps at Abouthis, I write the truth.

I, Harmachis, Hereditary Priest of the Temple, reared by the divine Sethi, afore-time a Pharaoh of Egypt, and now justified in Osiris and ruling in Amenti. I, Harmachis, by right Divine and by true descent of blood King of the Double Crown, and Pharaoh of the Upper and Lower Land. I, Harmachis, who cast aside the opening flower of our hope, who turned from the glorious path, who forgot the voice of God in hearkening to the voice of woman. I, Harmachis, the fallen, in whom are gathered up all woes as waters are gathered in a desert well, who have tasted of every shame, who through betrayal have betrayed, who in losing the glory that is here have lost of the glory which is to be, who am utterly undone—I write, and, by Him who sleeps at Abouthis, I write the truth.

O Egypt!—dear land of Khem, whose black soil nourished up my mortal part—land that I have betrayed—O Osiris!— Isis!—Horus!—ye Gods of Egypt whom I have betrayed!—

O ye temples whose pylons strike the sky, whose faith I
have betrayed!—O Royal blood of the Pharaohs of eld,
that yet runs within these withered veins—whose virtue
I have betrayed!—O Invisible Essence of all Good! and
O Fate, whose balance rested on my hand—hear me; and,
to the day of utter doom, bear me witness that I write
the truth.

Even while I write, beyond the fertile fields, the Nile is
running red, as though with blood. Before me the sunlight
beats upon the far Arabian hills, and falls upon the piles of
Abouthis. Still the priests make orison within the temples
at Abouthis that know me no more; still the sacrifice is
offered, and the stony roofs echo back the people's prayers.
Still from this lone cell within my prison-tower, I, the Word
of Shame, watch thy fluttering banners, Abouthis, flaunting
from thy pylon walls, and hear the chants as the long procession winds from sanctuary to sanctuary.

Abouthis, lost Abouthis! my heart goes out toward thee!
For the day comes when the desert sands shall fill thy
secret places! Thy Gods are doomed, O Abouthis! New
Faiths shall make a mock of all thy Holies, and Centurion
shall call upon Centurion across thy fortress-walls. I weep
—I weep tears of blood: for mine is the sin that brought
about these evils and mine for ever is their shame.

Behold, it is written hereafter.

Here in Abouthis I was born, I, Harmachis, and my father,
the justified in Osiris, was High Priest of the Temple of Sethi.
And on that same day of my birth Cleopatra, the Queen of
Egypt, was born also. I passed my youth in yonder fields
watching the baser people at their labours and going in and
out at will among the great courts of the temples. Of my

mother I knew naught, for she died when I yet hung at the breast. But before she died in the reign of Ptolemy Aulêtes, who is named the Piper, so the old wife, Atoua, told me, my mother took a golden uræus, the snake symbol of our Royalty of Egypt, from a coffer of ivory and laid it on my brow. And those who saw her do this believed that she was distraught of the Divinity, and in her madness foreshadowed that the day of the Macedonian Lagidæ was ended, and that Egypt's sceptre should pass again to the hand of Egypt's true and Royal race. But when my father, the old High Priest Amenemhat, whose only child I was, she who was his wife before my mother having been, for what crime I know not, cursed with barrenness by Sekhet: I say when my father came in and saw what the dying woman had done, he lifted up his hands towards the vault of heaven and adored the Invisible, because of the sign that had been sent. And as he adored, the Hathors [1] filled my dying mother with the Spirit of Prophecy, and she rose in strength from the couch and prostrated herself thrice before the cradle where I lay asleep, the Royal asp upon my brow, crying aloud :

'Hail to thee, fruit of my womb! Hail to thee, Royal child! Hail to thee, Pharaoh that shalt be! Hail to thee, God that shalt purge the land, Divine seed of Nekt-nebf, the descended from Isis. Keep thee pure, and thou shalt rule and deliver Egypt and not be broken. But if thou dost fail in thy hour of trial, then may the curse of all the Gods of Egypt rest upon thee, and the curse of thy Royal forefathers, the justified, who ruled the land before thee from the age of Horus. Then in life mayst thou be wretched, and after death may Osiris refuse thee, and the judges of Amenti give judgment against thee, and Set and Sekhet torment thee, till such time as thy sin is purged, and the Gods of Egypt, called by

[1] The Egyptian *Parcæ* or *Fates.*—ED.

C

strange names, are once more worshipped in the Temples of Egypt, and the staff of the Oppressor is broken, and the footsteps of the Foreigner are swept clean, and the thing is accomplished as thou in thy weakness shalt cause it to be done.'

When she had spoken thus, the Spirit of Prophecy went out of her, and she fell dead across the cradle where I slept, so that I awoke with a cry.

But my father, Amenemhat, the High Priest, trembled, and was very fearful both because of the words which had been said by the Spirit of the Hathors through the mouth of my mother, and because what had been uttered was treason against Ptolemy. For he knew that, if the matter should come to the ears of Ptolemy, Pharaoh would send his guards to destroy the life of the child concerning whom such things were prophesied. Therefore, my father shut the doors, and caused all those who stood by to swear upon the holy symbol of his office, and by the name of the Divine Three, and by the Soul of her who lay dead upon the stones beside them, that nothing of what they had seen and heard should pass their lips.

Now among the company was the old wife, Atoua, who had been the nurse of my mother, and loved her well; and in these days, though I know not how it has been in the past, nor how it shall be in the future, there is no oath that can bind a woman's tongue. And so it came about that by-and-by, when the matter had become homely in her mind, and her fear had fallen from her, she spoke of the prophecy to her daughter, who nursed me at the breast now that my mother was dead. She did this as they walked together in the desert carrying food to the husband of the daughter, who was a sculptor, and shaped effigies of the holy Gods in the tombs that are fashioned in the rock—telling the daughter, my nurse, how great must be her care and love toward the child that should one day be Pharaoh, and drive the Ptolemies from Egypt. But the daughter, my nurse, was so filled with wonder at what she heard that she could not keep the tale locked within her breast, and in the night she awoke her husband, and, in her turn, whispered it to him, and thereby compassed her own destruction, and the destruction of her child, my foster-brother. For the man told his friend, and the friend was a spy of Ptolemy's, and thus the tale came to Pharaoh's ears.

Now, Pharaoh was much troubled thereat, for though when he was full of wine he would make a mock of the Gods of the Egyptians, and swear that the Roman Senate was the only God to whom he bowed the knee, yet in his heart he was terribly afraid, as I have learned from one who was his physician. For when he was alone at night he would scream and cry aloud to the great Serapis, who indeed is no true God, and to other Gods, fearing lest he should be murdered and his soul handed over to the tormentors. Also, when he felt his throne tremble under him, he would send large presents to the temples, asking a message from the oracles, and more especially from the oracle that is at Philæ. Therefore, when it came to his ears that the wife of the High Priest of the great and ancient Temple of Abouthis had been filled with the Spirit of Prophecy before she died, and foretold that her son should be Pharaoh, he was much afraid, and summoning some trusty guards—who, being Greeks, did not fear to do sacrilege—he despatched them by boat up the Nile, with orders to come to Abouthis and cut off the head of the child of the High Priest and bring it to him in a basket.

But, as it chanced, the boat in which the guards came was of deep draught, and, the time of their coming being at the lowest ebb of the river, it struck and remained fast upon a

bank of mud that is opposite the mouth of the road running
across the plains to Abouthis, and, as the north wind was
blowing very fiercely, it was like to sink.　Thereon the guards
of Pharaoh called out to the common people, who laboured at
lifting water along the banks of the river, to come with boats
and take them off; but, seeing that they were Greeks of
Alexandria, the people would not, for the Egyptians do not
love the Greeks.　Then the guards cried that they were on
Pharaoh's business, and still the people would not, asking what
was their business.　Whereon a eunuch among them who had
made himself drunk in his fear, told them that they came to
slay the child of Amenemhat, the High Priest, of whom it was
prophesied that he should be Pharaoh and sweep the Greeks
from Egypt.　And then the people feared to stand longer in
doubt, but brought boats, not knowing what might be meant
by the man's words.　But there was one among them—a
farmer and an overseer of canals—who was a kinsman of my
mother's and had been present when she prophesied; and he
turned and ran swiftly for three parts of an hour, till he came
to where I lay in the house that is without the north wall of
the great Temple.　Now, as it chanced, my father was away
in that part of the Place of Tombs which is to the left of the
large fortress, and Pharaoh's guards, mounted on asses, were
hard upon us.　Then the messenger cried to the old wife, Atoua,
whose tongue had brought about the evil, and told how the
soldiers drew near to slay me.　And they looked at each other,
not knowing what to do; for, had they hid me, the guards
would not have stayed their search till I was found.　But the
man, gazing through the doorway, saw a little child at play:—

'Woman,' he said, 'whose is that child?'

'It is my grandchild,' she answered, 'the foster-brother
of the Prince Harmachis; the child to whose mother we owe
this evil case.'

' Woman,' he said, ' thou knowest thy duty, do it !' and he again pointed at the child. ' I command thee, by the Holy Name ! '

Atoua trembled exceedingly, because the child was of her own blood ; but, nevertheless, she took the boy and washed him and set a robe of silk on him, and laid him on my cradle. And me she took and smeared with mud to make my fair skin darker, and, drawing my garment from me, set me to play in the dirt of the yard, which I did right gladly.

Then the man hid himself, and presently the soldiers rode up and asked of the old wife if this were the dwelling of the High Priest Amenemhat ? And she told them yea, and, bidding them enter, offered them honey and milk, for they were thirsty.

When they had drunk, the eunuch who was with them asked if that were the son of Amenemhat who lay in the cradle ; and she said ' Yea—yea,' and began to tell the guards how he would be great, for it had been prophesied of him that he should one day rule them all.

But the Greek guards laughed, and one of them, seizing the child, smote off his head with a sword ; and the eunuch drew forth the signet of Pharaoh as warrant for the deed and showed it to the old wife, Atoua, bidding her tell the High Priest that his son should be a King without a head.

And as they went one of their number saw me playing in the dirt and called out that there was more breeding in yonder brat than in the Prince Harmachis ; and for a moment they wavered, thinking to slay me also, but in the end they passed on, bearing the head of my foster-brother, for they loved not to murder little children.

After a while, the mother of the dead child returned from the market-place, and when she found what had been done, she and her husband would have killed Atoua the old wife, her mother, and given me up to the soldiers of Pharaoh. But my father came in also and learned the truth, and he caused the man and his wife to be seized by night and hidden away in the dark places of the temple, so that none saw them more.

But I would to-day it had been the will of the Gods that I had been slain of the soldiers and not the innocent child.

Thereafter it was given out that the High Priest Amen-emhat had taken me to be as a son to him in the place of that Harmachis who was slain of Pharaoh.

CHAPTER II.

OF THE DISOBEDIENCE OF HARMACHIS; OF THE SLAYING OF THE LION; AND OF THE SPEECH OF THE OLD WIFE, ATOUA.

after these things Ptolemy the Piper troubled us no more, nor did he again send his soldiers to Abouthis to seek for him of whom it was prophesied that he should be Pharaoh. For the head of the child, my foster-brother, was brought to him by the eunuch as he sat in his palace of marble at Alexandria, flushed with Cyprian wine, and played upon the flute before his women. And at his bidding the eunuch lifted up the head by the hair for him to look on. Then he laughed and smote it on the cheek with his sandal, bidding one of the girls crown Pharaoh with flowers. And he bowed the knee, and mocked the head of the innocent child. But the girl, who was sharp of tongue —for all of this I heard in after years—said to him that ' he did well to bow the knee, for this child was indeed Pharaoh, the greatest of Pharaohs, and his name was the *Osiris* and his throne was *Death.*'

Aulêtes was much troubled at these words, and trembled, for, being a wicked man, he greatly feared the entering into

Amenti. So he caused the girl to be slain because of the evil omen of her saying; crying that he would send her to worship that Pharaoh whom she had named. And the other women he sent away, and played no more upon the flute till he was once again drunk on the morrow. But the Alexandrians made a song on the matter, which is still sung about the streets. And this is the beginning of it—

> Ptolemy the Piper played
>   Over dead and dying;
> Piped and played he well.
>   Sure that flute of his was made
> Of the dank reed sighing
>   O'er the streams of Hell.
>
> There beneath the shadows grey.
>   With the sisters three,
> Shall he pipe for many a day.
>   May the Frog his butler be!
>   And his wine the water of that countrie—
>   Ptolemy the Piper!

After this the years passed on, nor did I, being very little, know anything of the great things that came to pass in Egypt; nor is it my purpose to set them out here. For I, Harmachis, having little time left to me, will only speak of those things with which I have been concerned.

And as the time went on, my father and the teachers instructed me in the ancient learning of our people and in such matters appertaining to the Gods as it is meet that children should know. So I grew strong and comely, for my hair was black as the hair of the divine Nout, and my eyes were blue as the blue lotus, and my skin was like the alabaster within the sanctuaries. For now that these glories have passed from me I may speak of them without shame. I was strong also. There was no youth of my years in Abouthis who could stand against me to wrestle with me, nor could any throw so far with the sling or spear. And I much yearned to hunt the lion; but he whom I called my father forbade me, telling me that my life was of too great worth to be so lightly hazarded. But when I bowed before him and prayed he would make his meaning clear to me, the old man frowned and answered that the Gods made all things clear in their own season. For my part, however, I went away wroth, for there was a youth in Abouthis who with others had slain a lion which fell upon his father's herds, and, being envious of my strength and beauty, he set it about that I was cowardly at heart, in that when I went out to hunt I only slew jackals and gazelles. Now, this was when I had reached my seventeenth year and was a man grown.

It chanced, therefore, that as I went sore at heart from the presence of the High Priest, I met this youth, who called to me and mocked me, bidding me know the country people had told him that a great lion was down among the rushes by the banks of the canal which runs past the Temple, lying at a distance of thirty stadia from Abouthis. And, still mocking me, he asked me if I would come and help him slay this lion, or would I go and sit among the old women and bid them comb my side lock? This bitter word so angered me that I was near to falling on him; but in place thereof, forgetting my father's saying, I answered that if he would come alone, I would go with him and seek this lion, and he should learn if I were indeed a coward. And at first he would not, for, as men know, it is our custom to hunt the lion in companies; so it was my hour to mock. Then he went and fetched his bow and arrows and a sharp knife. And I brought forth my heavy spear, which had a shaft of thorn-wood, and at its end a pomegranate in silver, to hold the hand from slipping; and, in silence, we went, side by side, to where the lion lay. When we came to the place, it was near sundown; and there, upon the mud of the canal-bank, we found the lion's slot, which ran into a thick clump of reeds.

'Now, thou boaster,' I said, 'wilt thou lead the way into yonder reeds, or shall I?' And I made as though I would lead the way.

'Nay, nay,' he answered, 'be not so mad! The brute will spring upon thee and rend thee. See! I will shoot among the reeds. Perchance, if he sleeps, it will arouse him.' And he drew his bow at a venture.

How it chanced I know not, but the arrow struck the sleeping lion, and, like a flash of light from the belly of a cloud, he bounded from the shelter of the reeds, and stood before us with bristling mane and yellow eyes, the arrow quivering in his flank. He roared aloud in fury, and the earth shook.

'Shoot with the bow,' I cried, 'shoot swiftly ere he spring!'

But courage had left the breast of the boaster, his jaw dropped down and his fingers unloosed their hold so that the bow fell from them; then, with a loud cry he turned and fled behind me, leaving the lion in my path. But while I stood waiting my doom, for though I was sore afraid I would not fly, the lion crouched himself, and, turning not aside, with one great bound swept over me, touching me not. He lit, and again he bounded full on the boaster's back, striking him such a blow with his great paw that his head was crushed as an egg thrown against a stone. He fell down dead, and the lion stood and roared over him. Then I was mad with horror, and, scarce knowing what I did, I grasped my spear and with a shout I charged. As I charged the lion lifted himself up on his hinder legs, to greet me, so that his head stood up above me. He smote at me with his paw; but with all my strength I drove the broad spear into his throat, and, shrinking from the agony of the steel, his blow fell short and did no more than rip my skin. Back he fell, the great spear far in his throat; then rising, he roared in pain and leapt twice the height of a man straight into the air, smiting at the spear with his fore-paws. Twice he leapt thus, horrible to see, and twice he fell upon his back. Then his strength spent itself with his rush-ing blood, and, groaning like a bull, he died; while I, being but a lad, stood and trembled with fear now that all cause of fear had passed.

But as I stood and gazed at the dead body of him who had taunted me, and at the carcass of the lion, a woman came running towards me, even the same old wife, Atoua, who, though I knew it not as yet, had offered up her flesh and blood that I might be saved alive. For she had been gather-ing simples, in which she had great skill, by the water's edge, not knowing that there was a lion near (and, indeed, the lions, for the most part, are not found in the tilled land, but rather in the desert and the Libyan mountains), and had seen from a distance that which I have set down. Now, when she was come, she knew me for Harmachis, and, bending herself, she made obeisance to me, and saluted me, calling me Royal, and worthy of all honour, and beloved, and chosen of the Holy Three, ay, and by the name of the Pharaoh! the Deliverer!

But I, thinking that terror had made her sick of mind, asked her of what she would speak.

'Is it a great thing,' I asked, 'that I should slay a lion? Is it a matter worthy of such talk as thine? There live, and have lived, men who have slain many lions. Did not the Divine Amen-hetep the Osirian slay with his own hand more than a hundred lions? Is it not written on the scarabæus that hangs within my father's chamber, that he slew lions afore-time? And have not others done likewise? Why then, speakest thou thus, O foolish woman?'

All of which I said, because, having now slain the lion, I was minded, after the manner of youth, to hold it as a thing of no account. But she did not cease to make obeisance, and to call me by names that are too high to be written.

'O Royal One,' she cried, 'wisely did thy mother prophesy. Surely the Holy Spirit, the Knepth, was in her, O thou conceived by a God! See the omen. The lion there—he growls within the Capitol at Rome—and the dead man, he is the Ptolemy—the Macedonian spawn that, like a foreign weed, hath overgrown the land of Nile: with the Macedonian Lagidæ thou shalt go to smite the lion of Rome. But the Macedonian cur shall fly, and the Roman lion shall strike him down, and thou shalt strike down the lion, and the land of Khem shall once more be free! free! Keep thyself but pure, according to the commandment of the Gods, O son of the Royal House; O hope of Khemi! be but ware of Woman the Destroyer, and as I have said, so shall it be. I am poor and wretched; yea, stricken with sorrow. I have sinned in speaking of what should be hid, and for my sin I have paid in the coin of that which was born of my womb; willingly have I paid for thee. But I have still of the wisdom of our people, nor do the Gods, in whose eyes all are equal, turn their countenance from the poor; the Divine Mother Isis hath spoken to me—but last night she spake—bidding me come hither to gather herbs, and read to thee the signs that I should see. And as I have said, so it shall come to pass, if thou canst but endure the weight of the great temptation. Come hither, Royal One!' and she led me to the edge of the canal, where the water was deep, and still and blue. 'Now gaze upon that face as the water throws it back. Is not that brow fitted to bear the double crown? Do not those gentle eyes mirror the majesty of kings? Hath not the Ptah, the Creator, fashioned that form to fit the Imperial garb, and awe the glance of multitudes looking through thee to God ?

'Nay, nay!' she went on in another voice—a shrill old wife's voice—'I will—be not so foolish, boy—the scratch of a lion is a venomous thing, a terrible thing ; yea, as bad as the bite of an asp—it must be treated, else it will fester, and all thy days thou shalt dream of lions; ay, and snakes ; and, also, it will break out in sores. But I know of it—I know. I am not crazed for nothing. For mark ! everything has its balance—in madness is much wisdom, and in wisdom much madness. *La ! la ! la !* Pharaoh himself can't say where the one begins and the other ends. Now, don't stand gazing there, looking as silly as a cat in a crocus-coloured robe, as they say in Alexandria ; but just let me stick these green things on the place, and in six days you'll heal up as white as a three-year child. Never mind the smart of it, lad. By Him who sleeps at Philæ, or at Abouthis, or at Abydus—as our divine masters have it now—or wherever He does sleep, which is a thing we shall all find out before we want to—by Osiris, I say, you'll live to be as clean from scars as a sacrifice to Isis at the new moon, if you'll but let me put it on.

'Is it not so, good folk ? '—and she turned to address some people who, while she prophesied, had assembled unseen by me—' I've been speaking a spell over him, just to make a way for the virtue of my medicine—*la ! la !* there's nothing like a spell. If you don't believe it, just you come to me next time your wives are barren ; it's better than scraping every pillar in the Temple of Osiris, I warrant. I 'll make 'em bear like a twenty-year-old palm. But then, you see, you must know what to say—that's the point—everything comes to a point at last. *La! la!*'

Now, when I heard all this, I, Harmachis, put my hand to my head, not knowing if I dreamed. But presently looking

D

up, I saw a grey-haired man among those who were gathered
together, who watched us sharply, and afterwards I learned
that this man was the spy of Ptolemy, the very man, indeed,
who had wellnigh caused me to be slain of Pharaoh when I
was in my cradle.   Then I understood why Atoua spoke so
foolishly.

'Thine are strange spells, old wife,' the spy said.   'Thou
didst speak of Pharaoh and the double crown and of a
form fashioned by Ptah to bear it ; is it not so ? '

'Yea, yea—part of the spell, thou fool ; and what can one
swear by better nowadays than by the Divine Pharaoh the
Piper, whom, and whose music, may the Gods preserve to
charm this happy land ?—what better than by the double
crown he wears—grace to great Alexander of Macedonia ?
By the way, you know about everything : have they got back
his chlamys yet, which Mithridates took to Cos ?   Pompey
wore it last, didn't he ?—in his triumph, too—just fancy
Pompey in the cloak of Alexander !—a puppy-dog in a lion's
skin !   And talking of lions—look what this lad hath done—
slain a lion with his own spear ; and right glad you village
folks should be to see it, for it was a very fierce lion—just see
his teeth and his claws—his claws !—they are enough to make
a poor silly old woman like me shriek to look at them !   And
the body there, the dead body—the lion slew it.   Alack ! he's
an Osiris [1] now, the body—and to think of it, but an hour ago
he was an everyday mortal like you or me !   Well, away with
him to the embalmers.   He'll soon swell in the sun and burst,
and that will save them the trouble of cutting him open.   Not
that they will spend a talent of silver over him anyway.
Seventy days in natron—that's all he's likely to get.   *La !
la !* how my tongue does run, and it's getting dark.   Come,
aren't you going to take away the body of that poor lad, and

---

[1] The soul when it has been absorbed in the Godhead.—ED.

the lion, too ? There, my boy, you keep those herbs on, and you'll never feel your scratches. I know a thing or two for all I'm crazy, and you, my own grandson ! Dear, dear, I'm glad his Holiness the High Priest adopted you when Pharaoh —Osiris bless his holy name—made an end of his son ; you look so bonny. I warrant the real Harmachis could not have killed a lion like that. Give me the common blood, say I—it's so lusty.'

'You know too much and talk too fast,' grumbled the spy, now quite deceived. ' Well, he is a brave youth. Here, you men, bear this body back to Abouthis, and some of you stop and help me skin the lion. We'll send the skin to you, young man,' he went on ; 'not that you deserve it : to attack a lion like that was the act of a fool, and a fool deserves what he gets—destruction. Never attack the strong until you are stronger.'

But for my part I went home wondering.

CHAPTER III.

OF THE REBUKE OF AMENEMHAT; OF THE PRAYER OF HARMACHIS; AND OF THE SIGN GIVEN BY THE HOLY GODS.

OR a while as I, Harmachis, went, the juice of the green herbs which the old wife, Atoua, had placed upon my wounds caused me much smart, but presently the pain ceased. And, of a truth, I believe that there was virtue in them, for within two days my flesh healed up, so that after a time no marks remained. But I bethought me that I had disobeyed the word of the old High Priest, Amenemhat, who was called my father. For till this day I knew not that he was in truth my father according to the flesh, having been taught that his own son was slain as I have written; and that he had been pleased, with the sanction of the Divine ones, to take me as an adopted son and rear me up, that I might in due season fill an office about the Temple. Therefore I was much troubled, for I feared the old man, who was very terrible in his anger, and ever spoke with the cold voice of Wisdom. Nevertheless, I determined to go in to him and confess my fault and bear such punishment as he should be pleased to put upon me. So with the red spear in my hand, and the red wounds on my breast, I passed through the outer court of the great temple and came to the door of the place where the High Priest dwelt. It is a great chamber, sculptured round about with the images of the solemn Gods, and the sunlight comes to it in the daytime by an opening cut through the stones of the massy roof. But at night it was lit by a swinging lamp of bronze. I passed in without noise, for the door was not altogether shut, and, pushing my way through the heavy curtains that were beyond, I stood with a beating heart within the chamber.

The lamp was lit, for the darkness had fallen, and by its light I saw the old man seated in a chair of ivory and ebony at a table of stone on which were spread mystic writings of the words of Life and Death. But he read no more, for he slept, and his long white beard rested upon the table like the beard of a dead man. The soft light from the lamp fell on him, on the papyri and the gold ring upon his hand, where were graven the symbols of the Invisible One, but all around was shadow. It fell on the shaven head, on the white robe, on the cedar staff of priesthood at his side, and on the ivory of the lion-footed chair ; it showed the mighty brow of power, the features cut in kingly mould, the white eyebrows, and the dark hollows of the deep-set eyes. I looked and trembled, for there was about him that which was more than the dignity of man. He had lived so long with the Gods, and so long kept company with them and with thoughts divine, he was so deeply versed in all those mysteries which we do but faintly discern, here in this upper air, that even now, before his time, he partook of the nature of the Osiris, and was a thing to shake humanity with fear.

I stood and gazed, and as I stood he opened his dark eyes, but looked not on me, nor turned his head ; and yet he saw me and spoke.

'Why hast thou been disobedient to me, my son ?' he

said. ' How came it that thou wentest forth against the lion when I bade thee not ? '

' How knowest thou, my father, that I went forth ? ' I asked in fear.

' How know I ?   Are there, then, no other ways of knowledge than by the senses ?   Ah, ignorant child ! was not my Spirit with thee when the lion sprang upon thy companion ? Did I not pray Those set about thee to protect thee, to make sure thy thrust when thou didst drive the spear into the lion's throat !   How came it that thou wentest forth, my son ? '

' The boaster taunted me.' I answered, ' and I went.'

' Yes, I know it ; and, because of the hot blood of youth, I forgive thee, Harmachis.   But now listen to me, and let my words sink into thy heart like the waters of Sihor into the thirsty sand at the rising of Sirius.[1]   Listen to me.   The boaster was sent to thee as a temptation, he was sent as a trial of thy strength, and see ! it has not been equal to the burden.   Therefore thy hour is put back.   Hadst thou been strong in this matter, the path had been made plain to thee even now.   But thou hast failed, and therefore thy hour is put back.'

' I understand thee not, my father,' I answered.

' What was it, then, my son, that the old wife, Atoua, said to thee down by the bank of the canal ? '

Then I told him all that the old wife had said.

' And thou believest, Harmachis, my son ? '

' Nay,' I answered ; ' how should I believe such tales ? Surely she is mad.   All the people know her for mad.'

Now for the first time he looked towards me, who was standing in the shadow.

' My son ! my son !' he cried ; ' thou art wrong.   She is not mad.   The woman spoke the truth ; she spoke not of

---

[1] The dog-star, whose appearance marked the commencement of the overflow of the Nile.—ED.

herself, but of the voice within her that cannot lie. For this Atoua is ̄a prophetess and holy. Now learn thou the destiny that the Gods of Egypt have given to thee to fulfil, and woe be unto thee if by any weakness thou dost fail therein! Listen: thou art no stranger adopted into my house and the worship of the Temple; thou art my very son, saved to me by this same woman. But, Harmachis, thou art more than this, for in thee and me alone yet flows the Imperial blood of Egypt. Thou and I alone of men alive are descended, without break or flaw, from that Pharaoh Nekt-nebf whom Ochus the Persian drove from Egypt. The Persian came and the Persian went, and after the Persian came the Macedonian, and now for nigh upon three hundred years the Lagidæ have usurped the double crown, defiling the land of Khem and corrupting the worship of its Gods. And mark thou this: but now, two weeks since, Ptolemy Neus Dionysus, Ptolemy Aulêtes the Piper, who would have slain thee, is dead; and but now hath the Eunuch Pothinus, that very eunuch who came hither, years ago, to cut thee off, set at naught the will of his master, the dead Aulêtes, and placed the boy Ptolemy upon the throne. And therefore his sister Cleopatra, that fierce and beautiful girl, has fled into Syria; and there, if I err not, she will gather her armies and make war upon her brother Ptolemy: for by her father's will she was left joint-sovereign with him. And, meanwhile, mark thou this, my son: the Roman eagle hangs on high, waiting with ready talons till such time as he may fall upon the fat wether Egypt and rend him. And mark again: the people of Egypt are weary of the foreign yoke, they hate the memory of the Persians, and they are sick at heart of being named " Men of Macedonia " in the markets of Alexandria. The whole land mutters and murmurs beneath the yoke of the Greek and the shadow of the Roman.

'Have we not been oppressed? Have not our children been butchered and our gains wrung from us to fill the bottomless greed and lust of the Lagidæ? Have not the temples been forsaken?—ay, have not the majesties of the Eternal Gods been set at naught by these Grecian babblers, who have dared to meddle with the immortal truths, and name the Most High by another name—by the name of Serapis—confounding the substance of the Invisible? Doth not Egypt cry aloud for freedom?—and shall she cry in vain? Nay, nay, for thou, my son, art the appointed way of deliverance. To thee, being sunk in eld, I have decreed my rights. Already thy name is whispered in many a sanctuary, from Abu to Athu; already priests and people swear allegiance, even by the sacred symbols, unto him who shall be declared to them. Still, the time is not yet; thou art too green a sapling to bear the weight of such a storm. But to-day thou wast tried and found wanting.

'He who would serve the Gods, Harmachis, must put aside the failings of the flesh. Taunts must not move him, nor any lusts of man. Thine is a high mission, but this thou must learn. If thou learn it not, thou shalt fail therein; and then, my curse be on thee! and the curse of Egypt, and the curse of Egypt's broken Gods! For know thou this, that even the Gods, who are immortal, may, in the interwoven scheme of things, lean upon the man who is their instrument, as a warrior on his sword. And woe be to the sword that snaps in the hour of battle, for it shall be thrown aside to rust or perchance be melted with fire! Therefore, make thy heart pure and high and strong; for thine is no common lot, and thine no mortal meed. Triumph, Harmachis, and in glory thou shalt go—in glory here and hereafter! Fail, and woe—woe be on thee!'

He paused and bowed his head, and then went on:

'Of these matters thou shalt hear more hereafter. Meanwhile, thou hast much to learn. To-morrow I will give thee letters, and thou shalt journey down the Nile, past white-walled Memphis to Annu. There thou shalt sojourn certain years, and learn more of our ancient wisdom beneath the shadow of those secret pyramids of which thou, too, art the Hereditary High Priest that is to be. And meanwhile, I will sit here and watch, for my hour is not yet, and, by the help of the Gods, spin the web of Death wherein thou shalt catch and hold the wasp of Macedonia.

'Come hither, my son; come hither and kiss me on the brow, for thou art my hope, and all the hope of Egypt. Be but true, soar to the eagle crest of destiny, and thou shalt be glorious here and hereafter. Be false, fail, and I will spit upon thee, and thou shalt be accursed, and thy soul shall remain in bondage till that hour when, in the slow flight of time, the evil shall once more grow to good and Egypt shall again be free.'

I drew near, trembling, and kissed him on the brow. 'May all these things come upon me, and more,' I said, 'if I fail thee, my father!'

'Nay!' he cried, 'not me, not me; but rather those whose will I do. And now go, my son, and ponder in thy heart, and in thy secret heart digest my words; mark what thou shalt see, and gather up the dew of wisdom, making thee ready for the battle. Fear not for thyself, thou art protected from all ill. No harm may touch thee from without; thyself alone can be thine own enemy. I have said.'

Then I went forth with a full heart. The night was very still, and none were stirring in the temple courts. I hurried through them, and reached the entrance to the pylon that is at the outer gate. Then, seeking solitude, and, as it were, to draw near to heaven, I climbed the pylon's two hundred steps,

until at length I reached the massive roof. Here I leaned
my breast against the parapet, and looked forth. As I
looked, the red edge of the full moon floated up over the
Arabian hills, and her rays fell upon the pylon where I stood
and the temple walls beyond, lighting the visages of the
carven Gods. Then the cold light struck the stretch of
well-tilled lands, now whitening to the harvest, and as the
heavenly lamp of Isis passed up the sky, her rays crept slowly
down to the valley, where Sihor, father of the land of Khem,
rolls on toward the sea.

Now the bright beams kissed the water that smiled an
answer back, and now mountain and valley, river, temple,
town, and plain were flooded with white light, for Mother Isis
was arisen, and threw her gleaming robe across the bosom of
the earth. It was beautiful, with the beauty of a dream,
and solemn as the hour after death. Mightily, indeed,
the temples towered up against the face of night. Never had
they seemed so grand to me as in that hour—those eternal
shrines, before whose walls Time himself shall wither.
And it was to be mine to rule this moonlit land; mine to
preserve those sacred shrines, and cherish the honour of their
Gods; mine to cast out the Ptolemy and free Egypt from the
foreign yoke ! In my veins ran the blood of those great Kings
who await the day of Resurrection, sleeping in the tombs of
the valley of Thebes. My spirit swelled within me as I
dreamed upon this glorious destiny, I closed my hands, and
there, upon the pylon, I prayed as I had never prayed before
to the Godhead, who is called by many names, and in many
forms made manifest.

'O Amen,' I prayed, ' God of Gods, who hast been from
the beginning; Lord of Truth, who art, and of whom all are,
who givest out thy Godhead and gatherest it up again; in the
circle of whom the Divine ones move and are, who wast from

all time the Self-begot, and who shalt be till time—hearken unto me.[1]

'O Amen—Osiris, the sacrifice by whom we are justified, Lord of the Region of the Winds, Ruler of the Ages, Dweller in the West, the Supreme in Amenti, hearken unto me.

'O Isis, great Mother Goddess, mother of the Horus— mysterious Mother, Sister, Spouse, hearken unto me. If, indeed, I am the chosen of the Gods to carry out the purpose of the Gods, let a sign be given me, even now, to seal my life to the life above. Stretch out your arms towards me, O ye Gods, and uncover the glory of your countenance. Hear! ah, hear me!' And I cast myself upon my knees and lifted up my eyes to heaven.

And as I knelt, a cloud grew upon the face of the moon covering it up, so that the night became dark, and the silence deepened all around—even the dogs far below in the city ceased to howl, while the silence grew and grew till it was heavy as death. I felt my spirit lifted up within me, and my hair rose upon my head. Then of a sudden the mighty pylon seemed to rock beneath my feet, a great wind beat about my brows and a voice spoke within my heart :

'Behold a sign! Possess thyself in patience, O Har-machis!'

And as the voice spoke, a cold hand touched my hand, and left somewhat within it. Then the cloud rolled from the face of the moon, the wind passed, the pylon ceased to tremble, and the night was as the night had been.

As the light came back, I gazed upon that which had been left within my hand. It was a bud of the holy lotus new breaking into bloom, and from it came a most sweet scent.

And while I gazed behold! the lotus passed from my grasp and was gone, leaving me astonished.

---

[1] For a somewhat similar definition of the Godhead see the funeral papyrus of Nesikhonsu, a Princess of the Twenty-first Dynasty.—ED.

CHAPTER IV.

OF THE DEPARTURE OF HARMACHIS AND OF HIS MEETING WITH
HIS UNCLE SEPA, THE HIGH PRIEST OF ANNU EL RA; OF
HIS LIFE AT ANNU, AND OF THE WORDS OF SEPA

IT the dawning of the next day I was awakened by a priest of the temple, who brought word to me to make ready for the journey of which my father had spoken, inasmuch as there was an occasion for me to pass down the river to Annu el Ra. Now this is the Heliopolis of the Greeks, whither I should go in the company of some priests of Ptah at Memphis who had come hither to Abouthis to lay the body of one of their great men in the tomb that had been prepared near the resting-place of the blessed Osiris.

So I made ready, and the same evening, having received letters and embraced my father and those about the temple who were dear to me, I passed down the banks of Sihor, and we sailed with the south wind. As the pilot stood upon the prow and with a rod in his hand bade the sailor-men loosen the stakes by which the vessel was moored to the banks, the old wife, Atoua, hobbled up, her basket of simples in her hand, and, calling out her farewell, threw a sandal after me for good chance, which sandal I kept for many years.

So we sailed, and for six days passed down the wonderful river, making fast each night at some convenient spot. But when I lost sight of the familiar things that I had seen day by day since I had eyes to see, and found myself alone among strange faces, I felt very sore at heart, and would have wept had I not been ashamed. And of all the wonderful things I saw I will not write here, for, though they were new to me, have they not been known to men since such time as the Gods ruled in Egypt ? But the priests who were with me showed me no little honour and expounded to me what were the things I saw.

On the morning of the seventh day we came to Memphis, the city of the White Wall. Here, for three days I rested from my journey and was entertained of the priests of the wonderful Temple of Ptah the Creator, and shown the beauties of the great and marvellous city. Also I was led in secret by the High Priest and two others into the holy presence of the God Apis, the Ptah who deigns to dwell among men in the form of a bull. The God was black, and on his forehead there was a white square, on his back was a white mark shaped like an eagle, beneath his tongue was the likeness of a scarabæus, in his tail were double hairs, and a plate of pure gold hung between his horns. I entered the place of the God and worshipped, while the High Priest and those with him stood aside, watching earnestly. And when I had worshipped, saying the words which had been told me, the God knelt, and lay down before me. Then the High Priest and those with him, who, as I heard in after time, were great men of Upper Egypt, approached wondering, and, saying no word, made obeisance to me because of the omen. And many other things I saw in Memphis that are too long to write of here.

On the fourth day some priests of Annu came to lead me to Sepa, my uncle, the High Priest of Annu. So, having bidden farewell to those of Memphis, we crossed the river and rode on asses two parts of a day's journey through many villages, which we found in great poverty because of the oppression of the tax-gatherers. Also, as we went, I saw for the first time the great pyramids that are beyond the image of the God Horemkhu, that Sphinx whom the Greeks name Harmachis, and the Temples of the Divine Mother Isis, Queen of the Memnonia, and the God Osiris, Lord of Rosatou, of which temples, together with the Temple of the worship of the Divine Menkau-ra, I, Harmachis, am by right Divine the Hereditary High Priest. I saw them and marvelled at their greatness and the white carven limestone, and red granite of Syene, that flashed the sun's rays back to heaven. But at this time I knew nothing of the treasure that was hid in *Her*, which is the third among the pyramids—would I had never known of it!

And so at last we came within sight of Annu, which after Memphis has been seen is no large town, but stands on raised ground, before which are lakes fed by a canal. Behind the town is the inclosed field of the Temple of the God Ra.

We dismounted at the pylon, and were met beneath the portico by a man not great of stature, but of noble aspect, having his head shaven, and with dark eyes that twinkled like the further stars.

'Hold!' he cried, in a great voice which fitted his weak body but ill. 'Hold! I am Sepa, who opens the mouth of the Gods!'

'And I,' I said, 'am Harmachis, son of Amenemhat, Hereditary High Priest and Ruler of the Holy City Abouthis; and I bear letters to thee, O Sepa!'

'Enter,' he said. 'Enter!' scanning me all the while with his twinkling eyes. 'Enter, my son!' And he took me and led me to a chamber in the inner hall, closed to the door, and then, having glanced at the letters that I brought, of a sudden he fell upon my neck and embraced me.

'Welcome,' he cried, 'welcome, son of my own sister, and hope of Khem! Not in vain have I prayed the Gods that I might live to look upon thy face and impart to thee the wisdom which perchance I alone have mastered of those who are left alive in Egypt. There are few whom it is lawful that I should teach. But thine is the great destiny, and thine shall be the ears to hear the lessons of the Gods.'

And he embraced me once more and bade me go bathe and eat, saying that on the morrow he would speak with me further.

This of a truth he did, and at such length that I will forbear to set down all he said both then and afterwards, for if I did so there would be no papyrus left in Egypt when the task was ended. Therefore, having much to tell and but little time to tell it, I will pass over the events of the years that followed.

For this was the manner of my life. I rose early, I attended the worship of the Temple, and I gave my days to study. I learnt of the rites of religion and their meaning, and of the beginning of the Gods and the beginning of the Upper World. I learnt of the mystery of the movements of the stars, and of how the earth rolls on among them. I was instructed in that ancient knowledge which is called magic, and in the way of interpretation of dreams, and of the drawing nigh to God. I was taught the language of symbols and their outer and inner secrets. I became acquainted with the eternal laws of Good and Evil, and with the mystery of that trust which is held of man; also I learnt the secrets of the pyramids—which I would that I had never known. Further, I read the records of the past, and of the acts and words of the ancient kings who were before me since the rule of Horus upon earth; and I was made to know all craft of state, the lore of earth, and with it the history of Greece and

H

Rome. Also I learnt the Grecian and the Roman tongues, of which indeed I already had some knowledge—and all this while, for five long years, I kept my hands clean and my heart pure, and did no evil in the sight of God or man ; but laboured heavily to acquire all things, and to prepare myself for the destiny that awaited me.

Twice every year greetings and letters came from my father Amenemhat, and twice every year I sent back my answers asking if the time had come to cease from labour. And so the days of my probation sped away till I grew faint and weary at heart, for being now a man, ay and learned, I longed to make a beginning of the life of men. And often I wondered if this talk and prophecy of the things that were to be was but a dream born of the brains of men whose wish ran before their thought. I was, indeed, of the Royal blood, that I knew : for my uncle, Sepa the Priest, showed me a secret record of the descent, traced without break from father to son, and graven in mystic symbols on a tablet of the stone of Syene. But of what avail was it to be Royal by right when Egypt, my heritage, was a slave—a slave to do the pleasure and minister to the luxury of the Macedonian Lagidæ—ay, and when she had been so long a serf that, perchance, she had forgotten how to put off the servile smile of Bondage and once more to look across the world with Freedom's happy eyes ?

Then I bethought me of my prayer upon the pylon tower of Abouthis and of the answer given to my prayer, and wondered if that, too, were a dream.

And one night, as, weary with study, I walked within the sacred grove that is in the garden of the temple, and mused thus, I met my uncle Sepa, who also was walking and thinking.

' Hold ! ' he cried in his great voice ; ' why is thy face so sad, Harmachis ? Has the last problem that we studied over-whelmed thee ? '

' Nay, my uncle,' I answered, ' I am overwhelmed indeed, but not of the problem : it was a light one. My heart is heavy, for I am weary of life within these cloisters, and the piled-up weight of knowledge crushes me. It is of no avail to store up force which cannot be used.'

' Ah, thou art impatient, Harmachis,' he answered; ' it is ever the way of foolish youth. Thou wouldst taste of the battle ; thou dost tire of watching the breakers fall upon the beach, thou wouldst plunge into them and venture the desperate hazard of the war. And so thou wouldst be going, Harmachis ? The bird would fly the nest as, when they are grown, the swallows fly from the eaves of the Temple. Well, it shall be as thou desirest; the hour is at hand. I have taught thee all that I have learned, and methinks that the pupil has outrun his master,' and he paused and wiped his bright black eyes, for he was very sad at the thought of my departure.

' And whither shall I go, my uncle ? ' I asked rejoicing ; ' back to Abouthis to be initiated in the mysteries of the Gods ? '

' Ay, back to Abouthis, and from Abouthis to Alexandria, and from Alexandria to the Throne of thy fathers, Harmachis ! Listen, now ; things are thus : Thou knowest how Cleopatra, the Queen, fled into Syria when that false eunuch Pothinus set the will of her father Aulêtes at naught and raised her brother Ptolemy to the sole lordship of Egypt. Thou knowest also how she came back, like a Queen indeed, with a great army in her train, and lay at Pelusium, and how at this juncture the mighty Cæsar, that great man, that greatest of all men, sailed with a weak company hither to Alexandria from Pharsalia's bloody field in hot pursuit of Pompey. But

E 2

he found Pompey already dead, having been basely murdered by Achillas, the General, and Lucius Septimius, the chief of the Roman legions in Egypt, and thou knowest how the Alexandrians were troubled at his coming and would have slain his lictors.   Then, as thou hast heard, Cæsar seized Ptolemy, the young King, and his sister Arsinoë, and bade the army of Cleopatra and the army of Ptolemy, under Achillas, which lay facing each other at Pelusium, disband and go their ways. And for answer Achillas marched on Cæsar, and besieged him straitly in the Bruchium at Alexandria, and so, for a while, things were, and none knew who should reign in Egypt. But then Cleopatra took up the dice, and threw them, and this was the throw she made—in truth, it was a bold one.   For, leaving the army at Pelusium, she came at dusk to the harbour of Alexandria, and alone with the Sicilian Apollodorus entered and landed.   Then Apollodorus bound her in a bale of rich rugs, such as are made in Syria, and sent the rugs as a present to Cæsar.   And when the rugs were unbound in the palace, behold! within them was the fairest girl on all the earth—ay, and the most witty and the most learned.   And she seduced the great Cæsar—even his weight of years did not avail to protect him from her charms—so that, as a fruit of his folly, he wellnigh lost his life, and all the glory he had gained in a hundred wars.'

'The fool!' I broke in—'the fool!   Thou callest him great; but how can the man be truly great who has no strength to stand against a woman's wiles? Cæsar, with the world hanging on his word! Cæsar, at whose breath forty legions marched and changed the fate of peoples!   Cæsar the cold! the far-seeing! the hero!—Cæsar to fall like a ripe fruit into a false girl's lap!   Why, in the issue, of what common clay was this Roman Cæsar, and how poor a thing!'

But Sepa looked at me and shook his head.   'Be not so

rash, Harmachis, and talk not with so proud a voice. Knowest thou not that in every suit of mail there is a joint, and woe to him who wears the harness if the sword should search it out! For Woman, in her weakness, is yet the strongest force upon the earth. She is the helm of all things human; she comes in many shapes and knocks at many doors; she is quick and patient, and her passion is not ungovernable like that of man, but as a gentle steed that she can guide e'en where she will, and as occasion offers can now bit up and now give rein. She has a captain's eye, and stout must be that fortress of the heart in which she finds no place of vantage. Does thy blood beat fast in youth? She will outrun it, nor will her kisses tire. Art thou set toward ambition? She will unlock thy inner heart, and show thee roads that lead to glory. Art thou worn and weary? She has comfort in her breast. Art thou fallen? She can lift thee up, and to the illusion of thy sense gild defeat with triumph. Ay, Harmachis, she can do these things, for Nature ever fights upon her side; and while she does them she can deceive and shape a secret end in which thou hast no part. And thus Woman rules the world. For her are wars; for her men spend their strength in gathering gains; for her they do well and ill, and seek for greatness, to find oblivion. But still she sits like yonder Sphinx, and smiles; and no man has ever read all the riddle of her smile, or known all the mystery of her heart. Mock not! mock not! Harmachis; for he must be great indeed who can defy the power of Woman, which, pressing round him like the invisible air, is often strongest when the senses least discover it.'

I laughed aloud. 'Thou speakest earnestly, my uncle Sepa,' I said; 'one might almost think that thou hadst not come unscathed through this fierce fire of temptation. Well, for myself, I fear not woman and her wiles; I know naught of them, and naught I wish to know; and I still hold that this Cæsar was a fool. Had I stood where Cæsar stood, to cool its wantonness that bale of rugs should have been rolled down the palace steps, into the harbour mud.'

'Nay, cease! cease!' he cried aloud. 'It is evil to speak thus; may the Gods avert the omen and preserve to thee this cold strength of which thou boastest. Oh! man, thou knowest not!—thou in thy strength and beauty that is without compare, in the power of thy learning and the sweetness of thy tongue—thou knowest not! The world where thou must mix is not a sanctuary as that of the Divine Isis. But there—it may be so! Pray that thy heart's ice may never melt, so thou shalt be great and happy and Egypt be delivered. And now let me take up my tale—thou seest, Harmachis, even in so grave a story woman claims her place. The young Ptolemy, Cleopatra's brother, being loosed of Cæsar, treacherously turned on him. Then Cæsar and Mithridates stormed the camp of Ptolemy, who took to flight across the river. But his boat was sunk by the fugitives who pressed upon it, and such was the miserable end of Ptolemy.

'Thereon, the war being ended, though she had but then borne him a son, Cæsarion, Cæsar appointed the younger Ptolemy to rule with Cleopatra, and be her husband in name, and he himself departed for Rome, bearing with him the beautiful Princess Arsinoë to follow his triumph in her chains. But the great Cæsar is no more. He died as he had lived, in blood, and right royally. And but now Cleopatra, the Queen, if my tidings may be trusted, has slain Ptolemy, her brother and her husband, by poison, and taken the child Cæsarion to be her fellow on the throne, which she holds by the help of the Roman legions, and, as they say, of young Sextus Pompeius, who has succeeded Cæsar in her love. But, Harmachis, the whole land boils and seethes against her. In every city the children of Khem talk of the deliverer who is to come—and thou art he, Harmachis. The time is almost ripe. The hour is nigh at hand. Go thou back to Abouthis and learn the last secrets of the Gods, and meet those who shall direct the bursting of the storm. Then act, Harmachis—act, I say, and strike home for Khem, rid the land of the Roman and the Greek, and take thy place upon the throne of thy divine fathers and be a King of men. For to this end thou wast born, O Prince!'

CHAPTER V.

OF THE RETURN OF HARMACHIS TO ABOUTHIS ; OF THE CELE-
BRATION OF THE MYSTERIES ; OF THE CHANT OF ISIS ;
AND OF THE WARNING OF AMENEMHAT.

the next day I embraced my uncle Sepa, and with an eager heart departed from Annu back to Abouthis. To be short, I came thither in safety, having been absent five years and a month, being now no more a boy but a man full grown and having my mind well stocked with the knowledge of men and the ancient wisdom of Egypt. So once again I saw the old lands and the known faces, though of these some few were wanting, having been gathered to Osiris. Now, as, riding across the fields, I came nigh to the enclosure of the Temple, the priests and people issued forth to bid me welcome, and with them the old wife, Atoua, who, but for a few added wrinkles that Time had cut upon her forehead, was just as she had been when she threw the sandal after me five long years before.

'*La! la! la!*' she cried; 'and there thou art, my bonny lad; more bonny even than thou wert! *La!* what a man! what shoulders! and what a face and form! Ah, it does an old woman credit to have dandled thee! But thou art over-

pale; those priests down there at Annu have starved thee,
surely? Starve not thyself: the Gods love not a skeleton.
"Empty stomach makes empty head," as they say at Alexandria. But this is a glad hour; ay, a joyous hour. Come
in—come in!' and as I lighted down she emb aced me.

But I thrust her aside. 'My father! where is my father?'
I cried; 'I see him not!'

'Nay, nay, have no fear,' she answered; 'his Holiness
is well; he waits thee in his chamber. There, pass on. O
happy day! O happy Abouthis!'

So I went, or rather ran, and reached the chamber of
which I have written, and there at the table sat my father,
Amenemhat, the same as he had been, but very old. I came
to him and, kneeling before him, kissed his hand, and he
blessed me.

'Look up, my son,' he said, 'let my old eyes gaze upon
thy face, that I may read thy heart.'

So I lifted up my head, and he looked upon me long and
earnestly.

'I read thee,' he said at length; 'thou art pure and strong
in wisdom; I have not been deceived in thee. Oh, the years
have been lonely; but I did well to send thee hence. Now,
tell me of thy life; for thy letters have told me little, and
thou canst not know, my son, how hungry is a father's heart.'

And so I told him; we sat far into the night and talked
together. And in the end he bade me know that I must now
prepare to be initiated into those last mysteries that are
learned of the chosen of the Gods.

And so it came about that for a space of three months
I prepared myself according to the holy customs. I ate no
meat. I was constant in the sanctuaries, in the study of the
secrets of the Great Sacrifice and of the woe of the Holy
Mother. I watched and prayed before the altars. I lifted

up my soul to God; ay, in dreams I communed with the Invisible, till at length earth and earth's desires seemed to pass from me. I longed no more for the glory of this world, my heart hung above it as an eagle on his outstretched wings, and the voice of the world's blame could not stir it, and the vision of its beauty brought no delight. For above me was the vast vault of heaven, where in unalterable procession the stars pass on, drawing after them the destinies of men; where the Holy Ones sit upon their burning thrones, and watch the chariot-wheels of Fate as they roll from sphere to sphere. O hours of holy contemplation! who, having once tasted of your joy could wish again to grovel on the earth? O vile flesh to drag us down! I would that thou hadst then altogether fallen from me, and left my spirit free to seek Osiris!

The months of probation passed but too swiftly, and now the holy day drew near when I was in truth to be united to the universal Mother. Never hath Night so longed for the promise of the Dawn; never hath the heart of a lover so passionately desired the sweet coming of his bride, as I longed to see Thy glorious face, O Isis! Even now that I have been faithless to Thee, and Thou art far from me, O Divine! my soul goes out to Thee, and once more I know—— But as it is bidden that I should draw the veil, and speak of things which have not been told since the beginning of this world, let me pass on and reverently set down the history of that holy morn.

For seven days the great festival had been celebrated, the suffering of the Lord Osiris had been commemorated, the grief of the Mother Isis had been sung and glory had been done to the memory of the coming of the Divine Child Horus, the Son, the Avenger, the God-begot. All these things had been carried out according to the ancient rites. The boats had floated on the sacred lake, the priests had scourged themselves before the sanctuaries, and the images had been borne through the streets at night.

And now, as the sun sank on the seventh day, once more the great procession gathered to chant the woes of Isis and tell how the evil was avenged. We went in silence from the temple, and passed through the city ways. First came those who clear the path, then my father Amenemhat in all his priestly robes, and the wand of cedar in his hand. Then, clad in pure linen, I, the neophyte, followed alone; and after me the white-robed priests, holding aloft banners and emblems of the Gods. Next came those who bear the sacred boat, and after them the singers and the mourners; while, stretching far as the eye could reach, all the people marched, clad in melancholy black because Osiris was no more. We went in silence through the city streets till at length we came to the wall of the temple and passed in. And as my father, the High Priest, entered beneath the gateway of the outer pylon, a sweet-voiced woman singer began to sing the Holy Chant, and thus she sang:

> *'Sing we Osiris dead,*
> *Lament the fallen head:*
> *The light has left the world, the world is grey.*
> *Athwart the starry skies*
> *The web of Darkness flies,*
> *And Isis weeps Osiris passed away.*
> *Your tears, ye stars, ye fires, ye rivers, shed,*
> *Weep, children of the Nile, weep for your Lord is dead!'*

She paused in her most sweet song, and the whole multitude took up the melancholy dirge:

> *'Softly we tread, our measured footsteps falling*
> *Within the Sanctuary Sevenfold;*
> *Soft on the Dead that liveth are we calling:*
> *" Return, Osiris, from thy Kingdom cold!*
> *Return to them that worship thee of old."'*

The chorus ceased, and once again she sang:

> *' Within the court divine*
> *The Sevenfold sacred shrine*
> *We pass, while echoes of the Temple walls*
> *Repeat the long lament*
> *The sound of sorrow sent*
> *Far up within the imperishable halls,*
> *Where, each in other's arms, the Sisters weep,*
> *Isis and Nephthys, o'er His unawaking sleep.'*

And then again rolled forth the solemn chorus of a thousand voices:

> *' Softly we tread, our measured footsteps falling*
> *Within the Sanctuary Sevenfold;*
> *Soft on the Dead that liveth are we calling:*
> *" Return, Osiris, from thy Kingdom cold !*
> *Return to them that worship thee of old." '*

It ceased, and sweetly she took up the song ·

> *' O dweller in the West,*
> *Lover and Lordliest,*
> *Thy love, thy Sister Isis, calls thee home !*
> *Come from thy chamber dun*
> *Thou Master of the Sun,*
> *Thy shadowy chamber far below the foam !*
> *With weary wings and spent*
> *Through all the firmament,*
> *Through all the horror-haunted ways of Hell,*
> *I seek thee near and far,*
> *From star to wandering star,*
> *Free with the dead that in Amenti dwell.*
> *I search the height, the deep, the lands, the skies,*
> *Rise from the dead and live, our Lord Osiris, rise !'*

> *' Softly we tread, our measured footsteps falling*
> *Within the Sanctuary Sevenfold;*
> *Soft on the Dead that liveth are we calling:*
> *" Return, Osiris, from thy Kingdom cold !*
> *Return to them that worship thee of old." '*

Now in a strain more high and glad the singer sang:

> *' He wakes—from forth the prison*
>> *We sing Osiris risen,*
> *We sing the child that Nout conceived and bare.*
>> *Thine own love, Isis, waits*
>> *The Warden of the Gates,*
> *She breathes the breath of Life on breast and hair,*
>> *And in her breast and breath*
>> *Behold! he wakeneth,*
> *Behold! at length he riseth out of rest;*
>> *Touched with her holy hands,*
>> *The Lord of all the Lands,*
> *He stirs, he rises from her breath, her breast!*
>> *But thou, fell Typhon, fly,*
>> *The judgment day drawn nigh,*
> *Fleet on thy track as flame speeds Horus from the sky.'*

> *' Softly we tread, our measured footsteps falling*
>> *Within the Sanctuary Sevenfold;*
> *Soft on the Dead that liveth are we calling :*
>> *" Return, Osiris, from thy Kingdom cold!*
>> *Return to them that worship thee of old."*

Once more, as we bowed before the Holy, she sang, and sent the full breath of her glad music ringing up the everlasting walls till the silence quivered with her round notes of melody, and the hearts of those who hearkened stirred strangely in the breast. And thus, as we walked, she sang the song of Osiris risen, the song of Hope, the song of Victory :

> *' Sing we the Trinity,*
>> *Sing we the Holy Three,*
> *Sing we, and praise we and worship the Throne,*
>> *Throne that our Lord hath set—*
>> *There peace and truth are met*
> *There in the Halls of the Holy alone!*
>> *There in the shadowings*
>> *Faint of the folded wings,*

> *There shall we dwell and rejoice in our rest,*
> *We that thy servants are !*
> *Horus drive ill afar !*
> *Far in the folds of the dark of the West ! '*

Again, as her notes died away, thundered forth the chorus of all the voices :

> *' Softly we tread, our measured footsteps falling*
> *Within the Sanctuary Sevenfold ;*
> *Soft on the Dead that liveth are we calling :*
> *" Return, Osiris, from thy Kingdom cold !*
> *Return to them that worship thee of old." '*

The chanting ceased, and as the sun sank the High Priest raised the statue of the living God and held it before the multitude that was now gathered in the court of the temple. Then, with a mighty and joyful shout of :

> *' Osiris our hope ! Osiris ! Osiris ! '*

the people tore their black wrappings from their dress, revealing the white robes they wore beneath, and, as one man, they bowed before the God, and the feast was ended.

But for me the ceremony was only begun, for to-night was the night of my initiation. Leaving the inner court I bathed myself, and, clad in pure linen, passed, as it is ordained, into an inner, but not the inmost, sanctuary, and laid the accustomed offerings on the altar. Then, lifting up my hands to heaven, I remained for many hours in contemplation, striving, by holy thoughts and prayer, to gather up my strength against the mighty moment of my trial.

The hours sped slowly in the silence of the temple, till at length the door opened and my father Amenemhat, the High Priest, came in, clad in white, and leading by the hand the Priest of Isis. For, having been married, he did not himself enter into the mysteries of the Holy Mother.

I rose to my feet and stood humbly before them.

'Art thou ready ? ' said the priest, lifting the lamp he held so that its light fell upon my face. 'O thou chosen one, art thou ready to see the glory of the Goddess face to face ? '

' I am ready,' I answered.

'Bethink thee.' he said again, in solemn tones, ' it is no small thing. If thou wilt carry out this thy last desire, understand, royal Harmachis, that now this very night thou must for a while die in the flesh, what time thy soul shall look on spiritual things. And if thou diest and any evil shall be found within thy heart, when thou comest at last into that awful presence, woe unto thee, Harmachis, for the breath of life shall no more enter in at the gateway of thy mouth, thy body shall utterly perish, and what shall befall thy other parts, if I know. I may not say.[1] Art thou, therefore, pure and free from the thought of sin ? Art thou prepared to be taken to the breast of Her who Was and Is and Shall Be, and in all things to do Her holy will ; for Her, while she shall so command, to put away the thought of earthly woman ; and to labour always for Her glory till at the end thy life is gathered to Her eternal life ? '

' I am.' I answered ; ' lead on.'

' It is well,' said the priest. ' Noble Amenemhat, we go hence alone.'

' Farewell, my son,' said my father ; ' be firm and triumph over things spiritual as thou shalt triumph over things earthly. He who would truly rule the world must first be lifted up above the world. He must be at one with God, for thus only shall he learn the secrets of the Divine. But beware ! The Gods demand much of those who dare to enter the circle of their

---

[1] According to the Egyptian religion the being Man is composed of four parts : the body, the double or astral shape (*ka*), the soul (*bi*), and the spark of life sprung from the Godhead (*khou*).—ED.

Divinity. If they go back therefrom, they shall be judged of a sharper law, and scourged with a heavier rod, for as their glory is, so shall their shame be. Therefore, make thy heart strong, royal Harmachis! And when thou speedest down the ways of Night and enterest the Holies, remember that from him to whom great gifts have been given shall gifts be required again. And now—if, indeed, thy mind be fixed—go whither it is not as yet given me to follow thee. Farewell!'

For a moment as my heart weighed these heavy words, I wavered, as well I might. But I was filled with longing to be gathered to the company of the Divine ones, and I knew that I had no evil in me, and desired to do only the thing that is just. Therefore, having with so much labour drawn the bow-string to my ear, I was fain to let fly the shaft. 'Lead on,' I cried with a loud voice; 'lead on, thou holy Priest! I follow thee!'

And we went forth.

CHAPTER VI.

OF THE INITIATION OF HARMACHIS; OF HIS VISIONS; OF HIS
PASSING TO THE CITY THAT IS IN THE PLACE OF DEATH;
AND OF THE DECLARATIONS OF ISIS, THE MESSENGER.

silence we passed into the Shrine of
Isis. It was dark and bare—only
the feeble light from the lamp
gleamed faintly upon the sculptured walls, where, in a hundred
effigies, the Holy Mother suckled the
Holy Child.

The priest closed the doors and bolted
them. 'Once again,' he said, 'art thou
ready, Harmachis?'

'Once again,' I answered, 'I am
ready.'

He spoke no more; but, having lifted up his hands in
prayer, led me to the centre of the Holy, and with a swift
motion put out the lamp.

'Look before thee, Harmachis!' he cried; and his voice
sounded hollow in the solemn place.

I gazed and saw nothing. But from the niche that is high
in the wall, where is hid that sacred symbol of the Goddess
on which few may look, there came a sound as of the rattling
rods of the sistrum.[1] And as I listened, awestruck, behold!

---

[1] A musical instrument peculiarly sacred to Isis of which the shape
and rods had a mystic significance.—ED.

I saw the outline of the symbol drawn as with fire upon the blackness of the air. It hung above my head, and rattled while it hung. And, as it turned, I clearly saw the face of the Mother Isis that is graven on the one side, and signifies unending Birth, and the face of her holy sister, Nephthys, that is graven on the other, and signifies the ending of all birth in Death.

Slowly it turned and swung as though some mystic dancer trod the air above me, and shook it in her hand. But at length the light went out, and the rattling ceased.

Then of a sudden the end of the chamber became luminous, and in that white light I beheld picture after picture. I saw the ancient Nile rolling through deserts to the sea. There were no men upon its banks, nor any signs of man, nor any temples to the Gods. Only wild birds moved on Sihor's lonely face, and monstrous brutes plunged and wallowed in his waters. The sun sank in majesty behind the Libyan Desert and stained the waters red; the mountains towered up towards the silent sky; but in mountain, desert, and river there was no sign of human life. Then I knew that I saw the world as it had been before man was, and a terror of its loneliness entered my soul.

The picture passed and another rose up in its place. Once again I saw the banks of Sihor, and on them crowded wild-faced creatures, partaking of the nature of the ape more than of the nature of mankind. They fought and slew each other. The wild birds sprang up in affright as the fire leapt from reed huts given by foemen's hands to flame and pillage. They stole and rent and murdered, dashing out the brains of children with axes of stone. And, though no voice told me, I knew that I saw man as he was tens of thousands of years ago, when first he marched across the earth.

Yet another picture. Again I beheld the banks of Sihor;

but on them fair cities bloomed like flowers. In and out
their gates went men and women, passing to and fro from
wide, well-tilled lands. But I saw no guards or armies, and
no weapons of war. All was wisdom, prosperity, and peace.
And while I wondered, a glorious Figure, clad in raiment that
shone as flame, came from the gates of a shrine, and the
sound of music went before and followed after him. He
mounted an ivory throne which was set in a market-place
facing the water : and as the sun sank called all the multitudes to prayer. With one voice they prayed, bending in
adoration. And I understood that herein was shown the
reign of the Gods on earth, which was long before the days
of Menes.

A change came over the dream. Still the same fair city,
but other men—men with greed and evil on their faces—
who hated the bonds of righteous doing, and set their hearts
on sin. The evening came ; the glorious Figure mounted the
throne and called to prayer, but none bowed themselves in
adoration.

' We are aweary of thee ! ' they cried. ' Make Evil King!
Slay him! slay him! and loose the bonds of Evil ! Make
Evil King ! '

The glorious Shape rose up, gazing with mild eyes upon
those wicked men.

' Ye know not what ye ask,' he cried ; ' but as ye will, so
be it ! For if I die, by me, after much travail, shall ye once
again find a path to the Kingdom of Good ! '

Even as he spoke, a Form, foul and hideous to behold,
leapt upon him, cursing, slew him, tore him limb from limb,
and amidst the clamour of the people sat himself upon the
throne and ruled. But a Shape whose face was veiled passed
down from heaven on shadowy wings, and with lamentations
gathered up the rent fragments of the Being. A moment she

bent herself upon them, then lifted up her hands and wept. And as she wept, behold! from her side there sprang a warrior armed and with a face like the face of Ra at noon. He, the Avenger, hurled himself with a shout upon the Monster who had usurped the throne, and they closed in battle, and, struggling ever in a strait embrace, passed upward to the skies.

Then came picture after picture. I saw Powers and Peoples clad in various robes and speaking many tongues. I saw them pass and pass in millions—loving, hating, struggling, dying. Some few were happy and some had woe stamped upon their faces; but most bore not the seal of happiness nor of woe, but rather that of patience. And ever as they passed from age to age, high above in the heavens the Avenger fought on with the Evil Thing, while the scale of victory swung now here now there. But neither conquered, nor was it given to me to know how the battle ended.

And I understood that what I had beheld was the holy vision of the struggle between the Good and the Evil Powers. I saw that man was created vile, but Those who are above took pity on him, and came down to him to make him good and happy, for the two things are one thing. But man returned to his wicked way, and then the bright Spirit of Good, who is of us called Osiris, but who has many names, offered himself up for the evil-doing of the race that had dethroned him. And from him and the Divine Mother, of whom all nature is, sprang another spirit who is the Protector of us on earth, as Osiris is our justifier in Amenti.

For this is the mystery of the Osiris.

Of a sudden, as I saw the visions, these things became clear to me. The mummy cloths of symbol and of ceremony that wrap Osiris round fell from him, and I understood the secret of religion, which is Sacrifice.

The pictures passed, and again the priest, my guide, spoke
to me.

' Hast thou understood. Harmachis, those things which it
has been granted thee to see ? '

' I have,' I said.   ' Are the rites ended ? '

' Nay, they are but begun.   That which follows thou must
endure alone !   Behold I leave thee, to return at the morning
light.   Once more I warn thee.   That which thou shalt see,
few may look upon and live.   In all my days I have known
but three who dared to face this dread hour, and of those
three at dawn but one was found alive.   Myself, I have not
trod this path.   It is too high for me.'

' Depart,' I said ; ' my soul is athirst for knowledge.   I
will dare it.'

He laid his hand upon my head and blessed me.   He went.
I heard the door shut to behind him, the echoes of his footsteps slowly died away.

Then I felt that I was alone, alone in the Holy Place with
Things which are not of the earth.   Silence fell—silence deep
and black as the darkness which was around me.   The silence
fell, it gathered as the cloud gathered on the face of the moon
that night when, a lad, I prayed upon the pylon towers.   It
gathered denser and yet more dense till it seemed to creep
into my heart and call aloud therein ; for utter silence has a
voice that is more terrible than any cry.   I spoke ; the echoes
of my words came back upon me from the walls and seemed
to beat me down.   The stillness was lighter to endure than an
echo such as this.   What was I about to see ?   Should I die,
even now, in the fulness of my youth and strength ?   Terrible
were the warnings that had been given to me.   I was fear-
stricken, and bethought me that I would fly.   Fly !—fly
whither ?   The temple door was barred ; I could not fly.   I
was alone with the Godhead, alone with the Power that I had

invoked. Nay, my heart was pure—my heart was pure. I would face the terror that was to come, ay, even though I died.

'Isis, Holy Mother,' I prayed. 'Isis, Spouse of Heaven, come unto me, be with me now; I faint! be with me now.'

And then I knew that things were not as things had been. The air around me began to stir, it rustled as the wings of eagles rustle, it took life. Bright eyes gazed upon me, strange whispers shook my soul. Upon the darkness were bars of light. They changed and interchanged, they moved to and fro and wove mystic symbols which I could not read. Swifter and swifter flew that shuttle of the light : the symbols grouped, gathered, faded. gathered yet again, faster and still more fast, till my eyes could count them no more. Now I was afloat upon a sea of glory ; it surged and rolled, as the ocean rolls ; it tossed me high, it brought me low. Glory was piled on glory, splendour heaped on splendour's head, and I rode above it all !

Soon the lights began to pale in the rolling sea of air. Great shadows shot across it, lines of darkness pierced it and rushed together on its breast, till, at length, I only was a Shape of Flame set like a star on the bosom of immeasurable night. Bursts of awful music gathered from far away. Miles and miles away I heard them, thrilling faintly through the gloom. On they came, nearer and more near, louder and more loud, till they swept past, above, below, around me, swept on rushing pinions, terrifying and enchanting me. They floated by, ever growing fainter, till they died in space. Then others came, and no two were akin. Some rattled as ten thousand sistra shaken all to tune. Some rang from the brazen throats of unnumbered clarions. Some pealed with a loud, sweet chant of voices that were more than human ; and some rolled along in the slow thunder of a million drums.

They passed; their notes were lost in dying echoes; and the silence once more pressed in upon me and overcame me.

The strength within me began to fail. I felt my life ebbing at its springs. Death drew near to me and his shape was *Silence.* He entered at my heart, entered with a sense of numbing cold, but my brain was still alive, I could yet think. I knew that I was drawing near the confines of the Dead. Nay, I was dying fast, and oh, the horror of it! I strove to pray and could not; there was no more time for prayer. One struggle and the stillness crept into my brain. The terror passed; an unfathomable weight of sleep pressed me down. I was dying, I was dying, and then—nothingness!

I was dead!

A change—life came back to me, but between the new life and the life that had been was a gulf and difference. Once again I stood in the darkness of fhe shrine, but it blinded me no more. It was clear as the light of day, although it still was black. I stood; and yet it was not I who stood, but rather my spiritual part, for at my feet lay my dead Self. There it lay, rigid and still, a stamp of awful calm sealed upon its face, while I gazed on it.

And as I gazed, filled with wonder, I was caught up on the Wings of Flame and whirled away! away! faster than the lightnings flash. Down I fell, through depths of empty space set here and there with glittering crowns of stars. Down for ten million miles and ten times ten million, till at length I hovered over a place of soft unchanging light, wherein were Temples, Palaces, and Abodes, such as no man ever saw in the visions of his sleep. They were built of Flame, and they were built of Blackness. Their spires pierced up and up; their great courts stretched around. Even as I hovered they changed continually to the eye; what was Flame became Blackness, what was Blackness became Flame. Here was the flash of crystal, and there the blaze of gems shone even through the glory that rolls around the city which is in the Place of Death. There were trees, and their voice as they rustled was the voice of music; there was air, and, as it blew, its breath was the sobbing notes of song.

Shapes, changing, mysterious, wonderful, rushed up to meet me, and bore me down till I seemed to stand upon another earth.

'Who comes?' cried a great Voice.

'Harmachis,' answered the Shapes, that changed continually. 'Harmachis who hath been summoned from the earth to look upon the face of Her that Was and Is and Shall Be. Harmachis, Child of Earth!'

'Throw back the Gates and open wide the Doors!' pealed the awful Voice. 'Throw back the Gates and open wide the Doors; seal up his lips in silence, lest his voice jar upon the harmonies of Heaven, take away his sight lest he see that which may not be seen, and let Harmachis, who hath been summoned, pass down the path that leads to the place of the Unchanging. Pass on, Child of Earth; but before thou goest look up that thou mayest learn how far thou art removed from Earth.'

I looked up. Beyond the glory that shone about the city was black night, and high on its bosom twinkled one tiny star.

'Behold the world that thou has left,' said the Voice, 'behold and tremble.'

Then my lips and eyes were touched and sealed with silence and with darkness, so that I was dumb and blind. The Gates rolled back, the Doors swung wide, and I was swept into the city that is in the Place of Death. I was swept swiftly I know not whither, till at length I stood upon my feet. Again the great Voice pealed:

'Draw the veil of blackness from his eyes, unseal the

silence on his lips, that Harmachis, Child of Earth, may see, hear, and understand, and make adoration at the Shrine of Her that Was and Is and Shall Be.'

And my lips and eyes were touched once more, so that my sight and speech came back.

Behold ! I stood within a hall of blackest marble, so lofty that even in the rosy light scarce could my vision reach the great groins of the roof. Music wailed about its spaces, and all adown its length stood winged Spirits fashioned in living fire, and such was the brightness of their forms that I could not look on them. In its centre was an altar, small and square, and I stood before the empty altar. Then again the Voice cried :

' O Thou that hast been, art, and shalt be; Thou who, having many names, art yet without a name; Measurer of Time ; Messenger of God , Guardian of the Worlds and the Races that dwell thereon ; Universal Mother born of Nothingness ; Creatrix uncreated ; Living Splendour without Form, Living Form without Substance ; Servant of the Invisible ; Child of Law ; Holder of the Scales and Sword of Fate ; Vessel of Life, through whom all Life flows, to whom it again is gathered ; Recorder of Things Done ; Executrix of Decrees —*Hear !*

' Harmachis the Egyptian, who by Thy will hath been summoned from the earth, waits before Thine Altar, with ears unstopped, with eyes unsealed, and with an open heart. Hear and descend ! Descend, O Many-shaped ! Descend in Flame! Descend in Sound ! Descend in Spirit ! Hear and descend ! '

The Voice ceased and there was silence. Then through the silence came a sound like the booming of the sea. It passed and presently, moved thereto by I know not what, I raised my eyes from between my hands with which I had covered them, and saw a small dark cloud hanging over the Altar in and out of which a fiery Serpent climbed.

Then all the Spirits clad in light fell upon the marble floor, and with a loud voice adored; but what they said I could not understand. Behold! the dark cloud came down and rested on the Altar, the Serpent of fire stretched itself towards me, touched me on the forehead with its forky tongue and was gone. From within the cloud a Voice sweet and low and clear spoke in heavenly accents:

'Depart, ye Ministers, leave Me with my son whom I have summoned.'

Then like arrows rushing from a bow the flame-clad Spirits leapt from the ground and sped away.

'O Harmachis,' said the Voice, 'be not afraid, I am She whom thou dost know as Isis of the Egyptians; but what else I am strive not thou to learn, it is beyond thy strength. For I am all things. Life is my spirit, and Nature is my raiment. I am the laughter of the babe, I am the maiden's love, I am the mother's kiss. I am the Child and Servant of the Invisible that is God, that is Law, that is Fate—though myself I be not God and Fate and Law. When winds blow and oceans roar upon the face of Earth thou hearest my voice; when thou gazest on the starry firmament thou seest my countenance; when the spring blooms out in flowers, that is my smile, Harmachis. For I am Nature's self, and all her shapes are shapes of Me. I breathe in all that breathes. I wax and wane in the changeful moon: I grow and gather in the tides: I rise with the suns: I flash with the lightning and thunder in the storms. Nothing is too great for the measure of my majesty, nothing is so small that I cannot find a home therein. I am in thee and thou art in Me, O Harmachis. That which bade thee be bade Me also be. There- fore, though I am great and thou art little, have no fear.

For we are bound together by the common bond of life—that life which flows through suns and stars and spaces, through Spirits and the souls of men, welding all Nature to a whole that, changing ever, is yet eternally the same.'

I bowed my head—I could not speak, for I was afraid.

'Faithfully hast thou served Me, O my son,' went on the low sweet Voice; 'greatly thou hast longed to be brought face to face with Me here in Amenti; and greatly hast thou dared to accomplish thy desire. For it is no small thing to cast off the tabernacle of the Flesh and before the appointed time, if only for an hour, put on the raiment of the Spirit. And greatly, O my servant and my son, have I, too, desired to look on thee here where I am. For the Gods love those who love them, but with a wider and a deeper love, and under One who is as far from Me as I am from thee, mortal, I am a God of Gods. Therefore I have caused thee to be brought hither, Harmachis; and therefore I speak to thee, my son, and bid thee commune with Me now face to face, as thou didst commune that night upon the temple towers of Abouthis. For I was there with thee, Harmachis, as I was in ten thousand other worlds. It was I, O Harmachis, who laid the lotus in thy hand, giving thee the sign which thou didst seek. For thou art of the kingly blood of my children who served Me from age to age. And if thou dost not fail thou shalt sit upon that kingly throne and restore my ancient worship in its purity, and sweep my temples from their defilements. But if thou dost fail, then shall the eternal Spirit Isis become but a memory in Egypt:

The Voice paused; and, gathering up my strength, at length I spoke aloud:

'Tell me, O Holy,' I said, 'shall I then fail?'

'Ask Me not,' answered the Voice, 'that which it is not lawful that I should answer thee. Perchance I can read that

G

which shall befall thee, perchance it doth not please Me so to read. What can it profit the Divine, that hath all time wherein to await the issues, to be eager to look upon the blossom that is not blown, but which, lying a seed in the bosom of the earth, shall blow in its season? Know, Harmachis, that I do not shape the Future; the Future is to thee and not to Me; for it is born of Law and of the rule ordained of the Invisible. Yet thou art free to act therein, and thou shalt win or thou shalt fail according to thy strength and the measure of thy heart's purity. Thine be the burden, Harmachis, as thine in the event shall be the glory or the shame. Little do I reck of the issue, I who am but the Minister of what is written. Now hear me: I will always be with thee, my son, for my love once given can never be taken away, though by sin it may seem lost to thee. Remember then this: if thou dost triumph, thy guerdon shall be great; if thou dost fail, heavy indeed shall be thy punishment both in the flesh and in the land that thou callest Amenti. Yet this for thy comfort: shame and agony shall not be eternal. For however deep the fall from righteousness, if but repentance holds the heart, there is a path—a stony and a cruel path—whereby the height may be climbed again. Let it not be thy lot to follow it, Harmachis!

'And now, because thou hast loved Me, my son, and, wandering through the maze of fable, wherein men lose themselves upon the earth, mistaking the substance for the Spirit, and the Altar for the God, hast yet grasped a clue of Truth the Many-faced; and because I love thee and look on to the day that, perchance, shall come when thou shalt dwell blessed in my light and in the doing of my tasks: because of this, I say, it shall be given to thee, O Harmachis, to hear the Word whereby I may be summoned from the Uttermost, by one who hath communed with Me, and to look upon the face of Isis—even into the eyes of the Messenger, and not die the death.

'*Behold !*'

The sweet Voice ceased ; the dark cloud upon the altar changed and changed—it grew white, it shone, and seemed at length to take the shrouded shape of woman. Then the golden Snake crept from its heart once more, and, like a living diadem, twined itself about the cloudy brows.

Now suddenly a Voice called aloud the awful Word, then the vapours burst and melted, and with my eyes I saw that Glory, at the very thought of which my spirit faints. But what I saw it is not lawful to utter. For, though I have been bidden to write what I have written of this matter, perchance that a record may remain, thereon I have been warned —ay, even now, after these many years. I saw, and what I saw cannot be imagined ; for there are Glories and there are Shapes which are beyond the reach of man's imagination. I saw—then, with the echo of that Word, and the memory of that sight stamped for ever on my heart, my spirit failed me, and I sank down before the Glory.

And, as I fell, it seemed that the great hall burst open and crumbled into flakes of fire round me. Then a great wind blew : there was a sound as the sound of Worlds rushing down the flood of Time—and I knew no more !

CHAPTER VII.

OF THE AWAKING OF HARMACHIS; OF THE CEREMONY OF
HIS CROWNING AS PHARAOH OF THE UPPER AND THE
LOWER LAND; AND OF THE OFFERINGS MADE TO
PHARAOH.

again I woke — to find myself stretched at length upon the stone flooring of the Holy Place of Isis that is at Abouthis. By me stood the old Priest of the Mysteries, and in his hand was a lamp. He bent over me, and gazed earnestly upon my face.

'It is day—the day of thy new birth, and thou hast lived to see it, Harmachis!' he said at length. 'I give thanks. Arise, royal Harmachis—nay, tell me naught of that which has befallen thee. Arise, beloved of the Holy Mother. Come forth, thou who hast passed the fire and learned what lies behind the darkness—come forth, O newly-born!'

I rose and, walking faintly, went with him, and, passing out of the darkness of the Shrines filled with thought and wonder, came once more into the pure light of the morning. And then I went to my own chamber and slept; nor did any dreams come to trouble me. But no man—not even my father—asked me aught of what I saw upon that dread night, or after what fashion I had communed with the Goddess.

After these things which have been written, I applied myself for a space to the worship of the Mother Isis, and to the further study of the outward forms of those mysteries to which I now held the key. Moreover, I was instructed in matters politic, for many great men of our following came secretly to see me from all quarters of Egypt, and told me much of the hatred of the people towards Cleopatra, the Queen, and of other things. At last the hour drew nigh; it was three months and ten days from the night when, for a while, I left the flesh, and yet living with our life, was gathered to the breast of Isis, on which it was agreed that with due and customary rites, although in utter secrecy, I should be called to the throne of the Upper and the Lower Land. So it came about that, as the solemn time drew nigh, great men of the party of Egypt gathered to the number of thirty-seven from every nome, and each great city of their nome, meeting together at Abouthis. They came in every guise—some as priests, some as pilgrims to the Shrine, and some as beggars. Among them was my uncle, Sepa, who, though he clad himself as a travelling doctor, had much ado to keep his loud voice from betraying him. Indeed, I myself knew him by it, meeting him as I walked in thought upon the banks of the canal, although it was then dusk and the great cape, which, after the fashion of such doctors, he had thrown about his head, half hid his face.

'A pest on thee!' he cried, when I greeted him by his name. 'Cannot a man cease to be himself for a single hour? Didst thou but know the pains that it has cost me to learn to play this part—and now thou readest who I am even in the dark!'

And then, still talking in his loud voice, he told me how

he had travelled hither on foot, the better to escape the spies
who ply to and fro upon the river. But he said he should
return by the water, or take another guise; for since he had
come as a doctor he had been forced to play a doctor's part,
knowing but little of the arts of medicine ; and, as he greatly
feared, there were many between Annu and Abouthis who
had suffered from it.[1]   And he laughed loudly and embraced
me, forgetting his part.   For he was too whole at heart to be
an actor and other than himself, and would have entered
Abouthis with me holding my hand, had I not chid him for
his folly.

At length all were gathered.

It was night, and the gates of the temple were shut.
None were left within them, except the thirty-seven ; my
father, the High Priest Amenemhat ; that aged priest who
had led me to the Shrine of Isis ; the old wife, Atoua, who,
according to ancient custom, was to prepare me for the
anointing ; and some five other priests, sworn to secrecy by
that oath which none may break.   They gathered in the
second hall of the great temple ; but I remained alone, clad
in my white robe, in the passage where are the names of six-
and-seventy ancient Kings, who were before the day of the
divine Sethi.   There I rested in darkness, till at length my
father, Amenemhat, came, bearing a lamp, and, bowing low
before me, led me by the hand forth into the great hall.
Here and there, between its mighty pillars, lights were burning that dimly showed the sculptured images upon the walls,
and dimly fell upon the long line of the seven-and-thirty Lords,
Priests, and Princes, who, seated upon carven chairs, awaited
my coming in silence.   Before them, facing away from the
seven Sanctuaries, a throne was set, around which stood the

---

[1] In Ancient Egypt an unskilful or negligent physician was liable to
very heavy penalties.—ED.

priests holding the sacred images and banners. As I came into the dim and holy place, the Dignitaries rose, and bowed before me, speaking no word; while my father led me to the steps of the throne, and in a low voice bade me stand before it.

Then he spoke :

' Lords, Priests, and Princes of the ancient orders of the land of Khem—Nobles from the Upper and the Lower Country, here gathered in answer to my summons, hear me : I present to you, with such scant formality as the occasion can afford, the Prince Harmachis, by right and true descent of blood the descendant and heir of the ancient Pharaohs of our most unhappy land. He is priest of the inmost circle of the Mysteries of the Divine Isis, Master of the Mysteries— Hereditary Priest of the Pyramids which are by Memphis, Instructed in the Solemn Rites of the Holy Osiris. Is there any among you who has aught to urge against the true line of his blood ? '

He paused, and my uncle, Sepa, rising from his chair, spoke : ' We have made examination of the records and there is none, O Amenemhat. He is of the Royal blood, his descent is true.'

' Is there any among you,' went on my father, ' who can deny that this royal Harmachis, by sanction of the very Gods, has been gathered to Isis, been shown the way of the Osiris, been admitted to be the Hereditary High Priest of the Pyramids which are by Memphis, and of the Temples of the Pyramids ? '

Then that old priest rose who had been my guide in the Sanctuary of the Mother and made answer : ' There is none ; O Amenemhat ; I know these things of my own knowledge.'

Once more my father spoke : ' Is there any among you who has aught to urge against this royal Harmachis, in that by wickedness of heart or life, by uncleanliness or falsity, it is not fit or meet that we should crown him Lord of all the Lands ? '

Then an aged Prince of Memphis arose and made answer :

' We have inquired of these matters : there is none, O Amenemhat.'

' It is well,' said my father; ' then naught is wanting in the Prince Harmachis, seed of Nekt-nebf, the Osirian. Let the woman Atoua stand forth and tell this company those things that came to pass when, at the hour of her death, she who was my wife prophesied over this Prince, being filled with the Spirit of the Hathors.'

Thereon old Atoua crept forward from the shadow of the columns, and earnestly told those things that have been written.

' Ye have heard,' said my father : ' do ye believe that the woman who was my wife spake with the Divine voice ? '

' We do,' they answered.

Now my uncle Sepa rose and spoke :

' Royal Harmachis, thou hast heard. Know now that we are gathered here to crown thee King of the Upper and the Lower Lands—thy holy father, Amenemhat, renouncing all his right on thy behalf. We are met, not, indeed, in that pomp and ceremony which is due to the occasion—for what we do must be done in secret, lest our lives, and the cause that is more dear to us than life, should pay the forfeit—but yet with such dignity and observance of the ancient rites as our circumstance may command. Learn, now, how this matter hangs, and if, after learning, thy mind consents thereto, then mount thy throne, O Pharaoh—and swear the oath !

' Long has Khemi groaned beneath the mailed heel of the Greek, and trembled at the shadow of the Roman's spear ; long has the ancient worship of its Gods been desecrated, and its people crushed with oppression. But we believe that the hour of deliverance is at hand, and with the solemn voice of Egypt and by the ancient Gods of Egypt, to whose cause thou art of all men bound, we call upon thee, Prince, to be the sword of our deliverance. Hearken! Twenty thousand good and leal men are sworn to wait upon thy word, and at thy signal to rise as one, to put the Grecian to the sword, and with their blood and substance to build thee a throne set more surely on the soil of Khem than are its ancient pyramids—such a throne as shall even roll the Roman legions back. And for the signal, it shall be the death of that bold harlot, Cleopatra. Thou must compass her death, Harmachis, in such fashion as shall be shown to thee, and with her blood anoint the Royal throne of Egypt.

'Canst thou refuse, O our Hope? Doth not the holy love of country swell within thy heart? Canst thou dash the cup of Freedom from thy lips and bear to drink the bitter draught of slaves? The emprise is great; maybe it shall fail, and thou with thy life, as we with ours, shalt pay the price of our endeavour. But what of it, Harmachis? Is life, then, so sweet? Are we so softly cushioned on the stony bed of earth? Is bitterness and sorrow in its sum so small and scant a thing? Do we here breathe so divine an air that we should fear to face the passage of our breath? What have we here but hope and memory? What see we here but shadows? Shall we then fear to pass pure-handed where Fulfilment is and memory is lost in its own source, and shadows die in the light which cast them? O Harmachis, that man alone is truly blest who crowns his life with Fame's most splendid wreath. For, since to all the Brood of Earth Death hands his poppy-flowers, he indeed is happy to whom there is occasion given to weave them in a crown of glory. And how can a man die better than in a great endeavour to strike the gyves from his

Country's limbs so that she again may stana in the face of Heaven and raise the shrill shout of Freedom, and, clad once more in a panoply of strength, trample under foot the fetters of her servitude, defying the tyrant nations of the earth to set their seal upon her brow?

'Khem calls thee, Harmachis. Come then, thou Deliverer; leap like Horus from the firmament, break her chains, scatter her foes, and rule a Pharaoh on Pharaoh's Throne——'

'Enough, enough!' I cried, while the long murmur of applause swept about the columns and up the massy walls. 'Enough; is there any need to adjure me thus? Had I a hundred lives, would I not most gladly lay them down for Egypt?'

'Well said, well said!' answered Sepa. 'Now go forth with the woman yonder, that she may make thy hands clean before they touch the sacred emblems, and anoint thy brow before it is encircled of the diadem.'

And so I went into a chamber apart with the old wife, Atoua. There, muttering prayers, she poured pure water over my hands into a ewer of gold, and having dipped a fine cloth into oil wiped my brow with it.

'O happy Egypt!' she said; 'O happy Prince, that art come to rule in Egypt! O Royal youth!—too Royal to be a priest—so shall many a fair woman think; but, perchance, for thee they will relax the priestly rule, else how shall the race of Pharaoh be carried on? O happy I, who dandled thee and gave my flesh and blood to save thee! O royal and beautiful Harmachis, born for splendour, happiness, and love!'

'Cease, cease,' I said, for her talk jarred upon me; 'call me not happy till thou knowest my end, and speak not to me of love, for with love comes sorrow, and mine is another and a higher way.'

Ay, ay, so thou sayest—and joy, too, that comes with love! Never talk lightly of love, my King, for it brought thee here! *La! la!* but it is always the way—" The goose on the wing laughs at crocodiles," so goes their saying down at Alexandria; " but when the goose is asleep on the water, it is the crocodiles that laugh." Not but what women are pretty crocodiles. Men worship the crocodiles at Anthribis—Crocodilopolis they call it now, don't they ?—but they worship women all the world over! *La!* how my tongue runs on, and thou about to be crowned Pharaoh! Did I not prophesy it to thee? Well, thou art clean, Lord of the Double Crown. Go forth!'

So I went from the chamber with the old wife's foolish talk ringing in my ears, though of a truth her folly had ever a grain of wit in it.

As I came, the Dignitaries rose once more and bowed before me. Then my father, without delay, drew near me, and placed in my hands a golden image of the divine Ma, the Goddess of Truth, and golden images of the arks of the God Amen-Ra, of the divine Mout, and the divine Khons, and spoke solemnly :

'Thou swearest by the living majesty of Ma, by the majesty of Amen-Ra, of Mout, and of Khons?'

' I swear,' I said.

'Thou swearest by the holy land of Khem, by Sihor's flood, by the Temples of the Gods and the eternal Pyramids?'

'I swear.'

'Remembering thy hideous doom if thou shouldst fail therein, thou swearest that thou wilt in all things govern Egypt according to its ancient laws, that thou wilt preserve the worship of its Gods, that thou wilt do equal justice, that thou wilt not oppress, that thou wilt not betray, that thou wilt make no alliance with the Roman or the Greek, that thou wilt cast out the foreign Idols, that thou wilt devote thy life to the liberty of the land of Khem ? '

' I swear.'

' It is well. Mount, then, the throne, that in the presence of these thy subjects, I may name thee Pharaoh.'

I mounted upon the throne, of which the footstool is a Sphinx, and the canopy the overshadowing wings of Ma. Then Amenemhat drew nigh once again and placed the Pshent upon my brow, and on my head the Double Crown, and the Royal Robe about my shoulders, and in my hands the Sceptre and the Scourge.

' Royal Harmachis,' he cried, ' by these outward signs and tokens, I, the High Priest of the Temple of Ra-Men-Ma at Abouthis, crown thee Pharaoh of the Upper and Lower Land. Reign and prosper, O Hope of Khemi ! '

' Reign and prosper, Pharaoh ! ' echoed the Dignitaries, bowing down before me.

Then, one by one, they swore allegiance, till all had sworn. And, having sworn, my father took me by the hand ; he led me in solemn procession into each of the seven Sanctuaries that are in this Temple of Ra-Men-Ma, and in each I made offerings, swung incense, and officiated as priest. Clad in the Royal robes I made offerings in the Shrine of Horus, in the Shrine of Isis, in the Shrine of Osiris, in the Shrine of Amen-Ra, in the Shrine of Horemku, in the Shrine of Ptah, till at length I reached the Shrine of the King's Chamber.

Here they made their offering to me, as the Divine Pharaoh, and left me very weary—but a King.

[*Here the first and smallest of the papyrus rolls comes to an end.*]

BOOK II.

The Fall of Harmachis

CHAPTER I.

OF THE FAREWELL OF AMENEMHAT TO HARMACHIS; OF THE COMING OF HARMACHIS TO ALEXANDRIA; OF THE EXHORTATION OF SEPA; OF THE PASSING OF CLEOPATRA ROBED AS ISIS; AND OF THE OVERTHROW OF THE GLADIATOR BY HARMACHIS.

the long days of preparation had passed, and the time was at hand. I was initiated, and I was crowned; so that although the common folk knew me not, or knew me only as Priest of Isis, there were in Egypt thousands who at heart bowed down to me as Pharaoh. The hour was at hand, and my soul went forth to meet it. For I longed to overthrow the foreigner, to set Egypt free, to mount the throne that was my heritage, and cleanse the temples of my Gods. I was fain for the struggle, and I never doubted of its end. I looked into the mirror, and saw triumph written on my brows. The future stretched a path of glory from my feet—ay, glittering with glory like Sihor in the sun. I communed with my Mother Isis; I sat within my chamber and took counsel with my heart; I planned new temples; I revolved great laws that I would put forth for my people's weal;

B

and in my ears rang the shouts of exultation which should greet victorious Pharaoh on his throne.

But still I tarried a little while at Abouthis, and, having been commanded to do so, let my hair, that had been shorn, grow again long and black as the raven's wing, instructing myself meanwhile in all manly exercises and feats of arms. Also, for a purpose which shall be seen, I perfected myself in the magic art of the Egyptians, and in the reading of the stars, in which things, indeed, I already had great skill.

Now, this was the plan that had been built up. My uncle Sepa had, for a while, left the Temple of Annu, giving out that his health had failed him. Thence he had moved down to a house in Alexandria, to gather strength, as he said, from the breath of the sea, and also to learn for himself the wonders of the great Museum and the glory of Cleopatra's Court There it was planned that I should join him, for there, at Alexandria, the egg of the plot was hatching. Accordingly, when at last the summons came, all things being prepared, I made ready for the journey, and passed into my father's chamber to receive his blessing before I went. There sat the old man, as once before he sat when he had rebuked me because I went out to slay the lion, his long white beard resting on the table of stone and sacred writings in his hand. When I came in he rose from his seat and would have knelt before me, crying ' Hail, Pharaoh ! ' but I caught him by the hand.

' It is not meet, my father,' I said.

' It is meet,' he answered, ' it is meet that I should bow before my King ; but be it as thou wilt. And so thou goest, Harmachis ; my blessing go with thee, O my son ! And may Those whom I serve grant to me that my old eyes may, indeed, behold thee on the throne ! I have searched long, striving, Harmachis, to read the future that shall be ; but I can learn naught by all my wisdom. It is hid

from me, and at times my heart fails. But hear this,
there is danger in thy path, and it comes in the form of
Woman. I have known it long, and therefore thou hast been
called to the worship of the heavenly Isis, who bids her
votaries put away the thought of woman till such time as
she shall think well to slacken the rule. Oh, my son, I
would that thou wert not so strong and fair—stronger and
fairer, indeed, than any man in Egypt, as a King should be
—for in that strength and beauty may lie a cause of stumbling. Beware, then, of those witches of Alexandria, lest, like
a worm, some one of them creep into thy heart and eat its
secret out.'

'Have no fear, my father,' I answered, frowning, 'my
thought is set on other things than red lips and smiling eyes.'

'It is good,' he answered; 'so may it befall. And now
farewell. When next we meet, may it be in that happy hour
when, with all the priests of the Upper Land, I move down
from Abouthis to do my homage to Pharaoh on his throne.'

So I embraced him, and went. Alas! I little thought
how we should meet again.

Thus it came about that once more I passed down the
Nile travelling as a man of no estate. And to such as were
curious about me it was given out that I was the adopted
son of the High Priest of Abouthis, having been brought up
to the priesthood, and that I had at the last refused the service of the Gods, and chosen to go to Alexandria, to seek my
fortune. For, be it remembered, I was still held to be the
grandson of the old wife, Atoua, by all those who did not
know the truth.

On the tenth night, sailing with the wind, we reached the
mighty city of Alexandria, the city of a thousand lights.
Above them all towered the white Pharos, that wonder of the

world, from the crown of which a light like the light of the
sun blazed out across the waters of the harbour to guide
mariners on their way across the sea.   The vessel having
been cautiously made fast to the quay, for it was night, I
disembarked and stood wondering at the vast mass of houses,
and confused by the clamour of many tongues.   For here all
peoples seemed to be gathered together, each speaking after
the fashion of his own land.   And as I stood a young man
came and touched me on the shoulder, asking me if I was
from Abouthis and named Harmachis.   I said 'Yea.'   Then,
bending over me, he whispered the secret pass-word into my
ear, and, beckoning to two slaves, bade them bring my baggage
from the ship.   This they did, fighting their way through the
crowd of porters who were clamouring for hire.   Then I followed him down the quay, which was bordered with drinking-
places, where all sorts of men were gathered, tippling wine
and watching the dancing of women, some of whom were but
scantily arrayed, and some not arrayed at all.

And so we went through the lamp-lit houses till at last we
reached the shore of the great harbour, and turned to the right
along a wide way paved with granite and bordered by strong
houses, having cloisters in front of them, the like of which I
had never seen.   Turning once more to the right we came to a
quieter portion of the city, where, except for parties of strolling
revellers, the streets were still.   Presently my guide halted at a
house built of white stone.   We passed in, and, crossing a small
courtyard, entered a chamber where there was a light.   And
here, at last, I found my uncle Sepa, most glad to see me safe.

When I had washed and eaten, he told me that all things
went well, and that as yet there was no thought of evil at the
Court.   Further, he said, it having come to the ears of the
Queen that the Priest of Annu was sojourning at Alexandria,
she sent for him and closely questioned him—not as to any

plot, for of that she never thought, but as to the rumour which had reached her, that there was treasure hid in the Great Pyramid which is by Annu. For, being ever wasteful, she was ever in want of money, and had bethought her of opening the Pyramid. But he laughed at her, telling her the Pyramid was the burying-place of the divine Khufu, and that he knew nothing of its secrets. Then she was angered, and swore that so surely as she ruled in Egypt she would tear it down, stone by stone, and discover the secret at its heart. Again he laughed, and, in the words of the proverb which they have here at Alexandria, told her that ' Mountains live longer than Kings.' Thereon she smiled at his ready answer, and let him go. Also my uncle Sepa told me that on the morrow I should see this Cleopatra. For it was her birthday (as, indeed, it was also mine), and, dressed in the robes of the Holy Isis, she would pass in state from her palace on the Lochias to the Serapeum to offer a sacrifice at the Shrine of the false God who sits in the Temple. And he said that thereafter the fashion by which I should gain entrance to the household of the Queen should be contrived.

Then, being very weary, I went to rest, but could sleep little for the strangeness of the place, the noises in the streets, and the thought of the morrow. While it was yet dark, I rose, climbed the stair to the roof of the house, and waited. Presently, the sun's rays shot out like arrows, and lit upon the white wonder of the marble Pharos, whose light instantly sank and died, as though, indeed, the sun had killed it. Now the rays fell upon the palaces of the Lochias where Cleopatra lay, and lit them up till they flamed like a jewel set on the dark, cool bosom of the sea. Away the light flew, kissing the Soma's sacred dome, beneath which Alexander sleeps, touching the high tops of a thousand palaces and temples; past the porticoes of the great museum that loomed near at hand, striking the lofty Shrine, where, carved of ivory, is the image of the false God Serapis, and at last seeming to lose itself in the vast and gloomy Necropolis. Then, as the dawn gathered into day, the flood of brightness, overbrimming the bowl of night, flowed into the lower lands and streets, and showed Alexandria red in the sunrise as the mantle of a king, and shaped as a mantle. The Etesian wind came up from the north, and swept away the vapour from the harbours, so that I saw their blue waters rocking a thousand ships. I saw, too, that mighty mole the Heptastadium; I saw the hundreds of streets, the countless houses, the innumerable wealth and splendour of Alexandria set like a queen between lake Mareotis and the ocean, and dominating both, and I was filled with wonder. This, then, was one city in my heritage of lands and cities! Well, it was worth the grasping. And having looked my full and fed my heart, as it were, with the sight of splendour, I communed with the Holy Isis and came down from the roof.

In the chamber beneath was my uncle Sepa. I told him that I had been watching the sun rise over the city of Alexandria.

'So!' he said, looking at me from beneath his shaggy eyebrows; 'and what thinkest thou of Alexandria?'

'I think it is like some city of the Gods,' I answered.

'Ay!' he replied fiercely, 'a city of the infernal Gods—a sink of corruption, a bubbling well of iniquity, a home of false faith springing from false hearts. I would that not one stone of it was left upon another stone, and that its wealth lay deep beneath yonder waters! I would that the gulls were screaming across its site, and that the wind, untainted by a Grecian breath, swept through its ruins from the ocean to Mareotis! O royal Harmachis, let not the luxury and beauty of Alexandria poison thy sense; for in their deadly air, Faith perishes, and Religion cannot spread her heavenly wings. When the hour comes for thee to rule, Harmachis, cast down this accursed city and, as thy fathers did, set up thy throne in the white walls of Memphis. For I tell thee that, for Egypt, Alexandria is but a splendid gate of ruin, and, while it endures, all nations of the earth shall march through it, to the plunder of the land, and all false Faiths shall nestle in it and breed the overthrow of Egypt's Gods.'

I made no answer, for there was truth in his words. And yet to me the city seemed very fair to look on. After we had eaten, my uncle told me it was now time to set out to view the march of Cleopatra, as she went in triumph to the Shrine of Serapis. For although she would not pass till within two hours of the midday, yet these people of Alexandria have so great a love of shows and idling that had we not presently set forth, by no means could we have come through the press of the multitudes who were already gathering along the highways where the Queen must ride. So we went out to take our place upon a stand, built of timber, that had been set up at the side of the great road which pierces through the city, to the Canopic Gate. For my uncle had already purchased a right to enter there, and that dearly.

We won our way with much struggle through the great crowds that were already gathered in the streets till we reached the scaffolding of timber, which was roofed in with an awning and gaily hung with scarlet cloths. Here we seated ourselves upon a bench and waited for some hours, watching the multitude press past shouting, singing, and talking loudly in many tongues. At length soldiers came to clear the road, clad, after the Roman fashion, in breast-plates of chain-armour. After them marched heralds enjoining silence (at which the populace sung and shouted all the more loudly), and crying that Cleopatra, the Queen, was coming. Then followed a thousand Cilician skirmishers, a thousand Thracians, a thousand Macedonians, and a thousand Gauls, each armed after the fashion of their country. Then passed five hundred men of those who are called the Fenced Horsemen, for both men and horses were altogether covered with mail. Next came youths and maidens sumptuously draped and wearing golden crowns, and with them images symbolising Day and Night, Morning and Noon, the Heavens and the Earth. After these walked many fair women, pouring perfumes on the road, and others scattering blooming flowers. Now there rose a great shout of ' Cleopatra ! Cleopatra ! ' and I held my breath and bent forward to see her who dared to put on the robes of Isis.

But at that moment the multitude so gathered and thickened in front of where I was that I could no longer clearly see. So in my eagerness I leapt over the barrier of the scaffolding, and, being very strong, pushed my way through the crowd till I reached the foremost rank. And as I did so, Nubian slaves armed with thick staves and crowned with ivy-leaves ran up, striking the people. One man I noted more especially, for he was a giant, and, being strong, was insolent beyond measure, smiting the people without cause, as, indeed, is the wont of low persons set in authority. For a woman stood near to me, an Egyptian by her face, bearing a child in her arms, whom the man, seeing that she was weak, struck on the head with his rod so that she fell prone, and the people murmured. But at the sight my blood rushed of a sudden through my veins and drowned my reason. I held in my hand a staff of olive-wood from Cyprus, and as the black brute laughed at the sight of the stricken woman and her babe rolling on the ground, I swung the staff aloft and smote. So shrewdly did I strike, that the tough rod split upon the giant's shoulders and the blood spurted forth, staining his trailing leaves of ivy.

Then, with a shriek of pain and fury—for those who smite love not that they be smitten—he turned and sprang at me! And all the people round gave back, save only the woman who could not rise, leaving us two in a ring as it were. On he came with a rush, and, as he came, being now mad, I smote him with my clenched fist between the eyes, having nothing else with which to smite, and he staggered like an ox beneath the first blow of the priest's axe. Then the people shouted, for they love to see a fight, and the man was known to them as a gladiator victorious in the games. Gathering up his strength, the knave came on with an oath, and, whirling his heavy staff on high, struck at me in such a fashion that, had I not avoided the blow by nimbleness, I had surely been slain. But, as it chanced, the staff hit upon the ground, and so heavily that it flew in fragments. Thereon the multitude shouted again, and the great man, blind with fury, rushed at me to smite me down. But with a cry I sprang straight at his throat—for he was so heavy a man that I knew I could not hope to throw him by strength—ay, and gripped it. There I clung, though his fists battered me like bludgeons, driving my thumbs into his throat. Round and round we turned, till at length he flung himself to the earth, trusting thus to shake me off. But I held on fast as we rolled over and over on the ground, till at last he grew faint for want of breath. Then I, being uppermost, drove my knee down upon his chest, and, as I believe, should thus have slain him in my rage had not my uncle, and others there gathered, fallen upon me and dragged me from him.

And meanwhile, though I knew it not, the chariot in which the Queen sat, with elephants going before and lions led after it, had reached the spot, and had been halted because of the tumult. I looked up, and thus torn, panting, my white garments stained with the blood that had rushed from the mouth and nostrils of the mighty Nubian, I for the first time saw Cleopatra face to face. Her chariot was all of gold, and drawn by milk-white steeds. She sat in it with two fair girls, clad in Greek attire, standing one on either side, fanning her with glittering fans. On her head was the covering of Isis, the golden horns between which rested the moon's round disk and the emblem of Osiris' throne, with the uræus twined around. Beneath this covering was the vulture cap of gold, the blue enamelled wings and the vulture head with gemmy eyes, under which her long dark tresses flowed towards her feet. About her rounded neck was a broad collar of gold studded with emeralds and coral. Round her arms and wrists were bracelets of gold studded with emeralds and coral, and in one hand she held the holy cross of Life fashioned of crystal, and in the other the golden rod of royalty. Her breast was bare, but under it was a garment that glistened like the scaly covering of a snake, everywhere sewn with gems. Beneath this robe was a skirt of golden cloth, half hidden by a scarf of the broidered silk of Cos, falling in folds to the sandals that, fastened with great pearls, adorned her white and tiny feet.

All this I discerned at a glance, as it were. Then I looked upon the face—that face which seduced Cæsar, ruined Egypt, and was doomed to give Octavian the sceptre of the world. I looked upon the flawless Grecian features, the rounded chin, the full, rich lips, the chiselled nostrils, and the ears fashioned like delicate shells. I saw the forehead, low, broad, and lovely, the crisped, dark hair falling in heavy waves that sparkled in the sun, the arched eyebrows, and the long, bent lashes. There before me was the grandeur of her Imperial shape. There burnt the wonderful eyes, hued like the Cyprian violet—eyes that seemed to sleep and brood on secret things as night broods upon the desert, and yet as the

night to shift, change, and be illumined by gleams of sudden
splendour born within their starry depths. All those wonders
I saw, though I have small skill in telling them. But even
then I knew that it was not in these charms alone that the
might of Cleopatra's beauty lay. It was rather in a glory and
a radiance cast through the fleshly covering from the fierce
soul within. For she was a Thing of Flame like unto which
no woman has ever been nor ever will be. Even when she
brooded, the fire of her quick heart shone through her. But
when she woke, and the lightning leapt suddenly from her
eyes, and the passion-laden music of her speech chimed upon
her lips, ah! then, who can tell how Cleopatra seemed? For
in her met all the splendours that have been given to woman
for her glory, and all the genius which man has won from
heaven. And with them dwelt every evil of that greater sort,
which fearing nothing, and making a mock of laws, has
taken empires for its place of play, and, smiling, watered the
growth of its desires with the rich blood of men. In her
breast they gathered, together fashioning that Cleopatra whom
no man may draw, and yet whom no man, having seen, ever
can forget. They fashioned her grand as the Spirit of Storm,
lovely as Lightning, cruel as Pestilence, yet with a heart; and
what she did is known. Woe to the world when such another
comes to curse it!

For a moment I met Cleopatra's eyes as she idly bent herself to find the tumult's cause. At first they were sombre and
dark, as though they saw indeed, but the brain read nothing.
Then they awoke, and their very colour seemed to change as
the colour of the sea changes when the water is shaken.
First, there was anger written in them; next an idle noting;
then, when she looked upon the huge bulk of the man whom
I had overcome, and knew him for the gladiator, something,
perchance, that was not far from wonder. At the least they

softened, though, indeed, her face changed no whit. But
he who would read Cleopatra's mind had need to watch her
eyes, for her countenance varied but a little. Turning, she
said some word to her guards. They came forward and led
me to her, while all the multitude waited silently to see me
slain.

I stood before her, my arms folded on my breast. · Overcome though I was by the wonder of her loveliness I hated
her in my heart, this woman who dared to clothe herself in
the dress of Isis, this usurper who sat upon my throne, this
wanton squandering the wealth of Egypt in chariots and
perfumes. When she had looked me over from the head to
the feet, she spake in a low full voice and in the tongue of
Khemi which she alone had learned of all the Lagidæ:

'And who and what art thou, Egyptian—for Egyptian I
see thou art—who darest to smite my slave when I make
progress through my city?'

'I am Harmachis,' I answered boldly. 'Harmachis, the
astrologer, adopted son of the High Priest and Governor of
Abouthis, who am come hither to seek my fortune. I smote
thy slave, O Queen, because for no fault he struck down the
woman yonder. Ask of those who saw, royal Egypt.'

'Harmachis,' she said, 'the name has a high sound—and
thou hast a high look;' and then, speaking to a soldier who
had seen all, she bade him tell her what had come to pass.
This he did truthfully, being friendly disposed towards me
because I had overcome the Nubian. Thereon she turned and
spoke to the girl bearing the fan who stood beside her—a
woman with curling hair and shy dark eyes, very beautiful
to see. The girl answered somewhat. Then Cleopatra bade
them bring the slave to her. So they led forward the giant,
who had found his breath again, and with him the woman
whom he had smitten down.

'Thou dog!' she said, in the same low voice; 'thou coward! who, being strong, didst smite down this woman, and, being a coward, wast overthrown of this young man. See, thou, I will teach thee manners. Henceforth, when thou smitest women it shall be with thy left arm. Ho, guards, seize this black slave and strike off his right hand.'

Her command given, she sank back in her golden chariot, and again the cloud gathered in her eyes. But the guards seized the giant, and, notwithstanding his cries and prayers for mercy, struck off his hand with a sword upon the wood of the scaffolding and he was carried away groaning. Then the procession moved on again. As it went the fair woman with the fan turned her head, caught my eye, and smiled and nodded as though she rejoiced, at which I wondered somewhat.

The people cheered also and made jests, saying that I should soon practise astrology in the palace. But, as soon as we might, I and my uncle escaped, and made our way back to the house. All the while he rated me for my rashness; but when we came to the chamber of the house he embraced me and rejoiced greatly, because I had overthrown the giant with so little hurt to myself.

CHAPTER II.

OF THE COMING OF CHARMION; AND OF THE WRATH OF SEPA.

HAT same night, while we sat at supper in the house, there came a knock upon the door. It was opened, and a woman passed in wrapped from head to foot in a large dark peplos or cloak in such fashion that her face could not be clearly seen.

My uncle rose, and as he did so the woman uttered the secret word.

'I am come, my father,' she said in a sweet clear voice, ' though of a truth it was not easy to escape the revels at the palace yonder. But I told the Queen that the sun and the riot in the streets had made me sick, and she let me go.'

'It is well,' he answered. 'Unveil thyself; here thou art safe.'

With a little sigh of weariness she unclasped the peplos and let it slip from her, giving to my sight the face and form of that beauteous girl who had stood to fan Cleopatra in the chariot. For she was very fair and pleasant to look upon, and her Grecian robes clung sweetly about her supple limbs and budding form. Her wayward hair, flowing in a hundred little curls, was bound in with a golden fillet, and on her feet were sandals fastened with studs of gold. Her cheeks blushed like a flower, and her dark soft eyes were downcast, as though with modesty, but smiles and dimples trembled about her lips.

My uncle frowned when his eyes fell upon her dress.

'Why comest thou in this garb, Charmion?' he asked sternly. 'Is not the dress thy mothers wore good enough for thee? This is no time or place for woman's vanities. Thou art not here to conquer, but to obey.'

'Nay, be not wroth, my father,' she answered softly; 'perchance thou knowest not that she whom I serve will have none of our Egyptian dress, it is out of fashion. To wear it would have been to court suspicion—also I came in haste.' And as she spoke I saw that all the while she watched me covertly through the long lashes which fringed her modest eyes.

'Well, well,' he said sharply, fixing his keen glance upon her face, 'doubtless thou speakest truth, Charmion. Be ever mindful of thy oath, girl, and of the cause to which thou art sworn. Be not light-minded, and I charge thee forget the beauty with which thou hast been cursed. For mark thou this, Charmion: fail us but one jot, and vengeance shall fall on thee —the vengeance of man and the vengeance of the Gods! To this service,' he continued, lashing himself to anger as he went on till his great voice rang in the narrow room, 'thou hast been bred; to this end thou hast been instructed and placed where thou art to gain the ear of that wicked wanton whom thou seemest to serve. See thou forget it not; see that the luxury of yonder Court does not corrupt thy purity and divert thy aim, Charmion,' and his eyes flashed and his small form seemed to grow till it attained to dignity—nay, almost to grandeur.

'Charmion,' he went on, advancing towards her with outstretched finger, 'I say that at times I do not trust thee.

I

But two nights gone I dreamed I saw thee standing in the desert. I saw thee laugh and lift thy hand to heaven, and from it fell a rain of blood ; then the sky sank down on the land of Khem and covered it. Whence came the dream, girl, and what is its meaning ? I have naught against thee as yet ; but hearken ! On the moment that I have, though thou art of my kin, and I have loved thee—on that moment, I say, I will doom those delicate limbs, which thou lovest so much to show, to the kite and the jackal, and the soul within thee to all the tortures of the Gods ! Unburied shalt thou lie, and bodiless and accursed shalt thou wander in Amenti !—ay, for ever and ever ! '

He paused, for his sudden burst of passion had spent itself. But by it, more clearly than before, I saw how deep a heart this man had beneath the cloak of his merriness and simplicity of mien, and how fiercely the mind within him was set upon his aim. As for the girl, she shrank from him terrified, and, placing her hands before her sweet face, began to weep.

'Nay, speak not so, my father,' she said. between her sobs ; 'for what have I done ? I know nothing of the evil wandering of thy dreams. I am no soothsayer that I should read dreams. Have I not carried out all things according to thy desire ? Have I not been ever mindful of that dread oath ? '—and she trembled. 'Have I not played the spy and told thee all ? Have I not won the heart of the Queen, so that she loves me as a sister, refusing me nothing—ay, and the hearts of those about her ? Why dost thou affright me thus with thy words and threats ? ' and she wept afresh, looking even more beautiful in her sorrow than she was before.

'Enough, enough,' he answered ; 'what I have said, I have said. Be warned, and affront our sight no more with this wanton dress. Thinkest thou that we would feed our eyes upon those rounded arms—we whose stake is Egypt and who are dedicated to the Gods of Egypt? Girl, behold thy cousin and thy King!'

She ceased weeping, wiping her eyes with her chiton, and I saw that they seemed but the softer for her tears.

'Methinks, most royal Harmachis and beloved Cousin,' she said, as she bent before me, 'that we are already made acquainted.'

'Yea, Cousin,' I answered, not without shamefacedness, for I had never before spoken to so fair a maid; 'thou wert in the chariot with Cleopatra this day when I struggled with the Nubian?'

'Assuredly,' she said, with a smile and a sudden lighting of the eyes, 'it was a gallant fight and gallantly didst thou overthrow that black brute. I saw the fray and, though I knew thee not, I greatly feared for one so brave. But I paid him for my fright, for it was I who put it into the mind of Cleopatra to bid the guards strike off his hand—now, knowing who thou art, I would I had said his head.' And she looked up shooting a glance at me and then smiled.

'Enough,' put in my uncle Sepa, 'the time draws on. Tell thou thy mission, Charmion, and be gone.'

Then her manner changed; she folded her hands meekly before her and spoke:

'Let Pharaoh hearken to his handmaiden. I am the daughter of Pharaoh's uncle, the brother of his father, who is now long dead, and therefore in my veins also flows the Royal blood of Egypt. Also I am of the ancient Faith, and hate these Greeks, and to see thee set upon the throne has been my dearest hope now for many years. To this end I, Charmion, have put aside my rank and become serving-woman to Cleopatra, that I might cut a notch in which thou couldst set thy foot when the hour came for thee to climb the throne. And, Pharaoh, the notch is cut.

I 2

'This then is our plot, royal Cousin. Thou must gain
an entrance to the Household and learn its ways and secrets,
and, so far as may be, suborn the eunuchs and captains, some
of whom I have already tempted.   This done, and all things
being prepared without, thou must slay Cleopatra, and, aided
by me with those whom I control, in the confusion that shall
ensue, throw wide the gates, and, admitting those of our party
who are in waiting, put such of the troops as remain faithful
to the sword and seize the Bruchium,   Which being finished,
within two days thou shalt hold this fickle Alexandria.   At
the same time those who are sworn to thee in every city in
Egypt shall rise in arms, and in ten days from the death
of Cleopatra thou shalt indeed be Pharaoh.   This is the counsel which has been taken, and thou seest, royal Cousin, that,
though our uncle yonder thinks so ill of me, I have learned
my part—ay, and played it.'

'I hear thee, Cousin,' I answered, marvelling that so young
a woman—she had but twenty years—could weave so bold a
plot, for in its origin the scheme was hers.   But in those days
I little knew Charmion.   'Go on; how then shall I gain
entrance to the palace of Cleopatra?'

'Nay, Cousin, as things are it is easy.   Thus: Cleopatra
loves to look upon a man, and—give me pardon—thy face
and form are fair.   To-day she noted them, and twice she
said she would she had asked where that astrologer might be
found, for she held that an astrologer who could wellnigh
slay a Nubian gladiator with his bare hands, must indeed be a
master of the fortunate stars.   I answered her that I would
cause inquiry to be made.   So hearken, royal Harmachis.   At
midday Cleopatra sleeps in her inner hall which looks over the
gardens to the harbour.   At that hour to-morrow, then, I will
meet thee at the gates of the palace, whither thou shalt come
boldly asking for the Lady Charmion.   I will make appointment

for thee with Cleopatra, so that she shall see thee alone when she wakes, and the rest shall be for thee, Harmachis. For much she loves to play with the mysteries of magic, and I have known her stand whole nights watching the stars and making a pretence to read them. And but lately she has sent away Dioscorides the physician, because, poor fool! he ventured on a prophecy from the conjunction of the stars, that Cassius would defeat Mark Antony. Thereon Cleopatra sent orders to the General Allienus, bidding him add the legions she had sent to Syria to help Antony to the army of Cassius, whose victory, forsooth, was—according to Dioscorides—written on the stars. But, as it chanced, Antony beat Cassius first and Brutus afterwards, and so Dioscorides has departed, and now he lectures on herbs in the museum for his bread, and hates the name of stars. But his place is empty, and thou shalt fill it, and then we will work in secret and in the shadow of the sceptre. Ay, we will work like the worm at the heart of a fruit, till the time of plucking comes, and at thy dagger's touch, royal Cousin, the fabric of this Grecian throne crumbles to nothingness, and the worm that rotted it bursts his servile covering, and, in the sight of empires, spreads his royal wings o'er Egypt.'

I gazed at this strange girl once more astonished, and saw that her face was lit up with such a light as I had never seen in the eyes of woman.

'Ah,' broke in my uncle, who was watching her, 'ah, I love to see thee so, girl; there is the Charmion that I knew and I bred up—not the Court girl whom I like not, draped in silks of Cos and fragrant with essences. Let thy heart harden in this mould—ay, stamp it with the fervid zeal of patriot faith, and thy reward shall find thee. And now cover up that shameless dress of thine and leave us, for it grows late.

To-morrow Harmachis shall come, as thou hast said, and so farewell.'

Charmion bowed her head, and, turning, wrapped her dark-hued peplos round her. Then, taking my hand, she touched it with her lips and went without any further word.

'A strange woman!' said Sepa, when she had gone; 'a most strange woman, and an uncertain!'

'Methought, my uncle,' I said, 'that thou wast somewhat harsh with her.'

'Ay,' he answered, 'but not without a cause. Look thou, Harmachis: beware of this Charmion. She is too wayward, and, I fear me, may be led away. In truth, she is a very woman; and, like a restive horse, will take the path that pleases her. She has brain and fire, and she loves our cause; but I pray that the cause come not face to face with her desires, for what her heart is set on that will she do, at any cost she will do it. Therefore I frightened her now while I may: for who can know but that she will pass beyond my power? I tell thee, that in this one girl's hand lie all our lives: and if she play us false, what then? Alas! and alas! that we must use such tools as these! But it was needful · there was no other way; and yet I misdoubt me. I pray that it may be well; still, at times, I fear my niece Charmion—she is too fair, and the blood of youth runs too warm in those blue veins of hers.

'Ah, woe to the cause that builds its strength upon a woman's faith; for women are faithful only where they love, and when they love their faithlessness becomes their faith. They are not fixed as men are fixed: they rise more high and sink more low—they are strong and changeful as the sea. Harmachis, beware of this Charmion: for, like the ocean, she may float thee home; or, like the ocean, she may wreck thee, and, with thee, the hope of Egypt!'

CHAPTER III.

OF THE COMING OF HARMACHIS TO THE PALACE; OF HOW HE DREW PAULUS THROUGH THE GATES; OF CLEOPATRA SLEEPING; AND OF THE MAGIC OF HARMACHIS WHICH HE SHOWED HER.

 HUS it came to pass that on the next day I arrayed myself in a long and flowing robe, after the fashion of a magician or astrologer. I placed a cap on my head, about which were broidered images of the stars, and in my belt a scribe's palette and a roll of papyrus written over with mystic spells and signs. In my hand I held a wand of ebony, tipped with ivory, such as is used by priests and masters of magic. Among these, indeed, I took high rank, filling by knowledge of their secrets which I had learned at Annu what I lacked in that skill which comes from use. And so with no small shame, for I love not such play and hold this common magic in contempt, I set forth through the Bruchium to the palace on the Lochias, being guided on my way by my uncle Sepa. At length, passing up the avenue of sphinxes, we came to the great marble gateway and the gates of bronze, within which

is the guard-house. Here my uncle left me, breathing many prayers for my safety and success. But I advanced with an easy air to the gate, where I was roughly challenged by the Gallic sentries, and asked of my name, following, and business. I gave my name, Harmachis, the astrologer, saying that my business was with the Lady Charmion, the Queen's lady. Thereon the man made as though to let me pass in, when a captain of the guard, a Roman named Paulus, came forward and forbade it. Now, this Paulus was a large limbed man, with a woman's face, and a hand that shook from wine-bibbing. Still he knew me again.

'Why,' he cried, in the Latin tongue, to one who came with him, 'this is the fellow who wrestled yesterday with the Nubian gladiator, that same who now howls for his lost hand underneath my window. Curses on the black brute! I had a bet upon him for the games! I have backed him against Caius, and now he'll never fight again, and I must lose my money, all through this astrologer. What is it thou sayest?— thou hast business with the Lady Charmion? Nay, then, that settles it. I will not let thee through. Fellow, I worship the Lady Charmion—ay, we all worship her, though she gives us more slaps than sighs. And dost thou think that we will suffer an astrologer with such eyes and such a chest as thine to cut in the game?—by Bacchus, no! She must come out to keep the tryst, for in thou shalt not go.'

'Sir,' I said humbly and yet with dignity, 'I pray that a message may be sent to the Lady Charmion, for my business will not brook delay.'

'Ye Gods!' answered the fool, 'whom have we here that he cannot wait? A Cæsar in disguise? Nay, be off—be off! if thou wouldst not learn how a spear-prick feels behind.'

'Nay,' put in the other officer, 'he is an astrologer; make him prophesy—make him play tricks.

'Ay,' cried the others who had sauntered up, 'let the fellow show his art. If he is a magician he can pass the gates, Paulus or no Paulus.'

'Right willingly, good Sirs,' I answered; for I saw no other means of entering. 'Wilt thou, my young and noble Lord'—and I addressed him who was with Paulus—'suffer that I look thee in the eyes; perhaps I may read what is written there?'

'Right,' answered the youth; 'but I wish that the Lady Charmion was the sorceress. I would stare her out of countenance, I warrant.'

I took him by the hand and gazed deep into his eyes. 'I see,' I said. 'a field of battle at night, and about it bodies stretched—among them is *thy* body, and a hyena tears its throat. Most noble Sir, thou shalt die by sword-thrusts within a year.'

'By Bacchus!' said the youth, turning white to the gills, 'thou art an ill-omened sorcerer!' And he slunk off—shortly afterwards, as it chanced, to meet this very fate. For he was sent on service and slain in Cyprus.

'Now for thee, great Captain!' I said, speaking to Paulus. 'I will show thee how I will pass those gates without thy leave—ay, and draw thee through them after me. Be pleased to fix thy princely gaze upon the point of this wand in my hand.'

Being urged by his comrades he did this, unwillingly; and I let him gaze till I saw his eyes grow empty as an owl's eyes in the sun. Then I suddenly withdrew the wand, and, shifting my countenance into the place of it, I seized him with my will and stare, and, beginning to turn round and round, drew him after me, his fierce drawn face fixed, as it were, almost to my own. Then I moved slowly backwards till I had passed the gates, still drawing him after me, and suddenly jerked my head away. He fell to the ground, to rise wiping his brow and looking very foolish.

'Art thou content, most noble Captain?' I said. 'Thou seest we have passed the gates. Would any other noble Sir wish that I should show more of my skill?'

'By Taranis, Lord of Thunder, and all the Gods of Olympus thrown in, no!' growled an old Centurion. a Gaul named Brennus, 'I like thee not, I say. The man who could drag our Paulus through those gates by the eye, as it were, is not a man to play with. Paulus, too, who always goes the way you don't want him—backwards, like an ass—Paulus! Why, sirrah, thou needst must have a woman in one eye and a wine-cup in the other to draw our Paulus thus.'

At this moment the talk was broken, for Charmion her-self came down the marble path, followed by an armed slave. She walked calm and carelessly, her hands folded behind her. and her eyes gazing at nothingness, as it were. But it was when Charmion thus looked upon nothing that she saw most. And as she came the officers and men of the guard made way for her bowing, for, as I learned afterwards, this girl. next to Cleopatra's self, wielded more power than anyone about the palace.

'What is this tumult, Brennus?' she said, speaking to the Centurion, and making as if she saw me not; 'knowest thou not that the Queen sleeps at this hour, and if she be awakened it is thou who must answer for it, and that dearly?'

'Nay, Lady,' said the Centurion, humbly; 'but it is thus. We have here'—and he jerked his thumb towards me—'a magician of the most pestilent—um, I crave his pardon—of the very best sort, for he hath but just now, only by placing his eyes close to the nose of the worthy Captain Paulus, dragged him, the said Paulus, through the gates that Paulus swore the magician should not pass. By the same token, Lady, the magician says that he has business with you—which grieves me for your sake.'

Charmion turned and looked at me carelessly. 'Ay, I remember,' she said; 'and so he has—at least, the Queen would see his tricks; but if he can do none better than cause a sot '—here she cast a glance of scorn at the wondering Paulus—' to follow his nose through the gates he guards, he had better go whence he came. Follow me, Sir Magician; and for thee, Brennus, I say, keep thy riotous crew more quiet. For thee, most honourable Paulus, get thee sober, and next time I am asked for at the gates give him who asks a hearing.' And, with a queenly nod of her small head, she turned and led the way, followed at a distance by myself and the armed slave.

We passed up the marble walk which runs through the garden grounds, and is set on either side with marble statues, for the most part of heathen Gods and Goddesses, with which these Lagidæ were not ashamed to defile their royal dwellings. At length we came to a beautiful portico with fluted columns of the Grecian style of art, where we found more guards, who made way for the Lady Charmion. Crossing the portico we reached a marble vestibule where a fountain splashed softly, and thence by a low doorway a second chamber, known as the Alabaster Hall, most beautiful to see. Its roof was upheld by light columns of black marble, but all its walls were panelled with alabaster, on which Grecian legends were engraved. Its floor was of rich and many-hued mosaic that told the tale of the passion of Psyche for the Grecian God of Love, and about it were set chairs of ivory and gold. Charmion bade the armed slave stay at the doorway of this chamber, so that we passed in alone, for the place was empty except for two eunuchs who stood with drawn swords before the curtain at the further end.

' I am vexed, my Lord,' she said, speaking very low and
shyly, ' that thou shouldst have met with such affronts at the
gate ; but the guard there served a double watch, and I had
given my commands to the officer of the company that should
have relieved it. Those Roman officers are ever insolent, who,
though they seem to serve, know well that Egypt is their
plaything. But it is not amiss, for these rough soldiers are
superstitious, and will fear thee. Now bide thou here while
I go into Cleopatra's chamber, where she sleeps I have but
just sung her to sleep, and if she be awake I will call thee,
for she waits thy coming.' And without more words she
glided from my side.

In a little time she returned, and coming to me spoke:

' Wouldst see the fairest woman in all the world, asleep ?'
she whispered ; ' if so, follow me. Nay, fear not ; when she
awakes she will but laugh, for she bade me be sure to bring
thee instantly, whether she slept or woke. See, I have her
signet.'

So we passed up the beautiful chamber till we came to
where the eunuchs stood with drawn swords, and these would
have barred my entry. But Charmion frowned, and drawing
the signet from her bosom held it before their eyes. Having
examined the writing that was on the ring, they bowed, dropping their sword points and we passed through the heavy
curtains broidered with gold into the resting-place of Cleopatra. It was beautiful beyond imagining—beautiful with
many coloured marbles, with gold and ivory, gems and flowers
—all art can furnish and all luxury can dream of were here.
Here were pictures so real that birds might have pecked the
painted fruits ; here were statues of woman's loveliness frozen
into stone ; here were draperies fine as softest silk, but woven
of a web of gold ; here were couches and carpets such as
I never saw. The air, too, was sweet with perfume, while

through the open window places came the far murmur of the
sea.   And at the further end of the chamber, on a couch of
gleaming silk and sheltered by a net of finest gauze, Cleopatra
lay asleep.   There she lay—the fairest thing that man ever
saw—fairer than a dream, and the web of her dark hair flowed
all about her.   One white, rounded arm made a pillow for
her head, and one hung down towards the ground.   Her rich
lips were parted in a smile, showing the ivory lines of teeth ;
and her rosy limbs were draped in so thin a robe of the silk of
Cos, held about her by a jewelled girdle, that the white gleam
of flesh shone through it.   I stood astonished, and though my
thoughts had little bent that way, the sight of her beauty
struck me like a blow, so that for a moment I lost myself as
it were in the vision of its power, and was grieved at heart
because I must slay so fair a thing.

Turning suddenly from the sight, I found Charmion
watching me with her quick eyes—watching as though she
would search my heart.   And, indeed, something of my thought
must have been written on my face in a language that she
could read, for she whispered in my ear :

'Ay, it is pity, is it not ?   Harmachis, being but a man,
methinks that thou wilt need all thy ghostly strength to nerve
thee to the deed ! '

I frowned, but before I could frame an answer she touched
me lightly on the arm and pointed to the Queen.   A change
had come upon her : her hands were clenched, and about her
face, all rosy with the hue of sleep, gathered a cloud of fear.
Her breath came quick, she raised her arms as though to ward
away a blow, then with a stifled moan sat up and opened the
windows of her eyes.   They were dark, dark as night ; but
when the light found them they grew blue as the sky grows
blue before the blushing of the dawn.

'Cæsarion ? ' she said ; ' where is my son Cæsarion ?—

K

Was it then a dream ?   I dreamed that Julius—Julius who is
dead—came to me, a bloody toga wrapped about his face, and
having thrown his arms about his child led him away.   Then
I dreamed I died—died in blood and agony ; and one I might
not see mocked me as I died !   *Ah !*—who is that man ? '

'Peace, Madam ! peace ! ' said Charmion.   'It is but the
magician Harmachis, whom thou didst bid me bring to thee at
this hour.'

'Ah ! the magician—that Harmachis who overthrew the
giant ?   I remember now.   He is welcome.   Tell me, Sir
Magician, can thy magic mirror forth an answer to this dream ?
Nay, how strange a thing is Sleep, that wrapping the mind in
a web of darkness, straightly compels it to its will !   Whence,
then, come those images of fear rising on the horizon of the
soul like some untimely moon upon a midday sky ?   Who
grants them power to stalk so lifelike from Memory's halls,
and, pointing to their wounds, thus confront the Present with
the Past ?   Are they, then, messengers ?   Does the half-
death of sleep give them foothold in our brains, and thus
upknit the cut thread of human kinship ?   That was Cæsar's
self, I tell thee, who but now stood at my side and murmured
through his muffled robe warning words of which the memory
is lost to me.   Read me this riddle, thou Egyptian Sphinx,[1]
and I'll show thee a rosier path to fortune than all thy stars
can point.   Thou hast brought the omen, solve thou its
problem.'

'I come in a good hour, most mighty Queen,' I answered,
'for I have some skill in the mysteries of Sleep, that is, as
thou hast rightly guessed, a stair by which those who are
gathered to Osiris may from time to time enter at the gate-
ways of our living sense, and, by signs and words that can be

[1] Alluding to his name. Harmachis was the Grecian title of the
divinity of the Sphinx, as Horemkhu was the Egyptian.—Ed.

read of instructed mortals, repeat the echoes of that Hall of Truth which is their habitation. Yes, Sleep is a stair by which the messengers of the guardian Gods may descend in many shapes upon the spirit of their choice. For, O Queen, to those who hold the key, the madness of our dreams can show a clearer purpose and speak more certainly than all the acted wisdom of our waking life, which is a dream indeed. Thou didst see great Cæsar in his bloody robe, and he threw his arms about the Prince Cæsarion and led him hence. Hearken now to the secret of thy vision. It was Cæsar's self thou sawest coming to thy side from Amenti in such a guise as might not be mistaken. When he embraced the child Cæsarion he did it for a sign that to him, and him alone, had passed his greatness and his love. When he seemed to lead him hence he led him forth from Egypt to be crowned in the Capitol, crowned the Emperor of Rome and Lord of all the Lands. For the rest, I know it not. It is hid from me.'

Thus, then, I read the vision, though to my sense it had a darker meaning. But it is not well to prophesy evil unto Kings.

Meanwhile Cleopatra had risen, and, having thrown back the gnat gauze, was seated upon the edge of her couch, her eyes fixed upon my face, while her fingers played with her girdle's jewelled ends.

'Of a truth,' she cried, 'thou art the best of all magicians, for thou readest my heart, and drawest a hidden sweet out of the rough shell of evil omen!'

'Ay, O Queen,' said Charmion, who stood by with downcast eyes, and I thought there was bitter meaning in her soft tones; 'may no rougher words ever affront thy ears, and no evil presage tread less closely upon its happy sense.'

Cleopatra placed her hands behind her head and, leaning back, looked at me with half-shut eyes.

'Come, show us of thy magic, Egyptian,' she said. 'It is yet hot abroad, and I am weary of those Hebrew Ambassadors and their talk of Herod and Jerusalem. I hate that Herod, as he shall find—and will have none of the Ambassadors to-day, though I yearn a little to try my Hebrew on them. What canst thou do? Hast thou no new trick? By Serapis! if thou canst conjure as well as thou canst prophesy, thou shalt have a place at Court, with pay and perquisites to boot, if thy lofty soul does not scorn perquisites.'

'Nay,' I answered, 'all tricks are old; but there are some forms of magic to be rarely used, and with discretion, that may be new to thee, O Queen! Art thou afraid to venture on the charm?'

'I fear nothing; go on and do thy worst. Come, Charmion, and sit by me. But, stay, where are all the girls?—Iras and Merira?—they, too, love magic.'

'Not so,' I said; 'the charms work ill before so many. Now behold!' and, gazing at the twain, I cast my wand upon the marble and murmured a spell. For a moment it was still, and then, as I muttered, the rod slowly began to writhe. It bent itself, it stood on end, and moved of its own motion. Next it put on scales, and behold it was a serpent that crawled and fiercely hissed.

'Fie on thee!' cried Cleopatra, clapping her hands; 'callest thou that magic? Why, it is an old trick that any wayside conjurer can do. I have seen it a score of times.'

'Wait, O Queen,' I answered, 'thou hast not seen all.' And, as I spoke, the serpent seemed to break in fragments, and from each fragment grew a new serpent. And these, too, broke in fragments and bred others, till in a little while the place, to their glamoured sight, was a seething sea of snakes, that crawled, hissed, and knotted themselves in knots. Then I made a sign, and the serpents gathered themselves round me, and seemed slowly to twine themselves about my body and my limbs, till, save my face, I was wreathed thick with hissing snakes.

'Oh, horrible! horrible!' cried Charmion, hiding her countenance in the skirt of the Queen's garment.

'Nay, enough, Magician, enough!' said the Queen: 'thy magic overwhelms us.'

I waved my snake-wrapped arms, and all was gone. There at my feet lay the black wand tipped with ivory, and naught beside.

The two women looked upon each other and gasped with wonder. But I took up the wand and stood with folded arms before them.

'Is the Queen content with my poor art?' I asked most humbly.

'Ay, that am I, Egyptian; never did I see its like! Thou art Court astronomer from this day forward, with right of access to the Queen's presence. Hast thou more of such magic at thy call?'

'Yea, royal Egypt; suffer that the chamber be a little darkened, and I will show thee one more thing.'

'Half am I afraid,' she answered; 'nevertheless do thou as this Harmachis says, Charmion.'

So the curtains were drawn and the chamber made as though the twilight were at hand. I came forward, and stood beside Cleopatra. 'Gaze thou there!' I said sternly, pointing with my wand to the empty space where I had been, 'and thou shalt behold that which is in thy mind.'

Then for a little space was silence, while the two women gazed fixedly and half fearful at the spot.

And as they gazed a cloud gathered before them. Very slowly it took shape and form, and the form it took was the form of a man, though as yet he was but vaguely mapped upon the twilight, and seemed now to grow and now to melt away.

Then I cried with a loud voice:

'Shade, I conjure thee, *appear!*'

And as I cried the Thing, perfect in every part, leapt into form before us, suddenly as the flash of day. His shape was the shape of royal Cæsar, the toga thrown about his face, and on his form a vestment bloody from a hundred wounds. An instant so he stood, then I waved my wand and he was gone.

I turned to the two women on the couch, and saw Cleopatra's lovely face all clothed in terror. Her lips were ashy white, her eyes stared wide, and the flesh was shaking on her bones.

'Man!' she gasped; 'man! who and what art thou who canst bring the dead before our eyes?'

'I am the Queen's astronomer, magician, servant—what the Queen wills,' I answered laughing. 'Was this the form that was on the Queen's mind?'

She made no answer, but, rising, left the chamber by another door.

Then Charmion rose also and took her hands from her face, for she, too, had been stricken with dread.

'How dost thou these things, royal Harmachis?' she said. 'Tell me; for of a truth I fear thee.'

'Be not afraid,' I answered. 'Perchance thou didst see nothing but what was in my mind. All things are shadows. How canst thou, then, know their nature, or what is and what only seems to be? But how goes it? Remember, Charmion, this sport is played to an end.'

'It goes well,' she said. 'By to-morrow's dawn these tales will have gone round, and thou wilt be more feared than any man in Alexandria. Follow me, I pray thee.'

CHAPTER IV.

OF THE WAYS OF CHARMION; AND OF THE CROWNING OF HARMACHIS AS THE KING OF LOVE.

 the following day I received the writing of my appointment as Astrologer and Magician-in-Chief to the Queen, with the pay and perquisites of that office, which were not small. Rooms were given me in the palace, also, through which I passed at night to the high watch-tower, whence I looked on the stars and drew their auguries. For at this time Cleopatra was much troubled about matters political, and not knowing how the great struggle among the Roman factions would end, but being very desirous to side with the strongest, she took constant counsel with me as to the warnings of the stars. These I read to her in such manner as best seemed to fit the high interest of my ends. For Antony, the Roman Triumvir, was now in Asia Minor, and, rumour ran, very wroth because it had been told him that Cleopatra was hostile to the Triumvirate, in that her General, Serapion, had aided Cassius. But Cleopatra protested loudly to me and others that Serapion had acted against her will. Yet Charmion told me that, as with Allienus, it was because of a prophecy of Dioscorides the unlucky that the

Queen herself had secretly ordered Serapion so to do. Still, this did not save Serapion, for to prove to Antony that she was innocent she dragged the General from the sanctuary and slew him. Woe be to those who carry out the will of tyrants if the scale should rise against them! And so Serapion perished.

Meanwhile all things went well with us, for the minds of Cleopatra and those about her were so set upon affairs abroad that neither she nor they thought of revolt at home. But day by day our party gathered strength in the cities of Egypt, and even in Alexandria, which is to Egypt as another land, all things being foreign there. Day by day, those who doubted were won over and sworn to the cause by that oath which cannot be broken, and our plans of action more firmly laid. And every other day I went forth from the palace to take counsel with my uncle Sepa, and there at his house met the Nobles and the great priests who were for the party of Khem.

I saw much of Cleopatra, the Queen, and I was ever more astonished at the wealth and splendour of her mind, that for richness and variety was as a woven cloth of gold throwing back all lights from its changing face. She feared me somewhat, and therefore wished to make a friend of me, asking me of many matters that seemed to be beyond the province of my office. I saw much of the Lady Charmion also—indeed, she was ever at my side, so that I scarce knew when she came and when she went. For she would draw nigh with that soft step of hers, and I would turn to find her at hand and watching me beneath the long lashes of her downcast eyes. There was no service that was too hard for her, and no task too long; for day and night she laboured for me and for our cause.

But when I thanked her for her loyalty, and said it should be had in mind in that time which was at hand, she stamped her foot, and pouted with her lips, like an angry child, saying that, among all the things which I had learned, this had I not learned—that Love's service asked no payment, and was its own guerdon. And I, being innocent in such matters, and, foolish that I was, holding the ways of women as of small account, read her sayings in the sense that her services to the cause of Khem, which she loved, brought with them their own reward. But when I praised so fine a spirit, she burst into angry tears and left me wondering. For I knew nothing of the trouble at her heart. I knew not then that, unsought, this woman had given me her love, and that she was rent and torn by pangs of passion fixed like arrows in her breast. I did not know—how should I know it, who never looked upon her otherwise than as an instrument of our joint and holy cause? Her beauty never stirred me—no, not even when she leaned over me and breathed upon my hair, I never thought of it otherwise than as a man thinks of the beauty of a statue. What had I to do with such delights, I who was sworn to Isis and dedicate to the cause of Egypt? O ye Gods, bear me witness that I am innocent of this thing which was the source of all my woe and the woe of Khem!

How strange a thing is this love of woman, that is so small in its beginning and in its ends so great! See, at the first it is as the little spring of water welling from a mountain's heart. And at the last what is it? It is a mighty river that floats argosies of joy and makes wide lands to smile. Or, perchance, it is a torrent to wash in a flood of ruin across the fields of Hope, bursting in the barriers of design, and bringing to tumbled nothingness the tenement of man's purity and the temples of his faith. For when the Invisible conceived the order of the universe He set this seed of woman's love within its plan, that by its most unequal growth is doomed to bring about equality of law. For now it lifts the low to heights untold, and now it brings the noble to the level of the dust.

And thus, while Woman, that great surprise of Nature, is, Good and Evil can never grow apart. For still She stands, and, blind with love, shoots the shuttle of our fate, and pours sweet water into the cup of bitterness, and poisons the wholesome breath of life with the doom of her desire. Turn this way and turn that, She is at hand to meet thee. Her weakness is thy strength, her might is thy undoing. Of her thou art, to her thou goest. She is thy slave, yet holds thee captive; at her touch honour withers, locks open, and barriers fall. She is infinite as ocean, she is variable as heaven, and her name is the Unforeseen. Man, strive not to escape from Woman and the love of woman; for, fly where thou wilt, She is yet thy fate, and whate'er thou buildest thou buildest it for her!

And thus it came to pass that I, Harmachis, who had put such matters far from me, was yet doomed to fall by the thing I held of no account. For, see, this Charmion: she loved me—why, I know not. Of her own thought she learned to love me, and of her love came what shall be told. But I, knowing naught, treated her like a sister. walking as it were hand in hand with her towards our common end.

And so the time passed on, till, at length, all things were made ready.

It was the night before the night when the blow should fall, and there were revellings in the palace. That very day I had seen Sepa, and with him the captains of a band of five hundred men, who should burst into the palace at midnight on the morrow, when I had slain Cleopatra the Queen, and put the Roman and the Gallic legionaries to the sword. That very day I had suborned the Captain Paulus, who, since I drew him through the gates, was my will's slave. Half by fear and half by promises of great reward I had prevailed upon him, for the watch was his, to unbar that small gate which faces to the East at the signal on the morrow night.

All was made ready—the flower of Freedom that had been five-and-twenty years in growth was on the point of bloom. Armed companies were gathered in every city from Abu to Athu, and spies looked out from their walls, awaiting the coming of the messenger who should bring tidings that Cleopatra was no more and that Harmachis, the royal Egyptian, had seized the throne.

All was prepared, triumph hung to my hand as a ripe fruit to the hand of the plucker. Yet as I sat at the royal feast my heart was heavy, and a shadow of coming woe lay cold within my mind. I sat there in a place of honour, near the majesty of Cleopatra, and looked down the lines of guests, bright with gems and garlanded with flowers, marking those whom I had doomed to die. There before me lay Cleopatra in all her beauty, which thrilled the beholder as he is thrilled by the rushing of the midnight gale, or by the sight of stormy waters. I gazed on her as she touched her lips with wine and toyed with the chaplet of roses on her brow, thinking of the dagger beneath my robe that I had sworn to bury in her breast. Again, and yet again, I gazed and strove to hate her, strove to rejoice that she must die—and could not. There, too, behind her—watching me now, as ever, with her deep-fringed eyes—was the lovely Lady Charmion. Who, to look at her innocent face, would believe that she was the setter of that snare in which the Queen who loved her should miserably perish? Who would dream that the secret of so much death was locked in her girlish breast? I gazed, and grew sick at heart because I must anoint my throne with blood, and by evil sweep away the evil of the land. At that hour I wished, indeed, that I was nothing but some humble husbandman, who in its season sows and in its season garners the golden grain! Alas! the seed that I had been doomed to sow was the seed of Death, and now I must reap the red fruit of the harvest!

'Why, Harmachis, what ails thee?' said Cleopatra, smiling her slow smile. 'Has the golden skein of stars got tangled, my astronomer? or dost thou plan some new feat of magic? Say what is it that thou dost so poorly grace our feast? Nay, now, did I not know, having made inquiry, that things so low as we poor women are far beneath thy gaze, why, I should swear that Eros had found thee out, Harmachis!'

'Nay, that I am spared, O Queen,' I answered. 'The servant of the stars marks not the smaller light of woman's eyes, and therein is he happy!'

Cleopatra leaned herself towards me, looking on me long and steadily in such fashion that, despite my will, the blood fluttered at my heart.

'Boast not, thou proud Egyptian,' she said in a low voice which none but I and Charmion could hear, 'lest perchance thou dost tempt me to match my magic against thine. What woman can forgive that a man should push us by as things of no account? It is an insult to our sex which Nature's self abhors,' and she leaned back again and laughed most musically. But, glancing up, I saw Charmion, her teeth on her lip and an angry frown upon her brow.

'Pardon, royal Egypt,' I answered coldly, but with such wit as I could summon, 'before the Queen of Heaven even stars grow pale!' This I said of the moon, which is the sign of the Holy Mother whom Cleopatra dared to rival, naming herself Isis come to earth.

'Happily said,' she answered, clapping her white hands. 'Why, here's an astronomer who has wit and can shape a compliment! Nay, such a wonder must not pass unnoted, lest the Gods resent it. Charmion, take this rose-chaplet from my hair and set it upon the learned brow of our Harmachis. He shall be crowned *King of Love*, whether he will it or will it not.

Charmion lifted the chaplet from Cleopatra's brows and, bearing it to where I was, with a smile set it upon my head yet warm and fragrant from the Queen's hair, but so roughly that she pained me somewhat. She did this because she was wroth, although she smiled with her lips and whispered, 'An omen, royal Harmachis.' For though she was so very much a woman, yet, when she was angered or suffered jealousy, Charmion had a childish way.

Having thus fixed the chaplet, she curtsied low before me, and with the softest tone of mockery named me, in the Greek tongue, 'Harmachis, King of Love.' Then Cleopatra laughed and pledged me as 'King of Love,' and so did all the company, finding the jest a merry one. For in Alexandria they love not those who live straitly and turn aside from women.

But I sat there, a smile upon my lips and black wrath in my heart. For, knowing who and what I was, it irked me to think myself a jest for the frivolous nobles and light beauties of Cleopatra's Court. But I was chiefly angered against Charmion, because she laughed the loudest, and I did not then know that laughter and bitterness are often the veils with which a sore heart wraps its weakness from the world. 'An omen' she said it was—that crown of flowers—and so it proved indeed. For I was fated to barter the Double Diadem of the Upper and the Lower Land for a wreath of passion's roses that fade before they fully bloom, and Pharaoh's ivory bed of state for the pillow of a faithless woman's breast.

'*King of Love!*' they crowned me in their mockery; ay, and King of Shame! And I, with the perfumed roses on my brow—I, by descent and ordination the Pharaoh of Egypt —thought of the imperishable halls of Abouthis and of that other crowning which on the morrow should be consummate.

But still smiling, I pledged them back, and answered with

a jest. For rising, I bowed before Cleopatra and craved leave to go. 'Venus,' I said, speaking of the planet that we know as Donaou in the morning and Bonou in the evening, 'was in the ascendant. Therefore, as new-crowned King of Love, I must now pass to do my homage to its Queen.' For these barbarians name Venus Queen of Love.

And so amidst their laughter I withdrew to my watch-tower, and, dashing that shameful chaplet down amidst the instruments of my craft, made pretence to note the rolling of the stars. There I waited, thinking on many things that were to be, until Charmion should come with the last lists of the doomed and the messages of my uncle Sepa, whom she had seen that evening.

At length the door opened softly, and she came jewelled and clad in her white robes, as she had left the feast.

CHAPTER V.

OF THE COMING OF CLEOPATRA TO THE CHAMBER OF
HARMACHIS; OF THE THROWING FORTH OF THE KERCHIEF
OF CHARMION; OF THE STARS; AND OF THE GIFT BY
CLEOPATRA OF HER FRIENDSHIP TO HER SERVANT
HARMACHIS.

length thou art come, Charmion," I
said. ' It is over-late.'

' Yea, my Lord; but by no
means could I escape Cleopatra.
Her mood is strangely crossed to-
night. I know not what it may
portend. Strange whims and fancies
blow across it like light and contrary
airs upon a summer sea, and I cannot read her
purpose.'

' Well, well; enough of Cleopatra. Hast
thou seen our uncle ?'

' Yes, royal Harmachis.'

' And hast thou the last lists ?'

' Yes; here they are,' and she drew them from her bosom.
' Here is the list of those who, after the Queen, must certainly
be put to the sword. Among them thou wilt note is the name
of that old Gaul Brennus. I grieve for him, for we are friends;
but it must be. It is a heavy list.'

' It is so,' I answered conning it; ' when men write out

L

their count they forget no item, and our count is long. What must be must be. Now for the next.'

'Here is the list of those to be spared, as friendly or uncertain ; and here that of the towns which will certainly rise as soon as the messenger reaches their gates with tidings of the death of Cleopatra.'

'Good. And now'—and I paused—' and now as to the manner of Cleopatra's death. How hast thou settled it? Must it be by my own hand?'

'Yea, my Lord,' she answered, and again I caught that note of bitterness in her voice. 'Doubtless Pharaoh will rejoice that his should be the hand to rid the land of this false Queen and wanton woman, and at one blow break the chains which gall the neck of Egypt.'

'Talk not thus, girl,' I said ; 'thou knowest well that I do not rejoice, being but driven to the act by deep necessity and the pressure of my vows. Can she not, then, be poisoned? Or can no one of the eunuchs be suborned to slay her? My soul turns from this bloody work! Indeed, I marvel, however heavy be her crimes, that thou canst speak so lightly of the death by treachery of one who loves thee!'

'Surely Pharaoh is over-tender, forgetting the greatness of the moment and all that hangs upon this dagger-stroke that shall cut the thread of Cleopatra's life. Listen, Harmachis. *Thou* must do the deed, and *thou* alone! Myself I would do it, had my arm the strength ; but it has not. It cannot be done by poison, for every drop she drinks and every morsel that shall touch her lips is strictly tasted by three separate tasters, who cannot be suborned. Nor may the eunuchs of the guard be trusted. Two, indeed, are sworn to us ; but the third cannot be come at. He must be cut down afterwards ; and, indeed, when so many men must fall, what matters a eunuch more or less? Thus it shall be, then. To-morrow night, at three hours before midnight thou dost cast the final augury of the issue of the war. And then thou wilt, as is agreed, descend alone with me, having the signet, to the outer chamber of the Queen's apartment. For the vessel bearing orders to the Legions sails from Alexandria at the following dawn; and alone with Cleopatra. since she wills that the thing be kept secret as the sea, thou wilt read the message of the stars. And as she pores over the papyrus, then must thou stab her in the back, so that she dies ; and see thou that thy will and arm fail thee not I The deed being done—and indeed it will be easy—thou wilt take the signet and pass out to where the eunuch is—for the others will be wanting. If by any chance there is trouble with him—but there will be no trouble, for he dare not enter the private rooms, and the sounds of death cannot reach so far—thou must cut him down. Then I will meet thee ; and, passing on, we will come to Paulus, and it shall be my care to see that he is neither drunk nor backward, for I know how to hold him to the task. And he and those with him shall throw open the side gate, when Sepa and the five hundred chosen men who are in waiting shall pour in and cast themselves upon the sleeping legionaries, putting them to the sword. Why, the thing is easy so thou rest true to thyself, and let no womanish fears creep into thy heart. What is this dagger's thrust ? It is nothing, and yet upon it hang the destinies of Egypt and the world.

'Hush I ' I said. 'What is that ?—I hear a sound.'

Charmion ran to the door, and, gazing down the long, dark passage, listened. In a moment she came back, her finger on her lips. 'It is the Queen,' she whispered hurriedly; 'the Queen who mounts the stair alone. I heard her bid Iras leave her. I may not be found alone with thee at this hour; it has a strange look, and she may suspect. What wants she here ? Where can I hide ? '

I glanced round. At the further end of the chamber was a heavy curtain that hid a little place built in the thickness of the wall which I used for the storage of rolls and instruments.

'Haste thee—there!' I said, and she glided behind the curtain, which swung back and covered her. Then I thrust the fatal scroll of death into the bosom of my robe and bent over the mystic chart. Presently I heard the sweep of woman's robes and there came a low knock upon the door.

'Enter, whoever thou art,' I said.

The latch lifted, and Cleopatra swept in, royally arrayed, her dark hair hanging about her and the sacred snake of royalty glistening on her brow.

'Of a truth, Harmachis,' she said with a sigh, as she sank into a seat, ' the path to heaven is hard to climb ! Ah ! I am weary, for those stairs are many. But I was minded, my astronomer, to see thee in thy haunts.'

'I am honoured overmuch, O Queen !' I said bowing low before her.

'Art thou now ? And yet that dark face of thine has a somewhat angry look—thou art too young and handsome for this dry trade, Harmachis. Why, I vow thou hast cast my wreath of roses down amidst thy rusty tools! Kings would have cherished that wreath along with their choicest diadems, Harmachis ! and thou dost throw it away as a thing of no account ! Why, what a man art thou ! But stay ; what is this ? A lady's kerchief, by Isis ! Nay, now, my Harmachis, how came *this* here ? Are our poor kerchiefs also instruments of thy high art ? Oh, fie, fie !—have I caught thee, then ? Art thou indeed a fox ? '

'Nay, most royal Cleopatra, nay !' I said, turning : for the kerchief which had fallen from Charmion's neck had an awkward look. ' I know not, indeed, how the frippery came here. Perhaps, some one of the women who keep the chamber may have let it fall.'

'Ah! so—so!' she said drily, and still laughing like a rippling brook. 'Yes, surely, the slave-women who keep chambers own such toys as this, of the very finest silk, worth twice its weight in gold, and broidered, too, in many colours. Why, myself I should not shame to wear it! Of a truth it seems familiar to my sight.' And she threw it round her neck and smoothed the ends with her white hand. 'But there; doubtless, it is a thing unholy in thine eyes that the scarf of thy beloved should rest upon my poor breast. Take it, Harmachis; take it, and hide it in thy bosom—nigh thy heart indeed!'

I took the accursed thing, and, muttering what I may not write, stepped on to the giddy platform whence I watched the stars. Then, crushing it into a ball, I threw it to the winds of heaven.

At this the lovely Queen laughed once more.

'Nay, think now,' she cried; 'what would the lady say could she see her love-gauge thus cast to all the world? Mayhap, Harmachis, thou wouldst deal thus with my wreath also? See, the roses fade; cast it forth,' and, stooping, she took up the wreath and gave it to me.

For a moment, so vexed was I, I had a mind to take her at her word and send the wreath to join the kerchief. But I thought better of it.

'Nay,' I said more softly, 'it is a Queen's gift, and I will keep it,' and, as I spoke, I saw the curtain shake. Often since that night I have sorrowed over those simple words.

'Gracious thanks be to the King of Love for this small mercy,' she answered, looking at me strangely. 'Now, enough of wit; come forth upon this balcony—tell me of the mystery of those stars of thine. For I always loved the stars, that

are so pure and bright and cold, and so far away from our
fevered troubling. There I would wish to dwell, rocked on
the dark bosom of the night, and losing the little sense of self
as I gazed for ever on the countenance of yon sweet-eyed
space. Nay—who can tell, Harmachis?—perhaps those stars
partake of our very substance, and, linked to us by Nature's
invisible chain, do, indeed, draw our destiny with them as
they roll. What says the Greek fable of him who became a
star? Perchance it has truth, for yonder tiny sparks may
be the souls of men, but grown more purely bright and placed
in happy rest to illume the turmoil of their mother-earth.
Or are they lamps hung high in the heavenly vault that night
by night some Godhead, whose wings are Darkness, touches
with his immortal fire so that they leap out in answering
flame? Give me of thy wisdom and open these wonders to
me, my servant, for I have little knowledge. Yet my heart
is large, and I would fill it, for I have the wit, could I but find
the teacher.'

Thereon, being glad to find footing on a safer shore, and
marvelling somewhat to learn that Cleopatra had a place for
lofty thoughts, I spoke and willingly told her such things
as are lawful. I told her how the sky is a liquid mass pressing round the earth and resting on the elastic pillars of the
air, and how above is the heavenly ocean Nout, in which the
planets float like ships as they rush upon their radiant way.
I told her many things, and amongst them how, through the
certain never-ceasing movement of the orbs of light, the planet
Venus, that was called Donaou when she showed as the Morning Star, became the planet Bonou when she came as the sweet
Star of Eve. And while I stood and spoke watching the
stars, she sat, her hands clasped upon her knee, and watched
my face.

'Ah!' she broke in at length, 'and so Venus is to be seen

both in the morning and the evening sky. Well, of a truth, she is everywhere, though she best loves the night. But thou lovest not that I should use these Latin names to thee. Come, we will talk in the ancient tongue of Khem, which I know well; I am the first, mark thou, of all the Lagidæ who know it. And now,' she went on, speaking in my own tongue, but with a little foreign accent that did but make her talk more sweet, ' enough of stars, for, when all is said, they are but fickle things, and perhaps may even now be storing up an evil hour for thee or me, or for us both together. Not but what I love to hear thee speak of them, for then thy face loses that gloomy cloud of thought which mars it and grows quick and human. Harmachis, thou art too young for such a solemn trade: methinks that I must find thee a better. Youth comes but once: why waste it in these musings? It is time to think when we can no longer act. Tell me how old art thou, Harmachis?'

'I have six-and-twenty years, O Queen,' I answered, 'for I was born in the first month of Shomou, in the summer season, and on the third day of the month.'

'Why, then, we are of an age even to a day,' she cried, - for I too have six-and-twenty years, and I too was born on the third day of the first month of Shomou. Well, this may we say: those who begot us need have no shame. For if I be the fairest woman in Egypt, methinks, Harmachis, that there is in Egypt no man more fair and strong than thou, ay, or more learned. Born of the same day, why, 'tis manifest that we were destined to stand together, I, as the Queen, and thou, perchance, Harmachis, as one of the chief pillars of my throne, and thus to work each other's weal.'

' Or maybe each other's woe,' I answered, looking up; for her sweet speeches stung my ears and brought more colour to my face than I loved that she should see there.

'Nay, never talk of woe. Be seated here by me. Harmachis, and let us talk, not as Queen and subject, but as friend to friend. Thou wast angered with me at the feast to-night because I mocked thee with yonder wreath—was it not so? Nay, it was but a jest. Didst thou know how heavy is the task of monarchs and how wearisome are their hours, thou wouldst not be wroth because I lit my dulness with a jest. Oh, they weary me, those princes and those nobles, and those stiff-necked pompous Romans. To my face they vow themselves my slaves, and behind my back they mock me and proclaim me the servant of their Triumvirate, or their Empire, or their Republic, as the wheel of Fortune turns, and each rises on its round! There is never a man among them— nothing but fools, parasites, and puppets—never a man since with their coward daggers they slew that Cæsar whom all the world in arms was not strong enough to tame. And I must play off one against the other, if maybe, by so doing, I can keep Egypt from their grip. And for reward, what? Why, this is my reward—that all men speak ill of me—and, I know it, my subjects hate me! Yes, I believe that, woman though I am, they would murder me could they find a means!"

She paused, covering her eyes with her hand, and it was well, for her words pierced me so that I shrank upon the seat beside her.

'They think ill of me, I know it; and call me wanton, who have never stepped aside save once, when I loved the greatest man of all the world, and at the touch of love my passion flamed indeed, but burnt a hallowed flame. These ribald Alexandrians swear that I poisoned Ptolemy, my brother—whom the Roman Senate would, most unnaturally, have forced on me, his sister, as a husband! But it is false: he sickened and died of fever. And even so they say that I would slay Arsinoë, my sister—who, indeed, would slay me!—

but that, too, is false ! Though she will have none of me, I love my sister. Yes, they all think ill of me without a cause; even thou dost think ill of me, Harmachis.

'O Harmachis, before thou judgest, remember what a thing is envy !—that foul sickness of the mind which makes the jaundiced eye of pettiness to see all things distraught—to read Evil written on the open face of Good, and find impurity in the whitest virgin's soul ! Think what a thing it is, Harmachis, to be set on high above the gaping crowd of knaves who hate thee for thy fortune and thy wit ; who gnash their teeth and shoot the arrows of their lies from the cover of their own obscureness, whence they have no wings to soar ; and whose hearts' quest it is to drag down thy nobility to the level of the groundling and the fool !

'Be not, then, swift to think evil of the Great, whose every word and act is searched for error by a million angry eyes, and whose most tiny fault is trumpeted by a thousand throats, till the world shakes with echoes of their sin ! Say not : "It is thus, 'tis certainly thus"—say, rather : "May it not be otherwise ? Have we heard aright ? Did she this thing of her own will ? " Judge gently, Harmachis, as wert thou I thou wouldst be judged. Remember that a Queen is never free. She is, indeed, but the point and instrument of those forces politic with which the iron books of history are graved. O Harmachis ! be thou my friend—my friend and counsellor !—my friend whom I can trust indeed !—for here, in this crowded Court, I am more utterly alone than any soul that breathes about its corridors. But *thee* I trust ; there is faith written in those quiet eyes, and I am minded to lift thee high, Harmachis. I can no longer bear my solitude of mind—I must find one with whom I may commune and speak that which lies within my heart. I have faults, I know it ; but I am not all unworthy of thy faith, for there

is good grain among the evil seed.   Say, Harmachis, wilt
thou take pity on my loneliness and befriend me, who have
lovers, courtiers, slaves, dependents, more thick than I can
count, but never one single *friend*? ' and she leant towards
me, touching me lightly, and gazed on me with her wonderful
blue eyes.

I was overcome ; thinking of the morrow night, shame
and sorrow smote me.   *I*, her friend !—*I*, whose assassin
dagger lay against my breast !   I bent my head, and a sob or
a groan, I know not which, burst from the agony of my heart.

But Cleopatra, thinking only that I was moved beyond
myself by the surprise of her graciousness, smiled sweetly,
and said :

' It grows late ; to-morrow night when thou bringest the
auguries we will speak again, O my friend Harmachis, and
thou shalt answer me."   And she gave me her hand to kiss.
Scarce knowing what I did, I kissed it, and in another moment
she was gone.

But I stood in the chamber, gazing after her like one
asleep.

CHAPTER VI.

OF THE WORDS AND JEALOUSY OF CHARMION; OF THE
LAUGHTER OF HARMACHIS; OF THE MAKING READY FOR
THE DEED OF BLOOD; AND OF THE MESSAGE OF THE OLD
WIFE, ATOUA.

STOOD still, plunged in thought. Then by hazard as it were I took up the wreath of roses and looked on it. How long I stood so I know not, but when next I lifted up my eyes they fell upon the form of Charmion, whom, indeed, I had altogether forgotten. And though at the moment I thought but little of it, I noted vaguely that she was flushed as though with anger, and beat her foot upon the floor.

'Oh, it is thou, Charmion!' I said. 'What ails thee? Art thou cramped with standing so long in thy hiding-place? Why didst not thou slip hence when Cleopatra led me to the balcony?'

'Where is my kerchief?' she asked, shooting an angry glance at me. 'I let fall my broidered kerchief.'

'Thy kerchief!—why, didst thou not see? Cleopatra twitted me about it, and I flung it from the balcony."

'Yes, I saw,' answered the girl, 'I saw but too well. Thou didst fling away my kerchief, but the wreath of roses —

that thou wouldst not fling away. It was "a Queen's gift," forsooth, and therefore the royal Harmachis, the Priest of Isis, the chosen of the Gods, the crowned Pharaoh wed to the weal of Khem, cherished it and saved it. But my kerchief, stung by the laughter of that light Queen, he cast away!'

'What meanest thou?' I asked, astonished at her bitter tone. 'I cannot read thy riddles.'

'What mean I?' she answered, tossing up her head and showing the white curves of her throat. 'Nay, I mean naught, or all; take it as thou wilt. Wouldst know what I mean, Harmachis, my cousin and my Lord?' she went on in a hard, low voice. 'Then I will tell thee—thou art in danger of the great offence. This Cleopatra has cast her fatal wiles about thee, and thou goest near to loving her, Harmachis—to loving her whom to-morrow thou must slay! Ay, stand and stare at that wreath in thy hand—the wreath thou couldst not send to join my kerchief—sure Cleopatra wore it but to-night! The perfume of the hair of Cæsar's mistress—Cæsar's and others'—yet mingles with the odour of its roses! Now, prithee, Harmachis, how far didst thou carry the matter on yonder balcony? for in that hole where I lay hid I could not hear or see. 'Tis a sweet spot for lovers, is it not?—ay, and a sweet hour, too? Venus surely rules the stars to-night?'

All of this she said so quietly and in so soft and modest a way, though her words were not modest, and yet so bitterly, that every syllable cut me to the heart, and angered me till I could find no speech.

'Of a truth thou hast a wise economy,' she went on, seeing her advantage: 'to-night thou dost kiss the lips that to-morrow thou shalt still for ever! It is frugal dealing with the occasion of the moment; ay, worthy and honourable dealing!'

Then at last I broke forth. 'Girl,' I cried, 'how darest

thou speak thus to me? Mindest thou who and what I am that thou loosest thy peevish gibes upon me?'

'I mind what it behoves thee to be,' she answered quick. 'What thou art, that I mind not now. Surely thou knowest alone—thou and Cleopatra!'

'What meanest thou?' I said. 'Am I to blame if the Queen——'

'The Queen! What have we here? Pharaoh owns a Queen!'

'If Cleopatra wills to come hither of a night and talk——'

'Of stars, Harmachis—surely of stars and roses, and naught beside!'

After that I know not what I said; for, troubled as I was, the girl's bitter tongue and quiet way drove me wellnigh to madness. But this I know: I spoke so fiercely that she cowered before me as she had cowered before my uncle Sepa when he rated her because of her Grecian garb. And as she wept then, so she wept now, only more passionately and with great sobs.

At length I ceased, half-shamed but still angry and smarting sorely. For even while she wept she could find a tongue to answer with—and a woman's shafts are sharp.

'Thou shouldst not speak to me thus!' she sobbed; 'it is cruel—it is unmanly! But I forget thou art but a priest, not a man—except, mayhap, for Cleopatra!'

'What right hast thou?' I said. 'What canst thou mean?'

'What right have I?' she asked, looking up, her dark eyes all aflood with tears that ran down her sweet face like the dew of morning down a lily's heart. 'What right have I? O Harmachis! art thou blind? Dost thou not know by what right I speak thus to thee? Then I must tell thee. Well, it is the fashion in Alexandria! By that first and holy right of woman—by the right of the great love I bear thee, and which, it seems, thou hast no eyes to see—by the right of my glory and my shame. Oh, be not wroth with me, Harmachis, nor set me down as light, because the truth at last has burst from me; for I am not so. I am what thou wilt make me. I am the wax within the moulder's hands, and as thou dost fashion me so I shall be. There breathes within me now a breath of glory, blowing across the waters of my soul, that can waft me to ends more noble than ever I have dreamed afore, if thou wilt be my pilot and my guide. But if I lose thee, then I lose all that holds me from my worse self—and let shipwreck come! Thou knowest me not, Harmachis! thou canst not see how big a spirit struggles in this frail form of mine! To thee I am a girl, clever, wayward, shallow. But I am more! Show me thy loftiest thought and I will match it, the deepest puzzle of thy mind and I will make it clear. Of one blood we are, and love can ravel up our little difference and make us grow one indeed. One end we have, one land we love, one vow binds us both. Take me to thy heart, Harmachis, set me by thee on the Double Throne, and I swear that I will lift thee higher than ever man has climbed. Reject me, and beware lest I pull thee down! And now, putting aside the cold delicacy of custom, stung to it by what I saw of the arts of that lovely living falsehood, Cleopatra, which for pastime she practises on thy folly, I have spoken out my heart, and answer thou!' And she clasped her hands and, drawing one pace nearer, gazed, all white and trembling, on my face.

For a moment I stood struck dumb, for the magic of her voice and the power of her speech, despite myself, stirred me like the rush of music. Had I loved the woman, doubtless she might have fired me with her flame; but I loved her not, and I could not play at passion. And so thought came, and with thought that laughing mood, which is ever apt to fasten upon nerves strained to the point of breaking. In a flash, as it were, I bethought me of the way in which she had that very night forced the wreath of roses on my head. I thought of the kerchief and how I had flung it forth. I thought of Charmion in the little chamber watching what she held to be the arts of Cleopatra, and of her bitter speeches. Lastly, I thought of what my uncle Sepa would say of her could he see her now, and of the strange and tangled skein in which I was immeshed. And I laughed aloud—the fool's laughter that was my knell of ruin !

She turned whiter yet—white as the dead—and a look grew upon her face that checked my foolish mirth. 'Thou findest, then, Harmachis,' she said in a low, choked voice, and dropping the level of her eyes, 'thou findest cause of merriment in what I have said ?'

'Nay,' I answered ; 'nay, Charmion ; forgive me if I laughed. It was rather a laugh of despair ; for what am I to say to thee ? Thou hast spoken high words of all thou mightest be : is it left for me to tell thee what thou art ?'

She shrank, and I paused.

'Speak,' she said.

'Thou knowest—none so well !—who I am and what my mission is : thou knowest—none so well !—that I am sworn to Isis, and may, by law Divine, have naught to do with thee.'

'Ay,' she broke in, in her low voice, and with her eyes still fixed upon the ground—'ay, and I know that thy vows are broken in spirit, if not in form—broken like wreaths of cloud ; for, Harmachis—*thou lovest Cleopatra !*'

'It is a lie !' I cried. 'Thou wanton girl, who wouldst seduce me from my duty and put me to an open shame !—who, led by passion or ambition, or the love of evil, hast not shamed to break the barriers of thy sex and speak as thou hast spoken —beware lest thou go too far ! And if thou wilt have an

M

answer, here it is, put straightly, as thy question. Charmion, outside the matter of my duty and my vows, thou art *naught* to me!—nor for all thy tender glances will my heart beat one pulse more fast! Hardly art thou now my friend—for, of a truth, I scarce can trust thee. But, once more : beware! To me thou mayest do thy worst ; but if thou dost dare to lift a finger against our cause, that day thou diest! And now, is this play done ? '

And as, wild with anger, I spoke thus, she shrank back, and·yet further back, till at length she rested against the wall, her eyes covered with her hand. But when I ceased she dropped her hand, glancing up, and her face was as the face of a statue, in which the great eyes glowed like embers, and round them was a ring of purple shadow.

'Not altogether done,' she answered gently ; ' the arena must yet be sanded!' This she said having reference to the covering up of the bloodstains at the gladiatorial shows with fine sand. ' Well,' she went on, ' waste not thine anger on a thing so vile. I have thrown my throw and I have lost. *Væ victis!*—ah! *Væ victis!* Wilt thou not lend me the dagger in thy robe, that here and now I may end my shame ? No ? Then one word more, most royal Harmachis : if thou canst, forget my folly ; but, at the least, have no fear from me. I am now, as ever, thy servant and the servant of our cause. Farewell! '

And she went, leaning her hand against the wall. But I, passing to my chamber, flung myself upon my couch, and groaned in bitterness of spirit. Alas! we shape our plans, and by slow degrees build up our house of Hope, never counting on the guests that time shall bring to lodge therein. For who can guard against—the Unforeseen ?

At length I slept, and my dreams were evil. When I woke the light of that day which should see the red fulfilment of the plot was streaming through the casement, and the birds sang merrily among the garden palms. I woke, and as I woke the sense of trouble pressed in upon me, for I remembered that before this day was gathered to the past I must dip my hands in blood—yes, in the blood of Cleopatra, who trusted me! Why could I not hate her as I should? There had been a time when I looked on to this act of vengeance with somewhat of a righteous glow of zeal. And now—and now—why, I would frankly give my royal birthright to be free from its necessity! But, alas! I knew that there was no escape. I must drain this cup or be for ever cast away. I felt the eyes of Egypt watching me, and the eyes of Egypt's Gods. I prayed to my Mother Isis to give me strength to do this deed, and prayed as I had never prayed before; and oh, wonder! no answer came. Nay, how was this? What, then, had loosed the link between us that, for the first time, the Goddess deigned no reply to her son and chosen servant? Could it be that I had sinned in heart against her? What had Charmion said—that I loved Cleopatra? Was this sickness love? Nay! a thousand times nay!—it was but the revolt of Nature against an act of treachery and blood. The Goddess did but try my strength, or perchance she also turned her holy countenance from murder?

I rose filled with terror and despair, and went about my task like a man without a soul. I conned the fatal lists and noted all the plans—ay, in my brain I gathered up the very words of that proclamation of my Royalty which, on the morrow, I should issue to the startled world.

'Citizens of Alexandria and dwellers in the land of Egypt,' it began, 'Cleopatra the Macedonian hath, by the command of the Gods, suffered justice for her crimes——'

All these and other things I did, but I did them as a man without a soul—as a man moved by a force from without and not from within. And so the minutes wore away. In the third hour of the afternoon I went as by appointment fixed to the house where my uncle Sepa lodged, that same house to which I had been brought some three months gone when I entered Alexandria for the first time. And here I found the leaders of the revolt in the city assembled in secret conclave to the number of seven. When I had entered, and the doors were barred, they prostrated themselves, and cried, ' Hail, Pharaoh ! ' but I bade them rise, saying that I was not yet Pharaoh, for the chicken was still in the egg.

' Yea, Prince,' said my uncle, ' but his beak shows through. Not in vain hath Egypt brooded all these years, if thou fail not with that dagger-stroke of thine to-night ; and how canst thou fail ? Nothing can now stop our course to victory ! '

' It is on the knees of the Gods,' I answered.

' Nay,' he said, ' the Gods have placed the issue in the hands of a mortal—in thy hands, Harmachis !—and there it is safe. See : here are the last lists. Thirty-one thousand men who bear arms are sworn to rise when the tidings come to them. Within five days every citadel in Egypt will be in our hands, and then what have we to fear ? From Rome but little, for her hands are full ; and, besides, we will make alliance with the Triumvirate, and, if need be, buy them off. For of money there is plenty in the land, and if more be wanted thou, Harmachis, knowest where it is stored against the need of Khem, and outside the Roman's reach of arm. Who is there to harm us ? There is none. Perchance, in this turbulent city, there may be struggle, and a counter-plot to bring Arsinoë to Egypt and set her on the throne. Therefore Alexandria must be severely dealt with—ay, even to destruction, if need be. As for Arsinoë, those go forth to-morrow on the news of the Queen's death who shall slay her secretly.'

'There remains the lad Cæsarion,' I said. 'Rome might claim through Cæsar's son, and the child of Cleopatra inherits Cleopatra's rights. Here is a double danger.'

'Fear not,' said my uncle; 'to-morrow Cæsarion joins those who begat him in Amenti. I have made provision. The Ptolemies must be stamped out, so that no shoot shall ever spring from that root blasted by Heaven's vengeance.'

'Is there no other means?' I asked sadly. 'My heart is sick at the promise of this red rain of blood. I know the child well; he has Cleopatra's fire and beauty and great Cæsar's wit. It were shame to murder him.'

'Nay. be not so chicken-hearted, Harmachis,' said my uncle, sternly. 'What ails thee, then? If the lad is thus, the more reason that he should die. Wouldst thou nurse up a young lion to tear thee from the throne?'

'Be it so.' I answered, sighing. 'At least he is spared much, and will go hence innocent of evil. Now for the plans.'

We sat long taking counsel, till at length, in face of the great emergency and our high emprise, I felt something of the spirit of former days flow back into my heart. At the last all was ordered, and so ordered that it could scarce miscarry, for it was fixed that if by any chance I could not come to slay Cleopatra on this night, then the plot should hang in the scale till the morrow, when the deed must be done upon occasion. For the death of Cleopatra was the signal. These matters being finished, once more we stood and, our hands upon the sacred symbol, swore the oath that may not be written. And then my uncle kissed me with tears of hope and joy standing in his keen black eyes. He blessed me, saying that he would gladly give his life, ay, and a hundred lives, if they were his, if he might but live to see Egypt once more a nation, and me, Harmachis, the descendant of its royal and ancient blood, seated on the throne. For he was a patriot indeed, asking nothing for himself, and giving all things to his cause. And I kissed him in turn, and thus we parted. Nor did I ever see him more in the flesh who has earned the rest that as yet is denied to me.

So I went, and, there being yet time, walked swiftly from place to place in the great city, taking note of the positions of the gates and of the places where our forces must be gathered. At length I came to that quay where I had landed, and saw a vessel sailing for the open sea. I looked, and in my heaviness of heart longed that I were aboard of her, to be borne by her white wings to some far shore where I might live obscure and die forgotten. Also I saw another vessel that had dropped down the Nile, from whose deck the passengers were streaming. For a moment I stood watching them, idly wondering if they were from Abouthis, when suddenly I heard a familiar voice beside me.

'*La! la!*' said the voice. 'Why, what a city is this for an old woman to seek her fortune in! And how shall I find those to whom I am known? As well look for the rush in the papyrus-roll.[1] Begone! thou knave! and let my basket of simples lie; or, by the Gods, I'll doctor thee with them!'

I turned, wondering, and found myself face to face with my foster-nurse, Atoua. She knew me instantly, for I saw her start, but in the presence of the people she checked her surprise.

'Good Sir,' she whined, lifting her withered countenance towards me, and at the same time making the secret sign. 'By thy dress thou shouldst be an astronomer, and I

---

[1] Papyrus was manufactured from the pith of rushes. Hence Atoua's saying.—ED.

was specially told to avoid astronomers as a pack of lying
tricksters who worship their own star only; and, therefore,
I speak to thee, acting on the principle of contraries, which
is law to us women. For surely in this Alexandria, where
all things are upside down, the astronomers may be the honest
men, since the rest are clearly knaves.' And then, being by
now out of earshot of the press, 'royal Harmachis, I am come
charged with a message to thee from thy father Amenemhat.'

'Is he well?' I asked.

'Yes, he is well, though waiting for the moment tries
him sorely.'

'And his message?'

'It is this. He sends greeting to thee and with it warning
that a great danger threatens thee, though he cannot read it.
These are his words : '' Be steadfast and prosper.'' '

I bowed my head and the words struck a new chill of fear
into my soul.

'When is the time?' she asked.

'This very night.   Where goest thou?'

'To the house of the honourable Sepa, Priest of Annu.
Canst thou guide me thither?'

'Nay, I may not stay; nor is it wise that I should be seen
with thee.   Hold!' and I called a porter who was idling on
the quay, and, giving him a piece of money, bade him guide
the old wife to the house.

'Farewell,' she whispered; 'farewell till to-morrow.   Be
steadfast and prosper.'

Then I turned and went my way through the crowded
streets, where the people made place for me, the astronomer
of Cleopatra, for my fame had spread abroad.

And even as I went my footsteps seemed to beat *Be steadfast, Be steadfast, Be steadfast,* till at last it was as though
the very ground cried out its warning to me.

CHAPTER VII.

OF THE VEILED WORDS OF CHARMION; OF THE PASSING OF
HARMACHIS INTO THE PRESENCE OF CLEOPATRA; AND OF
THE OVERTHROW OF HARMACHIS.

was night, and I sat alone in my chamber, waiting the moment when, as it was agreed, Charmion should summon me to pass down to Cleopatra. I sat alone, and there before me lay the dagger that was to pierce her. It was long and keen, and the handle was formed of a sphinx of solid gold. I sat alone, questioning the future, but no answer came. At length I looked up, and Charmion stood before me—Charmion, no longer gay and bright, but pale of face and hollow-eyed.

'Royal Harmachis,' she said, 'Cleopatra summons thee, presently to declare to her the voices of the stars.'

So the hour had fallen!

'It is well, Charmion,' I answered. 'Are all things in order?'

'Yea, my Lord; all things are in order: well primed with wine, Paulus guards the gates, the eunuchs are withdrawn save one, the legionaries sleep, and already Sepa and his force lie hid without. Nothing has been neglected, and no lamb skipping at the shamble doors can be more innocent of its doom than is Queen Cleopatra.'

' It is well,' I said again; ' let us be going,' and rising, I placed the dagger in the bosom of my robe. Taking a cup of wine that stood near, I drank deep of it, for I had scarce tasted food all that day.

' One word,' Charmion said hurriedly, ' for it is not yet time : last night—ah, last night—' and her bosom heaved, ' I dreamed a dream that haunts me strangely, and perchance thou also didst dream a dream. It was all a dream and 'tis forgotten : is it not so, my Lord ? '

' Yes, yes,' I said; ' why troublest thou me thus at such an hour ? '

' Nay, I know not ; but to-night, Harmachis, Fate is in labour of a great event, and in her painful throes mayhap she'll crush me in her grip—me or thee, or the twain of us, Harmachis. And if that be so—well, I would hear from thee, before it is done, that 'twas naught but a dream, and that dream forgot ——'

' Yes, it is all a dream,' I said idly ; ' thou and I, and the solid earth, and this heavy night of terror, ay, and this keen knife—what are these but dreams, and with what face shall the waking come ? '

' So now, thou fallest in my humour, royal Harmachis. As thou sayest, we dream ; and while we dream yet can the vision change. For the phantasies of dreams are wonderful, seeing that they have no stability, but vary like the vaporous edge of sunset clouds, building now this thing, and now that ; being now dark and heavy, and now alight with splendour. Therefore, before we wake to-morrow tell me one word. Is that vision of last night, wherein I *seemed* to be quite shamed, and thou didst *seem* to laugh upon my shame, a fixed phantasy, or can it, perchance, yet change its countenance? For remember, when that waking comes, the vagaries of our sleep will be more unalterable and more enduring than are the pyramids. Then they will be gathered into that changeless region of the past where all things, great and small—ay, even dreams, Harmachis—are, each in its own semblance, frozen to stone and built into the Tomb of Time immortal.'

'Nay, Charmion,' I replied, 'I grieve if I did pain thee; but over that vision comes no change. I said what was in my heart and there's an end. Thou art my cousin and my friend, I can never be more to thee.'

'It is well—'tis very well,' she said; 'let it be forgotten. And now on from dream—to dream,' and she smiled with such a smile as I had never seen her wear before; it was sadder and more fateful than any stamp that grief can set upon the brow.

For, though being blinded by my own folly and the trouble at my heart I knew it not, with that smile, the happiness of youth died for Charmion the Egyptian; the hope of love fled; and the holy links of duty burst asunder. With that smile she consecrated herself to Evil, she renounced her Country and her Gods, and trampled on her oath. Ay, that smile marks the moment when the stream of history changed its course. For had I never seen it on her face Octavianus had not bestridden the world, and Egypt had once more been free and great.

And yet it was but a woman's smile!

'Why lookest thou thus strangely, girl?' I asked.

'In dreams we smile,' she answered. 'And now it is time; follow thou me. Be firm and prosper, royal Harmachis!' and bending forward she took my hand and kissed it. Then, with one strange last look, she turned and led the way down the stair and through the empty halls.

In the chamber that is called the Alabaster Hall, the roof of which is upborne by columns of black marble, we stayed. For beyond was the private chamber of Cleopatra, the same in which I had seen her sleeping.

'Abide thou here,' she said, ' while I tell Cleopatra of thy coming,' and she glided from my side.

I stood for long, mayhap in all the half of an hour, counting my own heart-beats, and, as in a dream, striving to gather up my strength to that which lay before me.

At length Charmion came back, her head held low and walking heavily.

' Cleopatra waits thee,' she said : 'pass on, there is no guard.'

' Where do I meet thee when what must be done is done ? ' I asked hoarsely.

' Thou meetest me here, and then to Paulus. Be firm and prosper. Harmachis, fare thee well ! '

And so I went ; but at the curtain I turned suddenly, and there in the midst of that lonely lamplit hall I saw a strange sight. Far away, in such a fashion that the light struck full upon her, stood Charmion, her head thrown back, her white arms outstretched as though to clasp, and on her girlish face a stamp of anguished passion so terrible to see that, indeed, I cannot tell it ! For she believed that I, whom she loved, was passing to my death, and this was her last farewell to me.

But I knew naught of this matter ; so with another passing pang of wonder I drew aside the curtains, gained the doorway, and stood in Cleopatra's chamber. And there, upon a silken couch at the far end of the perfumed chamber, clad in wonderful white attire, rested Cleopatra. In her hand was a jewelled fan of ostrich plumes, with which she gently fanned herself, and by her side was her harp of ivory, and a little table whereon were figs and goblets and a flask of ruby-coloured wine. I drew near slowly through the soft dim light to where the Wonder of the World lay in all her glowing beauty. And, indeed, I have never seen her look so fair as she did upon that fatal night. Couched in her amber cushions, she seemed to shine as a star on the twilight's glow. Perfume came from her hair and robes, music fell from her lips, and in her heavenly eyes all lights changed and gathered as in the ominous opal's disc.

And this was the woman whom, presently, I must slay !

Slowly I drew near, bowing as I came ; but she took no heed. She lay there, and the jewelled fan floated to and fro like the bright wing of some hovering bird.

At length I stood before her, and she glanced up, the ostrich-plumes pressed against her breast as though to hide its beauty.

'What ! friend ; art thou come ? ' she said. ' It is well ; for I grew lonely here. Nay ; 'tis a weary world ! We know so many faces, and there are so few whom we love to see again. Well, stand not there so mute, but be seated.' And she pointed with her fan to a carven chair that was placed near her feet.

Once more I bowed and took the seat.

'I have obeyed the Queen's desire,' I said, ' and with much care and skill worked out the lessons of the stars ; and here is the record of my labour. If the Queen permits, I will expound it to her.' And I rose, in order that I might pass round the couch and, as she read, stab her in the back.

' Nay, Harmachis,' she said quietly, and with a slow and lovely smile. ' Bide thou where thou art, and give me the writing. By Serapis ! thy face is too comely for me to wish to lose the sight of it ! '

Checked in this design, I could do nothing but hand her the papyrus, thinking to myself that while she read I would arise suddenly and plunge the dagger to her heart. She took it, and as she did so touched my hand. Then she made pretence to read. But she read no word, for I saw that her eyes were fixed upon me over the edge of the scroll.

' Why placest thou thy hand within thy robe ? ' she asked presently ; for, indeed, I clutched the dagger's hilt. ' Is thy heart stirred ? '

' Yea, O Queen,' I said ; ' it beats high.'

She gave no answer, but once more made pretence to read, and the while she watched me.

I took counsel with myself. How should I do the hateful deed ? If I flung myself upon her now she would see me and scream and struggle. Nay, I must wait a chance.

' The auguries are favourable, then, Harmachis ? ' she said at length, though this she must have guessed.

' Yes, O Queen,' I answered.

' It is well,' and she cast the writing on the marble. ' The ships shall sail. For, good or bad, I am weary of weighing chances.

' This is a heavy matter, O Queen,' I said. ' I had wished to show upon what circumstance I base my forecast.'

' Nay, not so, Harmachis ; I have wearied of the ways of stars. Thou hast prophesied ; that is enough for me ; for, doubtless, being honest, thou hast written honestly. Therefore, save thou thy reasons and we'll be merry. What shall we do ? I could dance to thee—there are none who can dance so well !—but it would scarce be queenly. Nay, I have it, I will sing.' And, leaning forward, she raised herself, and, bending the harp towards her, struck some wandering chords. Then her low voice broke out in perfect and most sweet song.

And thus she sang:

> '*Night on the sea, and night upon the sky,*
> *And music in our hearts, we floated there,*
> *Lulled by the low sea voices, thou and I,*
> *And the wind's kisses in my cloudy hair :*
> *And thou didst gaze on me and call me fair—*
> *Enfolded by the starry robe of night—*
> *And then thy singing thrilled upon the air,*
> *Voice of the heart's desire and Love's delight.*'

> '*Adrift, with starlit skies above,*
> *With starlit seas below,*
> *We move with all the suns that move,*
> *With all the seas that flow ;*
> *For bond or free, Earth, Sky, and Sea,*
> *Wheel with one circling will,*
> *And thy heart drifteth on to me,*
> *And only time stands still.*

> *Between two shores of Death we drift,*
> *Behind are things forgot :*
> *Before the tide is driving swift*
> *To lands beholden not.*
> *Above, the sky is far and cold ;*
> *Below, the moaning sea*
> *Sweeps o'er the loves that were of old,*
> *But, oh, Love ! kiss thou me.*

> *Ah, lonely are the ocean ways,*
> *And dangerous the deep,*
> *And frail the fairy barque that strays*
> *Above the seas asleep !*
> *Ah, toil no more at sail nor oar,*
> *We drift, or bond or free ;*
> *On yon far shore the breakers roar,*
> *But, oh, Love ! kiss thou me.*'

' And ever as thou sangest I drew near,
  Then sudden silence heard our hearts that beat,
For now there was an end of doubt and fear,
  Now passion filled my soul and led my feet;
Then silent didst thou rise thy love to meet,
  Who, sinking on thy breast, knew naught but thee,
And in the happy night I kissed thee, Sweet;
  Ah. Sweet ! between the starlight and the sea.'

The last echoes of her rich notes floated down the chamber,
and slowly died away ; but in my heart they rolled on and on.
I have heard among the women-singers at Abouthis voices
more perfect than the voice of Cleopatra, but never have I
heard one so thrilling or so sweet with passion's honey-notes.
And indeed it was not the voice alone, it was the perfumed
chamber in which was set all that could move the sense ; it was
the passion of the thought and words, and the surpassing
grace and loveliness of that most royal woman who sang
them. For, as she sang, I seemed to think that we twain
were indeed floating alone with the night, upon the starlit
summer sea. And when she ceased to touch the harp, and,
rising, suddenly stretched out her arms towards me, and with
the last low notes of song yet quivering upon her lips, let fall
the wonder of her eyes upon my eyes, she almost drew me to
her. But I remembered, and would not.

'Hast thou, then, no word of thanks for my poor singing,
Harmachis ?' she said at length.

'Yea, O Queen,' I answered, speaking very low, for my
voice was choked ; 'but thy songs are not good for the sons
of men to hear—of a truth they overwhelm me !'

'Nay, Harmachis ; there is no fear for thee,' she said
laughing softly, 'seeing that I know how far thy thoughts
are set from woman's beauty and the common weakness of
thy sex. With cold iron we may safely toy.'

N

I thought within myself that coldest iron can be brought to whitest heat if but the fire be fierce enough. But I said nothing, and, though my hand trembled, I once more grasped the dagger's hilt, and, wild with fear at my own weakness, set myself to find a means to slay her while yet my sense remained.

'Come hither, Harmachis,' she went on, in her softest voice. 'Come, sit by me, and we will talk together; for I have much to tell thee,' and she made place for me at her side upon the silken seat.

And I, thinking that I might so more swiftly strike, rose and seated myself some little way from her on the couch, while, flinging back her head, she gazed on me with her slumbrous eyes.

Now was my occasion, for her throat and breast were bare, and, with a mighty effort, once again I lifted my hand to clutch the dagger-hilt. But, more quick than thought, she caught my fingers with her own and gently held them.

'Why lookest thou so wildly, Harmachis?' she said. 'Art sick?'

'Ay, sick indeed!' I gasped.

'Then lean thou on the cushions and rest thee,' she answered, still holding my hand, from which the strength had fled. 'The fit will surely pass. Too long hast thou laboured with thy stars. How soft is the night air that flows from yonder casement heavy with the breath of lilies! Hark to the whisper of the sea lapping against the rocks, that, though it is faint, yet, being so strong, doth almost drown the quick cool fall of yonder fountain. List to Philomel; how sweet from a full heart of love she sings her message to her dear! Indeed it is a lovely night, and most beautiful is Nature's music, sung with a hundred voices from wind and trees and birds and ocean's wrinkled lips, and yet sung all to tune.

Listen, Harmachis: I have guessed something concerning thee. Thou, too, art of a royal race; no humble blood pours in those veins of thine. Surely such a shoot could spring but from the stock of Princes? What! gazest thou at the leaf-mark on my breast? It was pricked there in honour of great Osiris, whom with thee I worship. See!'

'Let me hence,' I groaned, striving to rise; but all my strength had gone.

'Nay, not yet awhile. Thou wouldst not leave me yet? thou *canst* not leave me yet. Harmachis, hast thou never loved?'

'Nay, nay, O Queen! What have I to do with love? Let me hence!—I am faint—I am fordone!'

'Never to have loved—'tis strange! Never to have known some woman-heart beat all in tune to thine—never to have seen the eyes of thy adored aswim with passion's tears, as she sighed her vows upon thy breast!—Never to have loved!— never to have lost thyself in the mystery of another's soul; nor to have learned how Nature can overcome our naked loneliness. and with the golden web of love of twain weave one identity! Why. it is never to have lived, Harmachis!'

And ever as she murmured she drew nearer to me, till at last, with a long, sweet sigh, she flung one arm about my neck. and gazed upon me with blue, unfathomable eyes, and smiled her dark. slow smile, that, like an opening flower, revealed beauty within beauty hidden. Nearer she bent her queenly form, and still more near—now her perfumed breath played upon my hair, and now her lips met mine.

And woe is me! In that kiss, more deadly and more strong than the embrace of Death, were forgotten Isis, my heavenly Hope. Oaths. Honour, Country, Friends, all things— all things save that Cleopatra clasped me in her arms, and called me Love and Lord.

'Now pledge me,' she sighed; 'pledge me one cup of wine in token of thy love.'

I took the draught, and I drank deep; then too late I knew that it was drugged.

I fell upon the couch, and, though my senses still were with me, I could neither speak nor rise.

But Cleopatra, bending over me, drew the dagger from my robe.

'*I've won!*' she cried, shaking back her long hair. 'I've won, and for the stake of Egypt, why, 'twas a game worth playing! With this dagger, then, thou wouldst have slain me, O my royal Rival, whose myrmidons even now are gathered at my palace gate? Art still awake? Now what hinders me that I should not plunge it to *thy* heart?'

I heard and feebly pointed to my breast, for I was fain to die. She drew herself to the full of her imperial height, and the great knife glittered in her hand. Down it came till its edge pricked my flesh.

'Nay,' she cried again, and cast it from her, 'too well I like thee. It were pity to slay such a man! I give thee thy life. Live on, lost Pharaoh! Live on, poor fallen Prince, blasted by a woman's wit! Live on, Harmachis—to adorn my triumph!'

Then sight left me; and in my ears I only heard the song of the nightingale, the murmur of the sea, and the music of Cleopatra's laugh of victory. And as I sank away, the sound of that low laugh still followed me into the land of sleep, and still it follows me through life to death.

CHAPTER VIII.

OF THE AWAKING OF HARMACHIS; OF THE SIGHT OF DEATH;
OF THE COMING OF CLEOPATRA; AND OF HER COMFORT-
ABLE WORDS.

more I woke; it was to find myself in my own chamber. I started up. Surely, I, too, had dreamed a dream? It could be nothing but a dream? It could not be that I woke to know myself a *traitor!* That the opportunity had gone for ever! That I had betrayed the cause, and that last night those brave men, headed by my uncle, had waited in vain at the outer gate! That Egypt from Abu to Athu was even now waiting—waiting in vain! Nay, whatever else might be, this could not be! Oh, it was an awful dream which I had dreamed! a second such would slay a man. It were better to die than face such another vision sent from hell. But, though the thing was naught but a hateful phantasy of a mind o'erstrained, where was I now? Where was I now? I should be in the Alabaster Hall, waiting till Charmion came forth.

Where was I? and O ye Gods! what was that dreadful thing, whose shape was the shape of a man?—that thing

draped in bloodstained white and huddled in a hideous heap
at the foot of the couch on which I seemed to lie?

I sprang at it with a shriek, as a lion springs, and struck
with all my strength. The blow fell heavily, and beneath its
weight the thing rolled over upon its side. Half mad with
terror, I rent away the white covering; and there, his knees
bound beneath his hanging jaw, was the naked body of a man
—and that man the Roman Captain Paulus! There he lay,
through his heart a dagger—my dagger, handled with the
sphinx of gold!—and pinned by its blade to his broad breast
a scroll, and on the scroll, writing in the Roman character. I
drew near and read, and this was the writing:

HARMACHIDI · SALVERE · EGO · SUM · QUEM · SUBDERE · NORAS
PAULUS · ROMANUS · DISCE · HINC · QUID · PRODERE · PROSIT.

*' Greeting, Harmachis! I was that Roman Paulus whom thou
didst suborn. Learn now how blessed are traitors!'*

Sick and faint I staggered back from the sight of that
white corpse stained with its own blood. Sick and faint I
staggered back, till the wall stayed me, while without the
birds sang a merry greeting to the day. So it was no dream,
and I was lost! lost!

I thought of my aged father, Amenemhat. Yes, the vision
of him flashed into my mind, as he would be, when they came
to tell him his son's shame and the ruin of his hopes. I
thought of that patriot priest, my uncle Sepa, waiting the
long night through for the signal which never came. Ah, and
another thought followed swift! How would it go with them?
I was not the only traitor. I, too, had been betrayed. By
whom? By yonder Paulus, perchance. If it were Paulus, he
knew but little of those who conspired with me. But the
secret lists had been in my robe. O Osiris! they were gone!
and the fate of Paulus would be the fate of all the patriots in

Egypt. And at this thought my mind gave way. I sank and swooned even where I stood.

My sense came back to me, and the lengthening shadows told me that it was afternoon. I staggered to my feet; the corpse of Paulus was still there, keeping its awful watch above me. I ran desperately to the door. It was barred, and without I heard the tramp of sentinels. As I stood they challenged and grounded their spears. Then the bolts were shot back, the door opened, and radiant, clad in royal attire, came the conquering Cleopatra. She came alone, and the door was shut behind her. I stood like one distraught; but she swept on till she was face to face with me.

'Greeting, Harmachis,' she said, smiling sweetly. 'So, my messenger has found thee!' and she pointed to the corpse of Paulus. 'Pah! he has an ugly look. Ho! guards!'

The door was opened, and two armed Gauls stepped across the threshold.

'Take away this carrion,' said Cleopatra, 'and fling it to the kites. Stay, draw that dagger from his traitor breast.' The men bowed low, and the knife, rusted red with blood, was dragged from the heart of Paulus and laid upon the table. Then they seized him by the head and body and staggered thence, and I heard their heavy footfalls as they bore him down the stairs.

'Methinks, Harmachis, thou art in an evil case,' she said, when the sound of the footfalls had died away. 'How strangely the wheel of Fortune turns! But for that traitor,' and she nodded towards the door through which the corpse of Paulus had been carried, 'I should now be as ill a thing to look on as he is, and the red rust on yonder knife would have been gathered from *my* heart.'

So it was Paulus who had betrayed me.

'Ay,' she went on, 'and when thou camest to me last

night, I *knew* that thou camest to slay. When, time upon time, thou didst place thy hand within thy robe, I knew that it grasped a dagger hilt, and that thou wast gathering thy courage to the deed which thou didst little love to do. Oh ! it was a strange wild hour, well worth the living, and I wondered greatly, from moment to moment, which of us twain would conquer, as we matched guile with guile and force to force!

' Yea, Harmachis, the guards tramp before thy door, but be not deceived. Did I not know that I hold thee to me by bonds more strong than prison chains—did I not know that I am hedged from ill at thy hands by a fence of honour harder for thee to pass than all the spears of all my legions, thou hadst been dead ere now, Harmachis. See, here is thy knife,' and she handed me the dagger; ' now slay me if thou canst,' and she drew near, tore open the bosom of her robe, and stood waiting with calm eyes.

' Thou canst not slay me,' she went on ; ' for there are things, as I know well, that no man—no such man as thou art—may do and live : and this is the chief of them—to slay the woman who is all his own. Nay, stay thy hand! Turn not that dagger against thy breast, for if thou mayst not slay me, by how much the more mayst thou not slay thyself, O thou forsworn Priest of Isis ! Art thou, then, so eager to face that outraged Majesty in Amenti ? With what eyes, thinkest thou, will the Heavenly Mother look upon Her son, who, shamed in all things and false to his most sacred vow, comes to greet Her, his life-blood on his hands ? Where, then, will be the space for thy atonement ?—if, indeed, thou mayst atone ! '

Then I could bear no more, for my heart was broken. Alas! it was too true—I dared not die! I was come to such a pass that I did not even dare to die! I flung myself upon the couch and wept—wept tears of blood and anguish.

But Cleopatra came to me, and, seating herself beside me, she strove to comfort me, throwing her arms about my neck.

' Nay, love, look up,' she said ; ' all is not lost for thee, nor am I angered against thee. We did play a mighty game ; but, as I warned thee, I matched my woman's magic against thine, and I have conquered. But I will be open with thee. Both as Queen and woman thou hast my pity—ay, and more ; nor do I love to see thee plunged in sorrow. It was well and right that thou shouldst strive to win back that throne my fathers seized, and the ancient liberty of Egypt. Myself as lawful Queen had done the same, nor shrunk from the deed of darkness to which I was sworn. Therein, then, thou hast my sympathy, that goes ever out to what is great and bold. It is well also that thou shouldst grieve over the greatness of thy fall. Therein, then, as woman—as loving woman—thou hast my sympathy. Nor is all lost. Thy plan was foolish—for, as I hold, Egypt could never have stood alone—for though thou hadst won the crown and country—as without a doubt thou must have done—yet there was the Roman to be reckoned with. And for thy hope learn this : I am little known. There is no heart in this wide land that beats with a truer love for ancient Khem than does this heart of mine—nay, not thine own, Harmachis. Yet I have been heavily shackled heretofore— for wars, rebellions, envies, plots, have hemmed me in on every side, so that I might not serve my people as I would. But thou, Harmachis, shalt show me how. Thou shalt be my counsellor and my love. Is it a little thing, Harmachis, to have won the heart of Cleopatra ; that heart—fie on thee!—that thou wouldst have stilled ? Yes, *thou* shalt unite me to my people and we will reign together, thus linking in one the new kingdom and the old and the new thought and the old. So do all things work for good—ay, for the very best : and thus, by another and a gentler road, thou shalt climb to Pharaoh's throne.

'See thou this, Harmachis : thy treachery shall be cloaked about as much as may be. Was it, then, thy fault that a Roman knave betrayed thy plans? that, thereon, thou wast drugged, thy secret papers stolen and their key guessed? Will it, then, be a blame to thee, the great plot being broken and those who built it scattered, that thou, still faithful to thy trust, didst serve thee of such means as Nature gave thee, and win the heart of Egypt's Queen, that, through her gentle love, thou mightest yet attain thy ends and spread thy wings of power across the land of Nile? Am I an ill-counsellor, thinkest thou, Harmachis?'

I lifted my head, and a ray of hope crept into the darkness of my heart; for when men fall they grasp at feathers. Then, I spoke for the first time :

'And those with me—those who trusted me—what of them?'

'Ay,' she answered, 'Amenemhat, thy father, the aged Priest of Abydus; and Sepa, thy uncle, that fiery patriot, whose great heart is hid beneath so common a shell of form , and——'

I thought she would have said Charmion, but she named her not.

'And many others—oh, I know them all !'

'Ay !' I said, 'what of them?'

'Hear now, Harmachis,' she answered, rising and placing her hand upon my arm, 'for thy sake I will show mercy to them. I will do no more than must be done. I swear by my throne and by all the Gods of Egypt that not one hair of thy aged father's head shall be harmed by me : and, if it be not too late, I will also spare thy uncle Sepa, ay, and the others. I will not do as did my forefather Epiphanes, who, when the Egyptians rose against him, dragged Athinis, Pausiras, Chesuphus, and Irobashtus, bound to his chariot—not as

Achilles dragged Hector, but yet living—round the city walls.
I will spare them all, save the Hebrews, if there be any
Hebrews ; for the Jews I hate.'

'There are no Hebrews,' I said.

'It is well,' she said, 'for no Hebrew will I ever spare.
Am I then, indeed, so cruel a woman as they say ? In thy
list, Harmachis, were many doomed to die ; and I have but
taken the life of one Roman knave, a double traitor, for he
betrayed both me and thee.   Art thou not overwhelmed,
Harmachis, with the weight of mercy which I give thee,
because—such are a woman's reasons—thou pleasest me,
Harmachis ? Nay, by Serapis ! ' she added with a little laugh,
'I'll change my mind ; I will not give thee so much for
nothing. Thou shalt buy it from me, and the price shall be a
heavy one—it shall be a kiss, Harmachis.'

'Nay,' I said, turning from that fair temptress, 'the
price is too heavy ; I kiss no more.'

'Bethink thee,' she answered, with a heavy frown. 'Bethink thee and choose.   I am but a woman, Harmachis, and
one who is not wont to sue to men. Do as thou wilt ; but this
I say to thee—if thou dost put me away, I will gather up the
mercy I have meted out.   Therefore, most virtuous priest,
choose thou between the heavy burden of my love and the swift
death of thy aged father and of all those who plotted with
him.

I glanced at her and saw that she was angered, for her
eyes shone and her bosom heaved.   So, I sighed and kissed
her, thereby setting the seal upon my shame and bondage.
Then, smiling like the triumphant Aphrodité of the Greeks,
she went thence, bearing the dagger with her.

I knew not yet how deeply I was betrayed ; or why I was
still left to draw the breath of life ; or why Cleopatra, the
tiger-hearted, had grown merciful.   I did not know that she

o

feared to slay me, lest, so strong was the plot and so feeble her hold upon the Double Crown, the tumult that might tread hard upon the tidings of my murder should shake her from the throne—even when I was no more. I did not know that because of fear and the weight of policy only she showed scant mercy to those whom I had betrayed, or that because of cunning and not for the holy sake of woman's love—though, in truth, she liked me well enough—she chose rather to bind me to her by the fibres of my heart. And yet I will say this in her behalf: even when the danger-cloud had melted from her sky she kept her faith, nor, save Paulus and one other, did any suffer the utmost penalty of death for their part in the great plot against Cleopatra's crown and dynasty. But they suffered many other things.

And so she went, leaving the vision of her glory to strive with the shame and sorrow in my heart. Oh, bitter were the hours that could not now be made light with prayer. For the link between me and the Divine was snapped, and Isis communed with Her Priest no more. Bitter were the hours and dark, but ever through their darkness shone the starry eyes of Cleopatra, and came the echo of her whispered love. For not yet was the cup of sorrow full. Hope still lingered in my heart, and I could almost think that I had failed to some higher end, and that in the depths of ruin I should find another and more flowery path to triumph.

For thus those who sin deceive themselves, striving to lay the burden of their evil deeds upon the back of Fate, striving to believe their wickedness may compass good, and to murder Conscience with the sharp plea of Necessity. But it can avail nothing, for hand in hand down the path of sin rush Remorse and Ruin, and woe to him they follow ! Ay, and woe to me who of all sinners am the chief !

CHAPTER IX.

OF THE IMPRISONMENT OF HARMACHIS; OF THE SCORN **OF** CHARMION; OF THE SETTING FREE OF HARMACHIS; AND **OF** THE COMING OF QUINTUS DELLIUS.

a space of eleven days I was thus kept prisoned in my chamber; nor did I see anyone except the sentries at my doors, the slaves who in silence brought me food and drink, and Cleopatra's self, who came continually. But, though her words of love were many, she would tell me nothing of how things went without. She came in many moods—now gay and laughing, now full of wise thoughts and speech, and now passionate only, **and** to every mood she gave some new-found charm. She was full of talk as to how I should help her make Egypt great, **and** lessen the burdens on the people, and fright the Roman eagles back. And, though at first I listened heavily when she spoke thus, by slow advance as she wrapped me closer and yet more close in her magic web, from which there was no escape, **my** mind fell in time with hers. Then I, too, opened something of my heart, and somewhat also of the plans that I had formed for Egypt. She seemed to listen gladly, weighing them all, and spoke of means and methods, telling me how she would purify

o 2

the Faith and repair the ancient temples—ay, and build new
ones to the Gods. And ever she crept deeper into my heart,
till at length, now that every other thing had gone from me, I
learned to love her with all the unspent passion of my aching
soul. I had naught left to me but Cleopatra's love, and I
twined my life about it, and brooded on it as a widow over
her only babe. And thus the very author of my shame
became my all, my dearest dear, and I loved her with a
strong love that grew and grew, till it seemed to swallow up
the past and make the present as a dream. For she had
conquered me, she had robbed me of my honour, and steeped
me to the lips in shame, and I, poor fallen, blinded wretch, I
kissed the rod that smote me, and was her very slave.

Ay, even now, in those dreams which will come when
Sleep unlocks the secret heart, and sets its terrors free to
roam through the opened halls of Thought, I seem to see her
royal form, as erst I saw it, come with arms outstretched
and Love's own light shining in her eyes, with lips apart
and flowing locks, and stamped upon her face the look of
utter tenderness that she alone could wear. Ay, still, after
all the years, I seem to see her come as erst she came, and
still I wake to know her an unutterable lie !

And thus one day she came. She had fled in haste, she
said, from some great council summoned concerning the wars
of Antony in Syria, and she came, as she had left the council,
in all her robes of state, the sceptre in her hand, and on
her brow the uræus diadem of gold. There she sat before
me, laughing ; for, wearying of them, she had told the envoys
to whom she gave audience in the council that she was called
from their presence by a sudden message come from Rome ;
and the jest seemed merry to her. Suddenly she rose, took
the diadem from her brow, and set it on my hair, and on my
shoulders her royal mantle, and in my hand the sceptre,

and bowed the knee before me. Then, laughing again, she
kissed me on the lips, and said I was indeed her King. But,
remembering how I had been crowned in the halls of Abouthis,
and remembering also that wreath of roses of which the odour
haunts me yet, I rose, pale with wrath, and cast the trinkets
from me, asking how she dared to mock me—her caged bird.
And I think there was that about me which startled her,
for she fell back.

'Nay, Harmachis,' she said, 'be not wroth! How
knowest thou that I mock thee? How knowest thou that
thou shalt not be Pharaoh in fact and deed?'

'What meanest thou?' I said. 'Wilt thou, then, wed
me before Egypt? How else can I be Pharaoh now?'

She cast down her eyes. 'Perchance, love, it is in my
mind to wed thee,' she said gently. 'Listen,' she went on:
'Thou growest pale, here, in this prison, and thou dost eat
little. Gainsay me not! I know it from the slaves. I have
kept thee here, Harmachis, for thy own sake, that is so dear
to me; and for thy own sake, and thy honour's sake, thou
must still seem to be my prisoner. Else wouldst thou be
shamed and slain—ay, murdered secretly. But I can meet
thee here no more! therefore to-morrow I will free thee in
all, save in the name, and thou shalt once more be seen at
Court as my astronomer. And I will give this reason—that
thou hast cleared thyself; and, moreover, that thy auguries
as regards the war have been auguries of truth—as, indeed,
they have, though for this I have no cause to thank thee,
seeing that thou didst suit thy prophecies to fit thy cause.
Now, farewell; for I must return to those heavy-browed ambassadors; and grow not so sudden wroth, Harmachis, for
who knows what may come to pass betwixt thee and me?'

And, with a little nod, she went, leaving it on my mind
that she had it in her heart to wed me openly. And of a

truth, I believe that, at this hour, such was her thought. For, if she loved me not, still she held me dear, and as yet she had not wearied of me.

On the morrow Cleopatra came not, but Charmion came—Charmion, whom I had not seen since that fatal night of ruin. She entered and stood before me, with pale face and downcast eyes, and her first words were words of bitterness.

'Pardon me,' she said, in her gentle voice, 'in that I dare to come to thee in Cleopatra's place. Thy joy is not delayed for long, for thou shalt see her presently.'

I shrank at her words, as well I might, and, seeing her vantage, she seized it.

'I come, Harmachis—royal no more!—I come to say that thou art free! Thou art free to face thine own infamy, and see it thrown back from every eye which trusted thee, as shadows are from water. I come to tell thee that the great plot—the plot of twenty years and more—is at its utter end. None have been slain, indeed, unless it is Sepa, who has vanished. But all the leaders have been seized and put in chains, or driven from the land, and their party is broken and scattered. The storm has melted before it burst. Egypt is lost, and lost for ever, for her last hope is gone! No longer may she struggle—now for all time she must bow her neck to the yoke, and bare her back to the rod of the oppressor!'

I groaned aloud. 'Alas, I was betrayed!' I said, 'Paulus betrayed us.'

'Thou wast betrayed? Nay, thou thyself wast the betrayer! How came it that thou didst not slay Cleopatra when thou wast alone with her? Speak, thou forsworn!'

'She drugged me,' I said again.

'O Harmachis!' answered the pitiless girl, 'how low art thou fallen from that Prince whom once I knew!—thou who dost not scorn to be a liar! Yea, thou wast drugged—drugged with a love-philtre! Yea, thou didst sell Egypt and thy cause for the price of a wanton's kiss! Thou Sorrow and thou Shame!' she went on, pointing her finger at me and lifting her eyes to my face, 'thou Scorn!—thou Outcast!— and thou Contempt! Deny it if thou canst. Ay, shrink from me—knowing what thou art, well mayst thou shrink! Crawl to Cleopatra's feet, and kiss her sandals till such time as it pleases her to trample thee in thy kindred dirt; but from all honest folk *shrink !—shrink !'*

My soul quivered beneath the lash of her bitter scorn and hate, but I had no words to answer.

'How comes it,' I said at last in a heavy voice, 'that thou, too, art not betrayed, but art still here to taunt me, thou who once didst swear that thou didst love me? Being a woman, hast thou no pity for the frailty of man?'

'My name was not on the lists,' she said, dropping her dark eyes. 'Here is an opportunity: betray me also, Harmachis! Ay, it is because I once loved thee—dost thou, indeed, remember it?—that I feel thy fall the more. The shame of one whom we have loved must in some sort become our shame, and must ever cling to us, because we blindly held a thing so base close to our inmost heart. Art thou also, then, a fool? Wouldst thou, fresh from thy royal wanton's arms, come to me for comfort—to *me* of all the world?'

'How know I,' I said, 'that it was not thou who, in thy jealous anger, didst betray our plans? Charmion, long ago Sepa warned me against thee, and of a truth now that I recall——'

'It is like a traitor,' she broke in, reddening to her brow, ' to think that all are of his family, and hold a common mind! Nay, I betrayed thee not ; it was that poor knave, Paulus, whose heart failed him at the last, and who is rightly served. Nor will I stay to hear thoughts so base. Harmachis—royal no more !—Cleopatra, Queen of Egypt, bids me say that thou art free, and that she waits thee in the Alabaster Hall.'

And shooting one swift glance through her long lashes she curtsied and was gone.

So once more I came and went about the Court, though but sparingly, for my heart was full of shame and terror, and on every face I feared to see the scorn of those who knew me for what I was. But I saw nothing, for all those who had knowledge of the plot had fled, and Charmion had spoken no word, for her own sake. Also, Cleopatra had put it about that I was innocent. But my guilt lay heavy on me, and made me thin and wore away the beauty of my countenance. And though I was free in name, yet I was ever watched ; nor might I stir beyond the palace grounds.

And at length came the day which brought with it Quintus Dellius, that false Roman knight who ever served the rising star. He bore letters to Cleopatra from Marcus Antonius, the Triumvir. who, fresh from the victory of Philippi, was now in Asia wringing gold from the subject kings with which to satisfy the greed of his legionaries.

Well I mind me of the day. Cleopatra, clad in her robes of state, attended by the officers of her Court, among whom I stood, sat in the great hall on her throne of gold, and bade the heralds admit the Ambassador of Antony. the Triumvir. The great doors were thrown wide, and amidst the blare of trumpets and salutes of the Gallic guards the Roman came in, clad in glittering golden armour and a scarlet cloak of silk, and followed by his suite of officers. He was smooth-faced and fair to look upon, and with a supple form ; but his mouth was cold, and false were his shifting eyes. And while the heralds called out his name, titles, and offices, he fixed his gaze on Cleopatra—who sat idly on her throne all radiant with beauty—as a man who is amazed. Then when the heralds had made an end, and he still stood thus, not stirring, Cleopatra spoke in the Latin tongue :

'Greeting to thee, noble Dellius, envoy of the most mighty Antony, whose shadow lies across the world as though Mars himself now towered up above us petty Princes—greeting and welcome to our poor city of Alexandria. Unfold, we pray thee, the purpose of thy coming.'

Still the crafty Dellius made no answer, but stood as a man amazed.

'What ails thee, noble Dellius, that thou dost not speak ? ' asked Cleopatra. 'Hast thou, then, wandered so long in Asia that the doors of Roman speech are shut to thee? What tongue hast thou ? Name it, and We will speak in it—for all tongues are known to Us.'

Then at last he spoke in a soft full voice : 'Oh, pardon me, most lovely Egypt, if I have thus been stricken dumb before thee . but too great beauty, like Death himself, doth paralyse the tongue and steal our sense away. The eyes of him who looks upon the fires of the mid-day sun are blind to all beside, and thus this sudden vision of thy glory, royal Egypt, overwhelmed my mind, and left me helpless and unwitting of all things else.'

'Of a truth, noble Dellius,' answered Cleopatra, 'they teach a pretty school of flattery yonder in Cilicia.'

'How goes the saying here in Alexandria ? ' replied the courtly Roman: "The breath of flattery cannot waft a cloud," [1] does it not ? But to my task. Here, royal Egypt, are letters under the hand and seal of the noble Antony treating of certain matters of the State. Is it thy pleasure that I should read them openly ? '

' In other words, what is Divine is beyond the reach of human praise.—ED

'Break the seals and read,' she answered.

Then bowing, he broke the seals and read:

'The *Triumviri Reipublicæ Constituendæ*, by the mouth
of Marcus Antonius, the Triumvir, to Cleopatra, by grace
of the Roman People Queen of Upper and Lower Egypt, send
greeting.   Whereas it has come to our knowledge that thou,
Cleopatra, hast, contrary to thy promise and thy duty, both
by thy servant Allienus and by thy servant Serapion, the
Governor of Cyprus, aided the rebel murderer Cassius against
the arms of the most noble Triumvirate. And, whereas it has
come to our knowledge that thou thyself wast but lately
making ready a great fleet to this end. We summon thee that
thou dost without delay journey to Cilicia, there to meet the
noble Antony, and in person make answer concerning these
charges which are laid against thee.   And we warn thee that
if thou dost disobey this our summons it is at thy peril. Farewell.

The eyes of Cleopatra flashed as she hearkened to these
high words, and I saw her hands tighten on the golden
lions' heads whereon they rested.

'We have had the flattery,' she said; 'and now, lest we
be cloyed with sweets, we have its antidote! Listen thou,
Dellius: the charges in that letter, or, rather, in that writ of
summons, are false, as all folk can bear us witness.   But it is
not now, and it is not to thee, that We will make defence of
our acts of war and policy.   Nor will We leave our kingdom
to journey into far Cilicia, and there, like some poor suppliant
at law, plead our cause before the Court of the noble Antony.
If Antony will have speech with us, and inquire concerning
these high matters, the sea is open and his welcome shall be
royal. Let him come hither. That is our answer to thee and
to the Triumvirate, O Dellius!'

But Dellius smiled as one who would put away the weight of wrath, and once more spoke :

'Royal Egypt, thou knowest not the noble Antony. He is stern on paper, and ever he sets down his thoughts as though his stylus were a spear dipped in the blood of men. But face to face with him, thou, of all the world, shalt find him the gentlest warrior that ever won a battle. Be advised, O Egypt! and come. Send me not hence with such angry words, for if thou dost draw Antony to Alexandria, then woe to Alexandria, to the people of the Nile, and to thee. great Egypt ! For then he will come armed and breathing war, and it shall go hard with thee, who dost defy the gathered might of Rome. I pray thee, then, obey this summons. Come to Cilicia ; come with peaceful gifts and not in arms. Come in thy beauty, and tricked in thy best attire, and thou hast naught to fear from the noble Antony.' He paused and looked at her meaningly ; while I, taking his drift, felt the angry blood surge into my face.

Cleopatra, too, understood, for I saw her rest her chin upon her hand and the cloud of thought gathered in her eyes. For a time she sat thus, while the crafty Dellius watched her curiously. And Charmion, standing with the other ladies by the throne, she also read his meaning, for her face lit up, as a summer cloud lights in the evening when the broad lightning flares behind it. Then once more it grew pale and quiet.

At length Cleopatra spoke. 'This is a heavy matter,' she said, ' and therefore, noble Dellius, we must have time to let our judgment ripen. Rest thou here, and make thee as merry as our poor circumstance allows. Thou shalt have thy answer within ten days.'

The envoy thought awhile, then replied smiling : ' It is

well, O Egypt ; on the tenth day from now I will attend for
my answer, and on the eleventh I sail hence to join Antony
my Lord.'

Once more, at a sign from Cleopatra, the trumpets blared,
and he withdrew bowing.

CHAPTER X.

OF THE TROUBLE OF CLEOPATRA; OF HER OATH TO HAR-
MACHIS; AND OF THE TELLING BY HARMACHIS TO CLEO-
PATRA OF THE SECRET OF THE TREASURE THAT LAY
BENEATH THE MASS OF 'HER.'

HAT same night Cleopatra summoned me to her private chamber.
I went, and found her much
troubled in mind; never before
had I seen her so deeply moved.
She was alone, and, like some
trapped lioness, walked to and fro
across the marble floor, while
thought chased thought across
her mind, each, as clouds scudding over
the sea, for a moment casting its shadow
in her deep eyes.

'So thou art come, Harmachis.' she said, resting for a
while, as she took my hand. 'Counsel me, for never did I
need counsel more. Oh, what days have the Gods measured
out to me—days restless as the ocean! I have known no
peace from childhood up, and it seems none shall I ever
know. Scarce by a very little have I escaped thy dagger's
point, Harmachis, when this new trouble, that, like a
storm, has gathered beneath the horizon's rim, suddenly
bursts over me. Didst mark that tigerish fop? Well should

I love to trap him! How soft he spoke! Ay. he purred
like a cat, and all the time he stretched his claws. Didst
hear the letter, too ? it has an ugly sound. I know this
Antony. When I was but a child, budding into womanhood,
I saw him ; but my eyes were ever quick, and I took his measure. Half Hercules and half a fool, with a dash of genius
veining his folly through. Easily led by those who enter at
the gates of his voluptuous sense ; but if crossed, an iron foe.
True to his friends, if, indeed he loves them ; and ofttimes
false to his own interest. Generous, hardy, and in adversity
a man of virtue ; in prosperity a sot and a slave to woman.
That is Antony. How deal with such a man, whom fate and
opportunity, despite himself, have set on the crest of fortune's
wave ? One day it will overwhelm him ; but till that day he
sweeps across the world and laughs at those who drown.'

'Antony is but a man,' I answered, 'and a man with many
foes; and, being but a man, he can be overthrown.'

'Ay, he can be overthrown ; but he is one of three, Harmachis. Now that Cassius hath gone where all fools go,
Rome has thrown out a hydra head. Crush one, and another
hisses in thy face. There's Lepidus, and, with him, that
young Octavianus, whose cold eyes may yet with a smile of
triumph look on the murdered forms of empty, worthless
Lepidus, of Antony, and of Cleopatra. If I go not to Cilicia,
mark thou! Antony will knit up a peace with these Parthians,
and, taking the tales they tell of me for truth—and, indeed,
there is truth in them—will fall with all his force on Egypt.
And how then ?'

'How then ? Why, then we'll drum him back to Rome.'

'Ah! thou sayest so. and. perchance, Harmachis, had I
not won that game we played together some twelve days gone,
thou, being Pharaoh. mightest well have done this thing, for
round thy throne old Egypt would have gathered. But Egypt

loves not me nor my Greek blood; and I have but now scattered that great plot of thine, in which half the land was meshed. Will these men, then, arise to succour me? Were Egypt true to me, I could, indeed, hold my own against all the force that Rome may bring; but Egypt hates me, and had as lief be ruled by the Roman as the Greek. Still I might make defence had I the gold, for with money soldiers can be bought to feed the maw of mercenary battle. But I have none; my treasuries are dry, and though there is wealth in the land, yet debts perplex me. These wars have brought me ruin, and I know not how to find a talent. Perchance, Harmachis, thou who art, by hereditary right, Priest of the Pyramids,' and she drew near and looked me in the eyes, ' perchance, if long descended rumour does not lie, thou canst tell me where I can touch the gold to save thy land from ruin, and thy Love from the grasp of Antony? Say, is it so?'

I thought a while, and then I answered:

' And if such a tale were true, and if I could show thee treasure stored by the mighty Pharaohs of the most far off age against the needs of Khem, how can I know that thou wouldst indeed make use of that wealth to those good ends?'

' Is there, then, a treasure?' she asked curiously. ' Nay, fret me not, Harmachis; for of a truth the very name of gold at this time of want is like the sight of water in the desert.'

' I believe,' I said, ' that there is such a treasure, though I myself have never seen it. But I know this, that if it still lie in the place where it was set, it is because so heavy a curse will rest upon him who shall lay hands on it wickedly and for selfish ends, that none of those Pharaohs to whom it has been shown have dared to touch it, however sore their need.'

' So,' she said, ' they were cowardly aforetime, or else their need was not great. Wilt thou show me this treasure, then, Harmachis?'

P

'Perhaps,' I answered, 'I will show it to thee if it still be there, when thou hast sworn that thou wilt use it to defend Egypt from this Roman Antony and for the welfare of her people.'

'I swear it!' she said earnestly. 'Oh, I swear by every God in Khem that if thou showest me this great treasure, I will defy Antony and send Dellius back to Cilicia with sharper words than those he brought. Yes, I'll do more, Harmachis: so soon as may be, I will take thee to husband before all the world, and thou thyself shalt carry out thy plans and beat off the Roman eagles.'

Thus she spoke, gazing at me with truthful, earnest eyes. I believed her, and for the first time since my fall was for a moment happy, thinking that all was not lost to me, and that with Cleopatra, whom I loved thus madly, I might yet win my place and power back.

'Swear it, Cleopatra!' I said.

'I swear, beloved! and thus I seal my oath!' and she kissed me on the forehead. And I, too, kissed her; and we talked of what we would do when we were wed, and how we should overcome the Roman.

And thus I was again beguiled; though I believe that, had it not been for the jealous anger of Charmion—which, as shall be seen, was ever urging her forward to fresh deeds of shame—Cleopatra would have wedded me and broken with the Roman. And, indeed, in the issue, it had been better for her and Egypt.

We sat far into the night, and I revealed to her somewhat of that ancient secret of the mighty treasure hid beneath the mass of *Her*. Thither, it was agreed, we should go on the morrow, and the second night from now attempt its search. So, early on the next day, a boat was secretly made ready, and Cleopatra entered it, veiled as an Egyptian lady about

to make a pilgrimage to the Temple of Horemkhu. And I
also entered, cloaked as a pilgrim, and with us ten of her
most trusted servants disguised as sailors. But Charmion
went not with us. We sailed with a fair wind from the
Canopic mouth of the Nile; and that night, pushing on
with the moon, we reached Sais at midnight, and here rested
for a while. At dawn we once more loosed our craft, and
all that day sailed swiftly, till, at last, at the third hour
from the sunset, we came in sight of the lights of that
fortress which is called Babylon. Here, on the opposite
bank of the river, we moored our ship safely in a bed of
reeds.

Then, on foot and secretly, we set out for the pyramids,
which were at a distance of two leagues, Cleopatra, I and one
trusted eunuch, for we left the other servants with the boat.
Only I caught an ass for Cleopatra to ride that was wandering in a tilled field, and threw a cloak upon it. She sat
on it and I led the ass by paths I knew, the eunuch following
us on foot. And, within little more than an hour, having gained
the great causeway, we saw the mighty pyramids towering up
through the moonlit air and aweing us to silence. We passed
on in utter silence, through the haunted city of the dead, for
all around us stood the solemn tombs, till at length we climbed
the rocky hill, and stood in the deep shadow of Khufu Khut,
the splendid Throne of Khufu.

' Of a truth,' whispered Cleopatra, as she gazed up the
dazzling marble slope above her, everywhere blazoned over
with a million mystic characters—' of a truth, there were
Gods ruling in Khem in those days, and not men. This place
is sad as Death--ay, and as mighty and far from man. Is it
here that we must enter ?'

' Nay,' I answered, ' it is not here. Pass on.'

I led the way through a thousand ancient tombs, till we

stood in the shadow of Ur the Great, and gazed at his red, heaven-piercing mass.

'Is it here that we must enter?' she whispered once again.

'Nay,' I answered, 'it is not here. Pass on.'

We passed on through many more tombs, till we stood in the shadow of *Her*,[1] and Cleopatra gazed astonished at its polished beauty, which for thousands of years, night by night, had mirrored back the moon, and at the black girdle of Ethiopian stone that circled its base about. For this is the most beautiful of all pyramids.

'Is it here that we must enter?' she said.

I answered, 'It is here.'

We passed round between the Temple of the Worship of his Divine Majesty, Menkau-ra, the Osirian, and the base of the pyramid till we came to the north side. Here in the centre is graved the name of Pharaoh Menkau-ra, who built the pyramid to be his tomb, and stored his treasure in it against the need of Khem.

'If the treasure still remains,' I said to Cleopatra, 'as it remained in the days of my great-great-grandfather, who was Priest of this Pyramid before me, it is hid deep in the womb of the mass before thee, Cleopatra ; nor can it be come by without toil, danger, and terror of mind. Art thou prepared to enter — for thou thyself must enter and must judge?'

'Canst thou not go in with the eunuch, Harmachis, and bring the treasure forth?' she said, for a little her courage began to fail her.

'Nay, Cleopatra,' I answered, 'not even for thee and for the weal of Egypt can I do this thing, for of all sins it would be the greatest sin. But it is lawful for me to do this.

[1] The 'Upper,' now known as the Third Pyramid.—ED.

I, as hereditary holder of the secret, may, upon demand, show to the ruling monarch of Khem the place where the treasure lies, and show also the warning that is written. And if on seeing and reading, the Pharaoh deems that the need of Khem is so sore and strait that it is lawful for him to brave the curse of the Dead and draw forth the treasure, it is well, for on his head must rest the weight of this dread deed. Three monarchs—so say the records that I have read—have thus dared to enter in the time of need. They were the Divine Queen Hat-shepsu, that wonder known to the Gods alone; her Divine brother Tahutimes Men-Kheper-ra; and the Divine Rameses Mi-amen. But of these three Majesties, not one when they saw dared to touch; for, though sharp their need, it was not great enough to consecrate the act. So, fearing lest the curse should fall upon them, they went hence sorrowing.'

She thought a little, till at last her spirit overcame her fear.

'At the least I will see with mine own eyes,' she said.

'It is well,' I answered. Then, stones having been piled up by me and the eunuch who was with us on a certain spot at the base of the pyramid, to somewhat more than the height of a man, I climbed on them and searched for the secret mark, no larger than a leaf. I found it with some trouble, for the weather and rubbing of the wind-stirred sand had worn even the Ethiopian stone. Having found it, I pressed on it with all my strength in a certain fashion. Even after the lapse of many years the stone swung round, showing a little opening, through which a man might scarcely creep. As it swung, a mighty bat, white in colour as though with unreckoned age, and such as I had never seen before for bigness, for his measure was the measure of a hawk, flew forth and for a moment hovered over Cleopatra, then sailed slowly up and up in circles, till at last he was lost in the bright light of the moon.

But Cleopatra uttered a cry of terror, and the eunuch, who was watching, fell down in fear, believing it to be the guardian Spirit of the pyramid. And I, too, feared, though I said nothing. For even now I believe that it was the Spirit of Menkau-ra, the Osirian, who, taking the form of a bat, flew forth from his holy House in warning.

I waited a while, till the foul air should clear from the passage. Then I drew out the lamps, kindled them, and passed them, to the number of three, into the entrance of the passage. This done, I went to the eunuch, and, taking him aside, I swore him by the living spirit of Him who sleeps at Abouthis that he should not reveal those things which he was about to see.

This he swore, trembling sorely, for he was very much afraid. Nor, indeed, did he reveal them.

This done, I clambered through the opening, taking with me a coil of rope, which I wound around my middle, and beckoned to Cleopatra to come. Making fast the skirt of her robe, she came, and I drew her through the opening, so that at length she stood behind me in the passage which is lined with slabs of granite. After her came the eunuch, and he also stood in the passage. Then, having taken counsel of the plan of the passage that I had brought with me, and which, in signs that none but the initiated can read, was copied from those ancient writings that had come down to me through one-and-forty generations of my predecessors, the Priests of this Pyramid of *Her*, and of the worship of the Temple of the Divine Menkau-ra, the Osirian, I led the way through that darksome place towards the utter silence of the tomb. Guided by the feeble light of our lamps, we passed down the steep incline, gasping in the heat and the thick, stagnated air. Presently we had left the region of the masonry and were slipping down a gallery hewn in the living rock. For twenty paces or more it ran steeply. Then its slope lessened and shortly we found ourselves in a chamber painted white, so low that I, being tall, had scarcely room to stand ; but in length four paces, and in breadth three, and cased throughout with sculptured panels. Here Cleopatra sank upon the floor and rested awhile, overcome by the heat and the utter darkness.

'Rise ! ' I said. 'We must not linger here, or we faint.'

So she rose, and, passing hand in hand through that chamber, we found ourselves face to face with a mighty door of granite, let down from the roof in grooves. Once more I took counsel of the plan, pressed with my foot upon a certain stone, and waited. Then, suddenly and softly, I know not by what means, the mass heaved itself from its bed of living rock. We passed beneath, and found ourselves face to face with a second door of granite. Again I pressed on a certain spot, and this door swung wide of itself, and we went through, to find ourselves face to face with a third door, yet more mighty than the two through which we had won our way. Following the secret plan, I struck this door with my foot upon a certain spot, and it sank slowly as though at a word of magic till its head was level with the floor of rock. We crossed and gained another passage which, descending gently for a length of fourteen paces, led us into a great chamber, paved with black marble, more than nine cubits high, by nine cubits broad, and thirty cubits long. In this marble floor was sunk a great sarcophagus of granite, and on its lid were graved the name and titles of the Queen of Menkau-ra. In this chamber, too, the air was purer, though I know not by what means it came thither.

'Is the treasure here ? ' gasped Cleopatra.

'Nay,' I answered; 'follow me,' and I led the way to a gallery, which we entered through an opening in the floor of the great chamber. It had been closed by a trap-door of stone, but the door was open. Creeping along this shaft, or passage, for some ten paces, we came at length to a well, seven cubits in depth. Making fast one end of the rope that I had brought about my body and the other to a ring in the rock, I was lowered, holding the lamp in my hand, till I stood in the last resting-place of the Divine Menkau-ra. Then the rope was drawn up, and Cleopatra, being made fast to it, was let down by the eunuch, and I received her in my arms. But I bade the eunuch, sorely against his will, since he feared to be left alone, await our return at the mouth of the shaft. For it was not lawful that he should enter whither we went.

CHAPTER XI.

OF THE TOMB OF THE DIVINE MENKAU-RA; OF THE WRITING
ON THE BREAST OF MENKAU-RA; OF THE DRAWING FORTH
OF THE TREASURE; OF THE DWELLER IN THE TOMB; AND
OF THE FLIGHT OF CLEOPATRA AND HARMACHIS FROM THE
HOLY PLACE.

stood within a small arched chamber, paved and lined with great blocks of the granite stone of Syene. There before us— hewn from a single mass of basalt shaped like a wooden house and resting on a sphinx with a face of gold—was the sarcophagus of the Divine Menkau-ra.

We stood and gazed in awe, for the weight of the silence and the solemnity of that holy place seemed to crush us. Above us, cubit over cubit in its mighty measure, the pyramid towered up to heaven and was kissed of the night air. But we were deep in the bowels of the rock beneath its base. We were alone with the dead, whose rest we were about to break; and no sound of the murmuring air, and no sight of life came to dull the awful edge of solitude. I gazed on the sarcophagus: its heavy lid had been lifted and rested at its side, and around it the dust of ages had gathered thick.

'See,' I whispered, pointing to a writing, daubed with pigment upon the wall in the sacred symbols of ancient times.

'Read it, Harmachis,' answered Cleopatra, in the same low voice; 'for I cannot.'

Then I read: 'I, Rameses Mi-amen, in my day and in my hour of need, visited this sepulchre. But, though great my need and bold my heart, I dared not face the curse of Menkau-ra. Judge, O thou who shalt come after me, and, if thy soul is pure and Khem be utterly distressed, take thou that which I have left.'

'Where, then, is the treasure?' she whispered. 'Is that Sphinx-face of gold?'

'Even there,' I answered, pointing to the sarcophagus. 'Draw near and see.'

And she took my hand and drew near.

The cover was off, but the painted coffin of the Pharaoh lay in the depths of the sarcophagus. We climbed the Sphinx, then I blew the dust from the coffin with my breath and read that which was written on its lid. And this was written:

'Pharaoh Menkau-ra, the Child of Heaven.

'Pharaoh Menkau-ra, Royal Son of the Sun.

'Pharaoh Menkau-ra, who didst lie beneath the heart of Nout.

'Nout, thy Mother, wraps thee in the spell of Her holy name.

'The name of thy Mother, Nout, is the mystery of Heaven.

'Nout, thy Mother, gathers thee to the number of the Gods.

'Nout, thy Mother, breathes on thy foes and utterly destroys them.

'O Pharaoh Menkau-ra, who livest for ever!'

'Where, then, is the treasure?' she asked again. 'Here, indeed, is the body of the Divine Menkau-ra; but the flesh even of Pharaohs is not gold, and if the face of this Sphinx be gold how may we move it ? '

For answer I bade her stand upon the Sphinx and grasp the upper part of the coffin while I grasped its foot. Then, at my word, we lifted, and the lid of the case, which was not fixed, came away, and we set it upon the floor. And there in the case was the mummy of Pharaoh, as it had been laid three thousand years before. It was a large mummy, and somewhat ungainly. Nor was it adorned with a gilded mask, as is the fashion of our day, for the head was wrapped in cloths yellow with age, which were made fast with pink flaxen bandages, under which were pushed the stems of lotus-blooms. And on the breast, wreathed round with lotus-flowers, lay a large plate of gold closely written over with sacred writing. I lifted up the plate, and, holding it to the light, I read :

' *I, Menkau-ra, the Osirian, aforetime Pharaoh of the Land of Khem, who in my day did live justly and ever walked in the path marked for my feet by the decree of the Invisible, who was the beginning and is the end, speak from my tomb to those who after me shall for an hour sit upon my Throne. Behold, I, Menkau-ra, the Osirian, having in the days of my life been warned of a dream that a time will come when Khem shall fear to fall into the hands of strangers, and her monarch shall have great need of treasure wherewith to furnish armies to drive the barbarian back, have out of my wisdom done this thing. For it having pleased the protecting Gods to give me wealth beyond any Pharaoh who has been since the days of Horus—thousands of cattle and geese, thousands of calves and asses, thousands of measures of corn, and hundreds of measures of gold and gems ; this wealth I have used sparingly, and that which remains I have bartered for precious stones— even for emeralds, the most beautiful and largest that are in the world. These stones, then, I have stored up against that day of the need of Khem. But because as there have been, so there shall be, those who do wickedly on the earth, and who, in the lust of gain, might seize this wealth that I have stored, and put it to their uses ; behold, thou Unborn One, who in the fulness of time shalt stand above me and read this that I have caused to be written, I have stored the treasure thus— even among my bones. Therefore, O thou Unborn One, sleeping in the womb of Nout, I say this to thee ! If thou indeed hast need of riches to save Khem from the foes of Khem, fear not and delay not, but tear me, the Osirian, from my tomb, loose my wrappings and rip the treasure from my breast, and all shall be well with thee ; for this only do I command, that thou dost replace my bones within my hollow coffin. But if the need be passing and not great, or if there be guile in thy heart, then the curse of Menkau-ra be on thee ! On thee be the curse that shall smite him who breaks in upon the dead ! On thee be the curse that follows the traitor ! On thee be the curse that smites him who outrages the Majesty of the Gods ! Unhappy shalt thou live, in blood and misery shalt thou die, and in misery shalt thou be tormented for ever and for ever ! For, Wicked One, there in Amenti we shall come face to face !*

'And to the end of the keeping of this secret I, Menkau-ra, have set up a Temple of my Worship, which I have built upon the eastern side of this my House of Death. It shall be made known from time to time to the Hereditary High Priest of this my Temple. And if any High Priest that shall be do reveal this secret to another than the Pharaoh, or Her who wears the Pharaoh's crown and is seated upon the throne of Khem, accursed be he also. Thus have I, Menkau-ra, the Osirian, written. Now to thee, who, sleeping in the womb of Nout, yet shall upon a time stand over me and read, I say,

judge thou! and if thou judgest,evilly, on thee shall fall this the curse of Menkau-ra from which there is no escape. Greeting and farewell.'

'Thou hast heard, O Cleopatra,' I said solemnly; 'now search thy heart; judge thou, and for thine own sake judge justly.'

She bent her head in thought.

'I fear to do this thing,' she said presently. 'Let us hence.'

'It is well,' I said, with a lightening of the heart, and bent down to lift the wooden lid. For I, too, feared.

'And yet, what said the writing of the Divine Menkau-ra?—it was emeralds, was it not? And emeralds are now so rare and hard to come by. Ever did I love emeralds, and I can never find them without a flaw.

'It is not a matter of what thou dost love, Cleopatra,' I said; 'it is matter of the need of Khem and of the secret meaning of thy heart, which thou alone canst know.'

'Ay, surely, Harmachis; surely! And is not the need of Egypt great? There is no gold in the treasury, and how can I defy the Roman if I have no gold? And have I not sworn to thee that I will wed thee and defy the Roman; and do I not swear it again—yes, even in this solemn hour, with my hand upon dead Pharaoh's heart? Why, here is that occasion of which the Divine Menkau-ra dreamed. Thou seest it is so, for else Hat-shepsu or Rameses or some other Pharaoh had drawn forth the gems. But no; they left them to this hour because the time was not yet come. Now it must be come, for if I take not the gems the Roman will surely seize on Egypt, and then there will be no Pharaoh to whom the secret may be told. Nay, let us away with fears and to the work. Why dost look so frightened? Having pure hearts, there is naught to fear, Harmachis.'

'Even as thou wilt,' I said again; 'it is for thee to judge, since if thou judgest falsely on thee will surely fall the curse from which there is no escape.'

'So, Harmachis, take Pharaoh's head and I will take his——Oh, what an awful place is this!' and suddenly she clung to me. 'Methought I saw a shadow yonder in the darkness! Methought that it moved toward us and then straightway vanished! Let us be going! Didst thou see naught?'

'I saw nothing, Cleopatra; but mayhap it was the Spirit of the Divine Menkau-ra, for the spirit ever hovers round its mortal tenement. Let us, then, be going; I shall be right glad to go.'

She made as though to start, then turned back again and spoke once more.

'It was naught—naught but the mind that, in such a house of Horror, bodies forth those shadowy forms of fear it dreads to see. Nay, I must look upon these emeralds: indeed, if I die, I must look! Come—to the work!' and stooping, she with her own hands lifted from the tomb one of the four alabaster jars, each sealed with the graven likeness of the heads of the protecting Gods, that held the holy heart and entrails of the Divine Menkau-ra. But nothing was found in these jars, save only what should be there.

Then together we mounted on the Sphinx, and with toil drew forth the body of the Divine Pharaoh, laying it on the ground. Now Cleopatra took my dagger, and with it cut loose the bandages which held the wrappings in their place, and the lotus-flowers that had been set in them by loving hands, three thousand years before, fell down upon the pavement. Then we searched and found the end of the outer bandage, which was fixed in at the hinder part of the neck. This we cut loose, for it was glued fast. This done, we began to unroll the wrappings of the holy corpse. Setting my

shoulders against the sarcophagus, I sat upon the rocky floor,
the body resting on my knees, and, as I turned it, Cleopatra
unwound the cloths; and awesome was the task. Presently
something fell out; it was the sceptre of the Pharaoh, fashioned
of gold, and at its end was a pomegranate cut from a single
emerald.

Cleopatra seized the sceptre and gazed on it in silence. Then
once more we went on with our dread business. And ever as
we unwound, other ornaments of gold, such as are buried with
Pharaohs, fell from the wrappings—collars and bracelets,
models of sistra, an inlaid axe, and an image of the holy Osiris
and of the holy Khem. At length all the bandages were unwound, and beneath we found a covering of coarsest linen;
for in those very ancient days the craftsmen were not so skilled
in matters pertaining to the embalming of the body as they are
now. And on the linen was written in an oval, 'Menkau-ra,
Royal Son of the Sun.' We could in no wise loosen this linen,
it held so firm on to the body. Therefore, faint with the great
heat, choked with mummy dust and the odour of spices, and
trembling with fear of our unholy task, wrought in that most
lonesome and holy place, we laid the body down, and ripped
away the last covering with the knife. First we cleared
Pharaoh's head, and now the face that no man had gazed on
for three thousand years was open to our view. It was a great
face, with a bold brow, yet crowned with the royal uræus,
beneath which the white locks, stained yellow by the spices,
fell in long, straight wisps. Not the cold stamp of death, and
not the slow flight of three thousand years, had found power
to mar the dignity of those shrunken features. We gazed on
them, and then, made bold with fear, stripped the covering
from the body. There at last it lay before us, stiff, yellow,
and dread to see; and on the left side, above the thigh, was
the cut through which the embalmers had done their work,

but it was sewn up so deftly that we could scarcely find the
mark.

'The gems are within,' I whispered, for I felt that the
body was very heavy. 'Now, if thy heart fail thee not, thou
must make an entry to this poor house of clay that once was
Pharaoh,' and I gave her the dagger—the same dagger which
had drunk the life of Paulus.

'It is too late to doubt,' she answered, lifting her white
beauteous face and fixing her blue eyes all big with terror
upon my own. She took the dagger, and with set teeth the
Queen of this day plunged it into the dead breast of
Pharaoh of three thousand years ago. And even as she did
so there came a groaning sound from the opening to the shaft
where we had left the eunuch! We leapt to our feet, but
heard no more, and the lamp-light still streamed down
through the opening.

'It is nothing,' I said. 'Let us make an end.'

Then with much toil we hacked and rent the hard flesh
open, and as we did so I heard the knife point grate upon the
gems within.

Cleopatra plunged her hand into the dead breast and drew
forth somewhat. She held it to the light, and gave a little cry,
for from the darkness of Pharaoh's heart there flashed into
light and life the most beauteous emerald that ever man beheld. It was perfect in colour, very large, without a flaw, and
fashioned to a scarabæus form, and on the under side was an
oval, inscribed with the divine name of Menkau-ra, Son of the
Sun.

Again, again, and yet again, she plunged in her hand and
drew great emeralds from Pharaoh's breast bedded there in
spices. Some were fashioned and some were not; but all
were perfect in colour without a flaw, and in value priceless.
Again and again she plunged her white hand into that dread

breast, till at length all were found, and there were one hundred and forty and eight of such gems as are not known in the world. The last time that she searched she brought forth not emeralds, indeed, but two great pearls, wrapped in linen, such as never have been seen. And of these pearls more hereafter

So it was done, and all the mighty treasure lay glittering in a heap before us. There it lay, and there, too, lay the regalia of gold, the spiced and sickly-scented wrappings, and the torn body of white-haired Pharaoh Menkau-ra, the Osirian, the ever living in Amenti.

We rose, and a great awe fell upon us, now that the deed was done and our hearts were no more upborne by the rage of search—so great an awe, indeed, that we could not speak. I made a sign to Cleopatra. She grasped the head of Pharaoh and I grasped his feet, and together we lifted him, climbed the Sphinx, and placed him once more within his coffin. I piled the torn mummy cloths over him and on them laid the lid of the coffin.

And now we gathered up the great gems, and such of the ornaments as might be carried with ease, and I hid them as many as I could, in the folds of my robe. Those that were left Cleopatra hid upon her breast. Heavily laden with the priceless treasure, we gave one last look at the solemn place, at the sarcophagus and the Sphinx on which it rested, whose gleaming face of calm seemed to mock us with its everlasting smile of wisdom. Then we turned and went from the tomb.

At the shaft we halted. I called to the eunuch, who stayed above, and methought that a faint mocking laugh answered me. Too smitten with terror to call again, and fearing that, should we delay, Cleopatra would certainly swoon, I seized the rope, and being strong and quick mounted by it and gained the passage. There burnt the lamp: but the eunuch I saw

Q 2

not. Thinking, surely, that he was a little way down the passage, and slept—as, in truth, he did—I bade Cleopatra make the rope fast about her middle, and with much labour, drew her up. Then, having rested awhile, we moved with the lamps to seek for the eunuch.

'He was stricken with terror and has fled, leaving the lamp,' said Cleopatra. 'O ye Gods! who is *that* seated there?'

I peered into the darkness, thrusting out the lamps, and this was what their light fell on—this at the very dream of which my soul sickens! There, facing us, his back resting against the rock, and his hands splayed on either side upon the floor, sat the eunuch—*dead!* His eyes and mouth were open, his fat cheeks dropped down, his thin hair yet seemed to bristle, and on his countenance was frozen such a stamp of hideous terror as well might turn the beholder's brain. And lo! fixed to his chin, by its hinder claws, hung that grey and mighty bat, which, flying forth when we entered the pyramid, vanished in the sky, but, returning, had followed us to its depths. There it hung upon the dead man's chin slowly rocking itself to and fro, and we could see the fiery eyes shining in its head.

Aghast, utterly aghast, we stood and stared at the hateful sight; till presently the bat spread his huge wings and, loosing his hold, sailed to us. Now he hovered before Cleopatra's face, fanning her with his white wings. Then with a scream, like a woman's shriek of fury, the accursed Thing flittered on, seeking his violated tomb, and vanished down the well into the sepulchre. I fell against the wall. But Cleopatra sank in a heap upon the floor, and, covering her head with her arms, she shrieked till the hollow passages rang with the echoes of her cries, that seemed to grow and double and rush along the depths in volumes of shrill sound.

' Rise ! ' I cried, ' rise and let us hence before the Spirit shall return to haunt us ? If thou dost suffer thyself to be overwhelmed in this place thou art lost for ever.'

She staggered to her feet, and never may I forget the look upon her ashy face or in her glowing eyes. Seizing lamps with a rush, we passed the dead eunuch's horrid form, I holding her by the hand. We gained the great chamber, where was the sarcophagus of the Queen of Menkau-ra, and traversed its length. We fled along the passage. What if the Thing had closed the three mighty doors ? No ; they were open, and we sped through them ; the last only did I stay to close. I touched the stone, as I knew how, and the great door crashed down, shutting us off from the presence of the dead eunuch and the Horror that had hung upon the eunuch's chin. Now we were in the white chamber with the sculptured panels, and now we faced the last steep ascent. Oh that last ascent ! Twice Cleopatra slipped and fell upon the polished floor. The second time—it was when half the distance had been done—she let fall her lamp, and would, indeed, have rolled down the slide had I not saved her. But in doing thus I, too, let fall my lamp that bounded away into shadow beneath us, and we were in utter darkness. And perchance about us, in the darkness, hovered that awful Thing !

' Be brave ! ' I cried ; ' O love, be brave, and struggle on, or both are lost ! The way, though steep, is not far ; and, though it be dark, we can scarce come to harm in this straight shaft. If the gems weight thee, cast them away ! '

' Nay,' she gasped, ' that I will not; this shall not be endured to no end. I die with them ! '

Then it was that I saw the greatness of this woman's heart; for in the dark, and notwithstanding the terrors we had passed and the awfulness of our state, she clung to me and clambered on up that dread passage. On we clambered, hand in hand, with bursting hearts, till there, by the mercy or the anger of the Gods, at length we saw the faint light of the moon, creeping through the little opening in the pyramid. One struggle more, now the hole was gained, and like a breath from heaven, the sweet night air played upon our brows. I climbed through, and, standing on the pile of stones, lifted and dragged Cleopatra after me. She fell to the ground and then sank down upon it motionless.

I pressed upon the turning stone with trembling hands. It swung to and caught, leaving no mark of the secret place of entry. Then I leapt down and, having pushed away the pile of stones, looked on Cleopatra. She had swooned, and notwithstanding the dust and grime upon her face, it was so pale that at first I believed she must be dead. But placing my hand upon her heart I felt it stir beneath; and, being spent, I flung myself down beside her upon the sand, to gather up my strength again.

CHAPTER XII.

OF THE COMING BACK OF HARMACHIS; OF THE GREETING OF CHARMION; AND OF THE ANSWER OF CLEOPATRA TO QUINTUS DELLIUS, THE AMBASSADOR OF ANTONY THE TRIUMVIR.

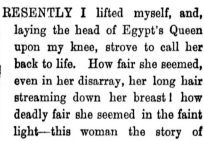 RESENTLY I lifted myself, and, laying the head of Egypt's Queen upon my knee, strove to call her back to life. How fair she seemed, even in her disarray, her long hair streaming down her breast! how deadly fair she seemed in the faint light—this woman the story of whose beauty and whose sin shall outlive the solid mass of the mighty pyramid that towered over us! The heaviness of her swoon had smoothed away the falseness of her face, and nothing was left but the divine stamp of Woman's richest loveliness, softened by shadows of the night and dignified by the cast of deathlike sleep. I gazed upon her and all my heart went out to her; it seemed that I did but love her more because of the depth of the treasons to which I had sunk to reach her, and because of the terrors we had outfaced together. Weary and spent with fears and the pangs of guilt, my heart sought hers for rest, for now she alone was left to me. She had sworn to wed me also, and with the treasure we had won we would

make Egypt strong and free her from her foes, and all should yet be well. Ah! could I have seen the picture that was to come, how, and in what place and circumstance, once again this very woman's head should be laid upon my knee, pale with that cast of death! Ah! could I have seen!

I chafed her hand between my hands. I bent down and kissed her on the lips, and at my kiss she woke. She woke with a little sob of fear—a shiver ran along her delicate limbs, and she stared upon my face with wide eyes.

'Ah! it is thou!' she said. 'I mind me—thou hast saved me from that horror-haunted place!' And she threw her arms about my neck, drew me to her and kissed me. 'Come, love,' she said, 'let us be going! I am sore athirst, and—ah! so very weary! The gems, too, chafe my breast! Never was wealth so hardly won! Come, let us be going from the shadow of this ghostly spot! See the faint lights glancing from the wings of Dawn. How beautiful they are, and how sweet to behold! Never, in those Halls of Eternal Night, did I think to look upon the blush of dawn again! Ah! I can still see the face of that dead slave, with the Horror hanging to his beardless chin! Bethink thee!— there he'll sit for ever—there—with the Horror! Come; where may we find water? I would give an emerald for a cup of water!'

'At the canal on the borders of the tilled land below the Temple of Horemkhu—it is close by,' I answered. 'If any see us, we will say that we are pilgrims who have lost our way at night among the tombs. Veil thyself closely, there-fore, Cleopatra; and beware lest thou dost show aught of those gems about thee.'

So she veiled herself, and I lifted her on to the ass which was tethered near at hand. We walked slowly through the plain till we came to the place where the symbol of the God

Horemkhu,[1] fashioned as a mighty Sphinx (whom the Greeks
call Harmachis), and crowned with the royal crown of Egypt,
looks out in majesty across the land, his eyes ever fixed upon
the East. As we walked the first arrow of the rising sun
quivered through the grey air, striking upon Horemkhu's
lips of holy calm, and the Dawn kissed her greeting to the
God of Dawn. Then the light gathered and grew upon the
gleaming sides of twenty pyramids, and, like a promise from Life
to Death, rested on the portals of ten thousand tombs. It
poured in a flood of gold across the desert sand—it pierced
the heavy sky of night, and fell in bright beams upon the
green of fields and the tufted crest of palms. Then from his
horizon bed royal Ra rose up in pomp and it was day.

Passing the temple of granite and of alabaster that was built
before the days of Khufu, to the glory of the Majesty of
Horemkhu, we descended the slope, and came to the banks of
the canal. There we drank; and that draught of muddy
water was sweeter than all the choicest wine of Alexandria.
Also we washed the mummy dust and grime from our hands
and brows and made us clean. As she bathed her neck,
stooping over the water, one of the great emeralds slipped
from Cleopatra's breast and fell into the canal, and it was but
by chance that at length I found it in the mire. Then, once
more, I lifted Cleopatra on to the beast, and slowly, for I was
very weary, we marched back to the banks of Sihor, where
our craft was. And having at length come thither, seeing no
one save some few peasants going out to labour on the lands,
I turned the ass loose in that same field where we had found
him, and we boarded the craft while the crew were yet sleeping. Then, waking them, we bade them make all sail, saying

[1] That is, 'Horus on the horizon'; and signifies the power of Light
and Good overcoming the power of Darkness and Evil incarnate in his
enemy, Typhon.—ED.

that we had left the eunuch to sojourn awhile behind us, as
in truth we had.   So we sailed, having first hidden away the
gems and such of the ornaments of gold as we could bring to
the boat.

We spent four days and more in coming to Alexandria,
for the wind was for the most part against us ; and they were
happy days !   At first, indeed, Cleopatra was somewhat silent
and heavy at heart, for what she had seen and felt in the
womb of the pyramid weighed her down.   But soon her
Imperial spirit awoke and shook the burden from her breast,
and she became herself again—now gay, now learned; now
loving, and now cold; now queenly, and now altogether
simple—ever changing as the winds of heaven, and as the
heaven, deep, beauteous, and unsearchable !

Night after night for those four perfect nights, the last
happy hours I ever was to know, we sat hand in hand upon
the deck and heard the waters lap the vessel's side, and
watched the soft footfall of the moon as she trod the depths
of Nile.   There we sat and talked of love, talked of our
marriage and all that we would do.   Also I drew up plans of
war and of defence against the Roman, which now we had
the means to carry out; and she approved them, sweetly
saying that what seemed good to me was good to her.   And
so the time passed all too swiftly.

Oh those nights upon the Nile ! their memory haunts me
yet !   Yet in my dreams I see the moonbeams break and
quiver, and hear Cleopatra's murmured words of love mingle
with the sound of murmuring waters.   Dead are those dear
nights, dead is the moon that lit them ; the waters which
rocked us on their breast are lost in the wide salt sea, and
where we kissed and clung there lips unborn shall kiss and
cling !   How beautiful was their promise, doomed, like an
unfruitful blossom, to wither, fall, and rot ! and their fulfil-

ment, ah, how drear ! For all things end in darkness and in
ashes, and those who sow in folly shall reap in sorrow. Ah !
those nights upon the Nile !

And so at length once more we stood within the hateful
walls of that fair palace on the Lochias, and the dream was
done.

'Whither hast thou wandered with Cleopatra, Harmachis?'
Charmion asked of me when I met her by chance on that day
of return. 'On some new mission of betrayal ? Or was it but
a love-journey ? '

'I went with Cleopatra upon secret business of the State,'
I answered sternly.

'So ! Those who go secretly, go evilly ; and foul birds love
to fly at night. Not but what thou art wise, for it would scarce
beseem thee, Harmachis, to show thy face openly in Egypt.'

I heard, and felt my passion rise within me, for I could ill
bear this fair girl's scorn.

'Hast thou never a word without a sting ? ' I asked
'Know, then, that I went whither thou hadst not dared to go,
to gather means to hold Egypt from the grasp of Antony.'

'So,' she answered, looking up swiftly. 'Thou foolish
man ! Thou hadst done better to save thy labour, for Antony
will grasp Egypt in thy despite. What power hast thou to-
day in Egypt ? '

'That he may do in my despite ; but in despite of Cleopatra
that he cannot do,' I said.

'Nay, but with the *aid* of Cleopatra he can and will do it,'
she answered with a bitter smile. 'When the Queen sails in
state up Cydnus stream she will surely draw this coarse
Antony thence to Alexandria, conquering, and yet, like thee,
a slave ! '

'It is false ! I say that it is false ! Cleopatra goes not

to Tarsus, and Antony comes not to Alexandria; or, if he come, it will be to take the chance of war.'

'Now, thinkest thou thus?' she answered with a little laugh. 'Well, if it please thee, think as thou wilt. Within three days thou shalt know. It is pretty to see how easily thou art fooled. Farewell! Go, dream on Love, for surely Love is sweet.'

And she went, leaving me angered and troubled at heart.

I saw Cleopatra no more that day, but on the day which followed I saw her. She was in a heavy mood, and had no gentle word for me. I spake to her of the defence of Egypt, but she put the matter away.

'Why dost thou weary me?' she said with anger; 'canst thou not see that I am lost in troubles? When Dellius has had his answer to-morrow then we will speak of these matters.'

'Ay,' I said, 'when Dellius has had his answer; and knowest thou that but yesterday, Charmion—whom about the palace they name the " Keeper of the Queen's secrets "—Charmion swore that the answer would be " Go in peace, I come to Antony ! " '

'Charmion knows nothing of my heart,' said Cleopatra, stamping her foot in anger, 'and if she talk so freely the girl shall be scourged out of my Court, as is her desert. Though, in truth,' she added, 'she has more wisdom in that small head of hers than all my privy councillors—ay, and more wit to use it. Knowest thou that I have sold a portion of those gems to the rich Jews of Alexandria, and at a great price, ay, at five thousand sestertia for each one?[1] But a few, in truth, for they could not buy more as yet. It was rare to see their eyes when they fell upon them : they grew large

---

[1] About forty thousand pounds of our money.—ED.

as apples with avarice and wonder. And now leave me, Harmachis, for I am weary. The memory of that dreadful night is with me yet.'

I bowed and rose to go, and yet stood wavering.

'Pardon me, Cleopatra; it is of our marriage.'

'Our marriage! Why, are we not indeed already wed?' she answered.

'Yes; but not before the world. Thou didst promise.'

'Ay, Harmachis, I promised; and to-morrow, when I have rid me of this Dellius, I will keep my promise, and name thee Cleopatra's Lord before the Court. See that thou art in thy place. Art content?'

And she stretched out her hand for me to kiss, looking on me with strange eyes, as though she struggled with herself. Then I went; but that night I strove once more to see Cleopatra, and could not. 'The Lady Charmion was with the Queen,' so said the eunuchs, and none might enter.

On the morrow the Court met in the great hall one hour before mid-day, and I went thither with a trembling heart to hear Cleopatra's answer to Dellius, and to hear myself also named King-consort to the Queen of Egypt. It was a full and splendid Court; there were councillors, lords, captains, eunuchs, and waiting-women, all save Charmion. The hour passed, but Cleopatra and Charmion came not. At length Charmion entered gently by a side entrance, and took her place among the waiting-ladies about the throne. Even as she did so she cast a glance at me, and there was triumph in her eyes, though I knew not over what she triumphed. I little guessed that she had but now brought about my ruin and sealed the fate of Egypt.

Then presently the trumpets blared, and, clad in her robes of state, the uræus crown upon her head, and on her breast,

flashing like a star, that great emerald scarabæus which she
had dragged from dead Pharaoh's heart, Cleopatra swept in
splendour to her throne, followed by a glittering guard of
Northmen. Her lovely face was dark, dark were her slumbrous
eyes, and none might read their message, though all that
Court searched them for a sign of what should come. She
seated herself slowly as one who may not be moved, and spoke
to the chief of the heralds in the Greek tongue:

'Does the Ambassador of the noble Antony wait?'

The herald bowed low and made assent.

'Let him come in and hear our answer.'

The doors were flung wide, and, followed by his train of
knights, Dellius, clad in his golden armour and his purple
mantle, walked with cat-like step up the great hall, and made
obeisance before the throne.

'Most royal and beauteous Egypt,' he said, in his soft
voice, 'as thou hast graciously been pleased to bid me, thy
servant, I am here to take thy answer to the letter of the noble
Antony the Triumvir, whom to-morrow I sail to meet at Tarsus,
in Cilicia. And I will say this, royal Egypt, craving pardon
the while for the boldness of my speech—bethink thee well
before words that cannot be unspoken fall from those sweet
lips. Defy Antony, and Antony will wreck thee. But, like
thy mother Aphrodité, rise glorious on his sight from the
bosom of the Cyprian wave, and for wreck he will give thee
all that can be dear to woman's royalty—Empire, and pomp
of place, cities and the sway of men, fame and wealth, and the
Diadem of rule made sure. For mark: Antony holds this
Eastern World in the hollow of his warlike hand; at his
will kings are, and at his frown they cease to be.'

And he bowed his head and, folding his hands meekly
on his breast, awaited answer.

For a while Cleopatra answered not, but sat like the Sphinx

Horemkhu, dumb and inscrutable, gazing with lost eyes down the length of that great hall.

Then, like soft music, her answer came; and trembling I listened for Egypt's challenge to the Roman:

'Noble Dellius,—We have bethought us much of the matter of thy message from great Antony to our poor Royalty of Egypt. We have bethought us much, and we have taken counsel from the oracles of the Gods, from the wisest among our friends, and from the teaching of our heart, that ever, like a nesting bird, broods over our people's weal. Sharp are the words that thou hast brought across the sea; methinks they had been better fitted to the ears of some petty half-tamed prince than to those of Egypt's Queen. Therefore we have numbered the legions that we can gather, and the triremes and the galleys wherewith we may breast the sea, and the moneys which shall buy us all things wanting to our war. And we find this, that, though Antony be strong, yet has Egypt naught to fear from the strength of Antony.'

She paused, and a murmur of applause of her high words ran down the hall. Only Dellius stretched out his hand as though to push them back. Then came the end!

'Noble Dellius,—Half are we minded there to bid our tongue stop, and, strong in our fortresses of stone, and our other fortresses built of the hearts of men, abide the issue. And yet thou shalt not go thus. We are guiltless of those charges against us that have come to the ears of noble Antony, and which now he rudely shouts in ours; nor will we journey into Cilicia to answer them.'

Here the murmur arose anew, while my heart beat high in triumph; and in the pause that followed, Dellius spoke once more.

'Then, royal Egypt, my word to Antony is word of War?'

'Nay,' she answered; 'it shall be one of Peace. Listen:

R

we said that we would not come to make answer to these
charges, nor will we. But '—and she smiled for the first time
—' we will gladly come, and that swiftly, in royal friendship
to make known our fellowship of peace upon the banks of
Cydnus.'

I heard, and was bewildered. Could I hear aright? Was
it thus that Cleopatra kept her oaths? Moved beyond the
hold of reason, I lifted up my voice and cried:

' O Queen, *remember!* '

She turned upon me like a lioness, with a flashing of the
eyes and a swift shake of her lovely head.

' Peace, Slave! ' she said; ' who bade thee break in upon
our counsels? Mind thou thy stars, and leave matters of the
world to the rulers of the world! '

I sank back shamed, and, as I did so, once more I saw the
smile of triumph on the face of Charmion, followed by what
was, perhaps, the shadow of pity for my fall.

' Now that yon brawling charlatan,' said Dellius, pointing
at me with his jewelled finger, ' has been rebuked, grant me
leave, O Egypt, to thank thee from my heart for these gentle
words——'

' We ask no thanks from thee, noble Dellius; nor lies it
in thy mouth to chide our servant,' broke in Cleopatra, frowning heavily; ' we will take thanks from the lips of Antony
alone. Get thee to thy master, and say to him that before he
can make ready a fitting welcome our keels shall follow in the
track of thine. And now, farewell! Thou shalt find some
small token of our bounty upon thy vessel.'

Dellius bowed thrice and withdrew, while the Court stood
waiting the Queen's word. And I, too, waited, wondering if
she would yet make good her promise, and name me royal
Spouse there in the face of Egypt. But she said nothing.
Only, still frowning heavily, she rose, and, followed by her

guards, left the throne, and passed into the Alabaster Hall. Then the Court broke up, and as the lords and councillors went by they looked on me with mockery. For though none knew all my secret, nor how it stood between me and Cleopatra, yet they were jealous of the favour shown me by the Queen, and rejoiced greatly at my fall. But I took no heed of their mocking as I stood dazed with misery and felt the world of Hope slip from beneath my feet.

CHAPTER XIII.

OF THE REPROACH OF HARMACHIS; OF THE STRUGGLE OF
HARMACHIS WITH THE GUARDS; OF THE BLOW OF
BRENNUS; AND OF THE SECRET SPEECH OF CLEOPATRA.

ND at length, all being gone, I, too, turned to go, when a eunuch struck me on the shoulder and roughly bade me wait on the presence of the Queen. An hour past this fellow would have crawled to me on his knees; but he had heard, and now he treated me —so brutish is the nature of such slaves —as the world treats the fallen, with scorn. For to come low after being great is to learn all shame. Unhappy, therefore, are the Great, for they may fall!

I turned upon the slave with so fierce a word that, cur-like, he sprang behind me; then I passed on to the Alabaster Hall, and was admitted by the guards. In the centre of the hall, near the fountain, sat Cleopatra, and with her were Charmion and the Greek girl Iras, and Merira and other of her waiting-ladies. 'Go,' she said to these, 'I would speak with my astrologer.' So they went, and left us face to face.

'Stand thou there,' she said, lifting her eyes for the first time. 'Come not nigh me, Harmachis: I trust thee not. Perchance thou hast found another dagger. Now, what hast

thou to say ? By what right didst thou dare to break in upon
my talk with the Roman ? '

I felt the blood rush through me like a storm ; bitterness
and burning anger took hold of my heart. 'What hast
thou to say, Cleopatra ? ' I answered boldly. 'Where is thy
vow, sworn on the dead heart of Menkau-ra, the ever-living ?
Where now thy challenge to this Roman Antony ? Where
thy oath that thou wouldest call me " husband " in the face
of Egypt ? ' And I choked and ceased.

'Well doth it become Harmachis, who never was forsworn,
to speak to me of oaths ! ' she said in bitter mockery. 'And
yet, O thou most pure Priest of Isis ; and yet, O thou most
faithful friend, who never didst betray thy friends ; and yet, O
thou most steadfast, honourable, and upright man, who never
bartered thy birthright, thy country, and thy cause for the
price of a woman's passing love—by what token knowest thou
that my word is void ? '

'I will not answer thy taunts, Cleopatra,' I said, holding
back my heart as best I might, 'for I have earned them all,
though not from thee. By this token, then, I know it. Thou
goest to visit Antony ; thou goest, as said that Roman knave,
" tricked in thy best attire," to feast with him whom thou
shouldst give to vultures for their feast. Perhaps, for aught
I know, thou art about to squander those treasures that thou
hast filched from the body of Menkau-ra, those treasures stored
against the need of Egypt, upon wanton revels which shall
complete the shame of Egypt. By these things, then, I know
that thou art forsworn, and I, who, loving thee, believed thee,
tricked ; and by this, also, that thou who didst but yesternight
swear to wed me, dost to-day cover me with taunts, and even
before that Roman put me to an open shame ! '

'To wed thee ? and I did swear to wed thee ? Well, and
what is marriage ? Is it the union of the heart, that bond

beautiful as gossamer and than gossamer more light, which
binds soul to soul, as they float through the dreamy night of
passion, a bond to be, perchance, melted in the dews of dawn?
Or is it the iron link of enforced, unchanging union whereby
if sinks the one the other must be dragged beneath the sea of
circumstance, there, like a punished slave, to perish of un-
avoidable corruption?[1]   Marriage!   *I* to marry! *I* to forget
freedom and court the worst slavery of our sex, which, by the
selfish will of man, the stronger, still binds us to a bed
grown hateful, and enforces a service that love mayhap no
longer hallows!   Of what use, then, to be a Queen, if thereby
I may not escape the evil of the meanly born?   Mark thou,
Harmachis: Woman being grown hath two ills to fear—Death
and Marriage; and of these twain is Marriage the more vile;
for in Death we may find rest, but in Marriage, should it fail
us, we must find hell.   Nay, being above the breath of common
slander that enviously would blast those who of true virtue
will not consent to stretch affection's links, I *love*, Harmachis; but I *marry* not!'

'And yesternight, Cleopatra, thou didst swear that thou
wouldst wed me, and call me to thy side before the face of
Egypt!'

'And yesternight, Harmachis, the red ring round the moon
marked the coming of the storm, and yet the day is fair! But
who knows that the tempest may not break to-morrow? Who
knows that I have not chosen the easier path to save Egypt
from the Roman? Who knows, Harmachis, that thou shalt
not still call me wife?'

Then I no longer could bear her falsehood, for I saw
that she but played with me. And so I spoke that which
was in my heart:

---

[1] Referring to the Roman custom of chaining a living felon to the
body of one already dead.—ED.

'Cleopatra!' I cried, 'thou didst swear to protect Egypt, and thou art about to betray Egypt to the Roman! Thou didst swear to use the treasures that I revealed to thee for the service of Egypt, and thou art about to use them to be her means of shame—to fashion them as fetters for her wrists! Thou didst swear to wed me, who loved thee, and for thee gave all, and thou dost mock me and reject me! Therefore I say—with the voice of the dread Gods I say it!—that on *thee* shall fall the curse of Menkau-ra, whom thou hast robbed indeed! Let me go hence and work out my fate! Let me go, O thou fair Shame! thou living Lie! whom I have loved to my doom, and who hast brought upon me the last curse of doom! Let me hide myself and see thy face no more!'

She rose in her wrath, and she was terrible to see.

'Let thee go to stir up evil against me! Nay, Harmachis, thou shalt not go to build new plots against my throne! I say to thee that thou, too, shalt come to visit Antony in Cilicia, and there, perchance, I will let thee go!' And ere I could answer, she had struck upon the silver gong that hung near her.

Before its rich echo had died away, Charmion and the waiting-women entered from one door, and from the other, a file of soldiers—four of them of the Queen's bodyguard, mighty men, with winged helmets and long fair hair.

'Seize that traitor!' cried Cleopatra, pointing to me. The captain of the guard—it was Brennus—saluted and came towards me with drawn sword.

But I, being mad and desperate, and caring little if they slew me, flew straight at his throat, and dealt him such a heavy blow that the great man fell headlong, and his armour clashed upon the marble floor. As he fell I seized his sword and targe, and, meeting the next, who rushed on me with a shout, caught his blow upon the shield, and in answer smote with all my strength. The sword fell where the neck is set into the shoulder and, shearing through the joints of his harness, slew him, so that his knees were loosened and he sank down dead. And the third, as he came, I caught upon the point of my sword before he could strike, and it pierced him and he died. Then the last rushed on me with a cry of 'Taranis!' and I, too, rushed on him, for my blood was aflame. Now the women shrieked—only Cleopatra said nothing, but stood and watched the unequal fray. We met. and I struck with all my strength, and it was a mighty blow, for the sword shore through the iron shield and shattered there, leaving me weaponless. With a shout of triumph the guard swung up his sword and smote down upon my head, but I caught the blow with my shield. Again he smote, and again I parried; but when he raised his sword a third time I saw this might not endure, so with a cry I hurled my buckler at his face. Glancing from his shield it struck him on the breast and staggered him. Then, before he could gain his balance, I rushed in beneath his guard and gripped him round the middle.

For a full minute the tall man and I struggled furiously, and then, so great was my strength in those days, I lifted him like a toy and dashed him down upon the marble floor in such fashion that his bones were shattered so that he spoke no more. But I could not save myself and fell upon him, and as I fell the Captain Brennus, whom I had smitten to earth with my fist, having once more found his sense, came up behind me and smote me upon the head and shoulders with the sword of one of those whom I had slain. But I being on the ground, the blow did not fall with all its weight, also my thick hair and broidered cap broke its force; and thus it came to pass that, though sorely wounded, the life was yet whole in me. But I could struggle no more.

Then the cowardly eunuchs, who had gathered at the sound of blows and stood huddled together like a herd of cattle, seeing that I was spent, threw themselves upon me, and would have butchered me with their knives. But Brennus, now that I was down, would strike no more, but stood waiting. And the eunuchs had surely slain me, for Cleopatra watched like one who watches in a dream and made no sign. Already my head was dragged back, and their knife-points were at my throat, when Charmion, rushing forward, threw herself upon me and, calling them 'Dogs!' desperately thrust her body before them in such fashion that they could not smite. Now Brennus with an oath seized first one and then another and cast them from me.

'Spare his life, Queen!' he cried in his barbarous Latin. 'By Jupiter, he is a brave man! Myself felled like an ox in the shambles, and three of my boys finished by a man without armour and taken unawares! I grudge them not to such a man! A boon, Queen! spare his life, and give him to me!'

'Ay, spare him! spare him!' cried Charmion, white and trembling.

Cleopatra drew near and looked upon the dead and him who lay dying as I had dashed him to the ground, and on me, her lover of two days gone, whose wounded head rested now on Charmion's white robes.

I met the Queen's glance. 'Spare not!' I gasped; '*væ victis!*' Then a flush gathered on her brow—methinks it was a flush of shame!

'Dost after all love this man at heart, Charmion,' she said with a little laugh, 'that thou didst thrust thy tender body between him and the knives of these sexless hounds?' and she cast a look of scorn upon the eunuchs.

'Nay!' the girl answered fiercely; 'but I cannot stand by to see a brave man murdered by such as these.'

'Ay!' said Cleopatra, 'he is a brave man, and he fought gallantly; I have never seen so fierce a fight even in the games

at Rome! Well, I spare his life, though it is weak of me—
womanish weak. Take him to his own chamber and guard
him there till he is healed or—dead.'

Then my brain reeled, a great sickness seized upon me,
and I sank into the nothingness of swoon.

Dreams, dreams, dreams! without end and ever-changing,
as for years and years I seemed to toss upon a sea of agony.
And through them a vision of a dark-eyed woman's tender
face and the touch of a white hand soothing me to rest.
Visions, too, of a royal countenance bending at times over my
rocking bed—a countenance that I could not grasp, but
whose beauty flowed through my fevered veins and was a part
of me—visions of childhood and of the Temple towers of
Abouthis, and of the white-haired Amenemhat, my father—
ay, and an ever-present vision of that dread hall in Amenti,
and of the small altar and the Spirits clad in flame! There
I seemed to wander everlastingly, calling on the Holy Mother,
whose memory I could not grasp; calling ever and in vain!
For no cloud descended upon the altar, only from time to time
the great Voice pealed aloud: 'Strike out the name of
Harmachis, child of Earth, from the living Book of Her who
Was and Is and Shall Be! *Lost! lost! lost!*'

And then another voice would answer:

'Not yet! not yet! Repentance is at hand; strike not
out the name of Harmachis, child of Earth, from the living
Book of Her who Was and Is and Shall Be! By suffering
may sin be wiped away!'

I woke to find myself in my own chamber in the tower of
the palace. I was so weak that I scarce could lift my hand,
and life seemed but to flutter in my breast as flutters a dying
dove. I could not turn my head; I could not stir; yet in my

heart there was a sense of rest and of dark trouble done. The light from the lamp hurt my eyes : I shut them, and, as I shut them, heard the sweep of a woman's robes upon the stair, and a swift, light step that I knew well. It was that of Cleopatra !

She entered and drew near. I felt her come ! Every pulse of my poor frame beat an answer to her footfall, and all my mighty love and hate rose from the darkness of my death-like sleep, and rent me in their struggle ! She leaned over me ; her ambrosial breath played upon my face : I could hear the beating of her heart ! Lower she leaned, till at last her lips touched me softly on the brow.

'Poor Man ! ' I heard her murmur. ' Poor, weak, dying Man ! Fate hath been hard to thee ! Thou wert too good to be the sport of such a one as I—the pawn that I must move in my play of policy ! Ah, Harmachis ! thou shouldst have ruled the game! Those plotting priests could give thee learning ; but they could not give thee knowledge of mankind, nor fence thee against the march of Nature's law. And thou didst love me with all thy heart—ah ! well I know it ! Manlike, thou didst love the eyes that, as a pirate's lights, beckoned thee to ship-wrecked ruin, and didst hang doting on the lips which lied thy heart away and called thee " slave " ! Well ; the game was fair, for thou wouldst have slain me : and yet I grieve. So thou dost die ? and this is my farewell to thee ! Never may we meet again on earth ; and, perchance, it is well, for who knows, when my hour of tenderness is past, how I might deal with thee, didst thou live ? Thou dost die, they say—those learned long-faced fools, who, if they let thee die, shall pay the price. And where, then, shall we meet again when my last throw is thrown ? We shall be equal there, in the king-dom that Osiris rules. A little time, a few years—perhaps to-morrow—and we shall meet; then, knowing all I am, how wilt thou greet me ? Nay, here, as there, still must thou worship me ! for injuries cannot touch the immortality of such a love as thine. Contempt alone, like acid, can eat away the love of noble hearts, and reveal the truth in its pitiful nakedness. Thou must still cling to me, Harmachis ; for, whatever my sins, yet I am great and set above thy scorn. Would that I could have loved thee as thou lovest me ! Almost I did so when thou slewest those guards ; and yet—not quite.

' What a fenced city is my heart, that none can take it, and, even when I throw the gates wide, no man may win its citadel ! Oh, to put away this loneliness and lose me in another's soul ! Oh, for a year, a month, an hour to quite forget policy, peoples, and my pomp of place, and be but a loving woman ! Harmachis, fare thee well ! Go join great Julius whom thy art called up from death before me, and take Egypt's greetings to him. Ah well ! I fooled thee, and I fooled Cæsar—perchance before all is done Fate will find me, and myself I shall be fooled. Harmachis, fare thee well ! '

She turned to go, and as she turned I heard the sweep of another dress and the light fall of another woman's foot.

' Ah ! it is thou, Charmion. Well, for all thy watching the man dies.'

' Ay,' she answered, in a voice thick with grief. ' Ay, O Queen, so the physicians say. Forty hours has he lain in stupor so deep that at times his breath could barely lift this tiny feather's weight, and hardly could my ear, placed against his breast, take notice of the rising of his heart. I have watched him now for ten long days, watched him day and night, till my eyes stare wide with want of sleep, and for faintness I can scarce keep myself from falling. And this is the end of all my labour ! The coward blow of that accursed Brennus has done its work, and Harmachis dies ! '

' Love counts not its labour, Charmion, nor can it weigh

its tenderness in the scale of purchase. That which it has it
gives, and craves for more to give and give, till the soul's
infinity be drained. Dear to thy heart are these heavy nights
of watching ; sweet to thy weary eyes is that sad sight of
strength brought so low that it hangs upon thy weakness like
a babe to its mother's breast ! For, Charmion, thou dost
love this man who loves thee not, and now that he is helpless
thou canst pour thy passion forth over the unanswering darkness of his soul, and cheat thyself with dreams of what yet
might be.'

'I love him not, as thou hast proof, O Queen ! How can
I love one who would have slain thee, who art as my heart's
sister ? It is for pity that I nurse him.'

She laughed a little as she answered, ' Pity is love's own
twin, Charmion. Wondrous wayward are the paths of woman's
love, and thou hast shown thine strangely, that I know. But
the more high the love, the deeper the gulf whereinto it can
fall—ay, and thence soar again to heaven, once more to fall !
Poor woman ! thou art thy passion's plaything : now tender as
the morning sky, and now, when jealousy grips thy heart,
more cruel than the sea. Well, thus are we made. Soon,
after all this troubling, nothing will be left thee but tears,
remorse, and —memory.'

And she went forth.

CHAPTER XIV.

OF THE TENDER CARE OF CHARMION; OF THE HEALING OF
HARMACHIS; OF THE SAILING OF THE FLEET OF CLEO-
PATRA FOR CILICIA; AND OF THE SPEECH OF BRENNUS
TO HARMACHIS.

CLEOPATRA went, and for a while
I lay silent, gathering up my
strength to speak. But Charmion
came and stood over me, and I
felt a great tear fall from her dark
eyes upon my face, as the first
heavy drop of rain falls from a
thunder cloud.

'Thou goest,' she whispered;
'thou goest fast whither I may not
follow! O Harmachis, how gladly
would I give my life for thine!'

Then at length I opened my eyes, and spoke as best I
could:

'Restrain thy grief, dear friend,' I said, 'I live yet; and,
in truth, I feel as though new life gathered in my breast!'

She gave a little cry of joy, and I never saw aught more
beautiful than the change that came upon her weeping face!
It was as when the first lights of the day run up the pallor
of that sad sky which veils the night from dawn. All rosy

grew her lovely countenance; her dim eyes shone out like
stars; and a smile of wonderment, more sweet than the
sudden smile of the sea as its ripples wake to brightness
beneath the kiss of the risen moon, broke through her rain of
tears.

'Thou livest!' she cried, throwing herself upon her knees
beside my couch. 'Thou livest—and I thought thee gone!
Thou art come back to me! Oh! what say I? How foolish
is a woman's heart! 'Tis this long watching! Nay; sleep
and rest thee, Harmachis!—why dost thou talk? Not one
more word, I command thee straitly! Where is the draught
left by that long-bearded fool? Nay thou shalt have
no draught! There, sleep, Harmachis; sleep!' and she
crouched down at my side and laid her cool hand upon my
brow, murmuring, '*Sleep! sleep!*'

And when I woke there she was still, but the lights of
dawn were peeping through the casement. There she knelt,
one hand upon my forehead, and her head, in all its dis-
array of curls, resting upon her outstretched arm.

'Charmion,' I whispered, 'have I slept?'

Instantly she was wide awake, and, gazing on me with
tender eyes, 'Yea, thou hast slept, Harmachis.'

'How long, then, have I slept?'

'Nine hours.'

'And thou hast held thy place there, at my side, for nine
long hours?'

'Yes, it is nothing; I also have slept—I feared to waken
thee if I stirred.'

'Go, rest,' I said; 'it shames me to think of this thing.
Go rest thee, Charmion!'

'Vex not thyself,' she answered; 'see, I will bid a slave
watch thee, and to wake me if thou needest aught; I sleep
there, in the outer chamber. Peace—I go!' and she strove

s

to rise, but, so cramped was she, fell straightway on the floor.

I can scarcely tell the sense of shame that filled me when I saw her fall. Alas! I could not stir to help her.

'It is naught,' she said; 'move not, I did but catch my foot. There!' and she rose, again to fall—'a pest upon my awkwardness! Why—I must be sleeping. 'Tis well now. I'll send the slave;' and she staggered thence like one overcome with wine.

And after that, I slept once more, for I was very weak. When I woke it was afternoon, and I craved for food, which Charmion brought me.

I ate. 'Then I die not,' I said.

'Nay,' she answered, with a toss of her head, 'thou wilt live. In truth, I did waste my pity on thee.'

'And thy pity saved my life,' I said wearily, for now I remembered.

'It is nothing,' she answered carelessly. 'After all, thou art my cousin; also, I love nursing—it is a woman's trade. Like enough I had done as much for any slave. Now, too, that the danger is past, I leave thee.'

'Thou hadst done better to let me die, Charmion,' I said after a while, 'for life to me can now be only one long shame. Tell me, then, when sails Cleopatra for Cilicia?'

'She sails in twenty days, and with such pomp and glory as Egypt has never seen. Of a truth, I cannot guess where she has found the means to gather in this store of splendour, as a husbandman gathers his golden harvest.'

But I, knowing whence the wealth came, groaned in bitterness of spirit, and made no answer.

'Goest thou also, Charmion?' I asked presently.

'Ay, I and all the Court. Thou, too—thou goest.'

'I go? Nay, why is this?'

'Because thou art Cleopatra's slave. and must march in gilded chains behind her chariot; because she fears to leave thee here in Khem; because it is her will, and there is an end.'

'Charmion, can I not escape?'

'Escape, thou poor sick man? Nay, how canst thou escape? Even now thou art most strictly guarded. And if thou didst escape, whither wouldst thou fly? There's not an honest man in Egypt but would spit on thee in scorn!'

Once more I groaned in spirit, and, being so very weak, I felt the tears roll adown my cheek.

'Weep not!' she said hastily, and turning her face aside. 'Be a man, and brave these troubles out. Thou hast sown, now must thou reap; but after harvest the waters rise and wash away the rotting roots, and then seed-time comes again. Perchance, yonder in Cilicia, a way may be found, when once more thou art strong, by which thou mayst fly—if in truth thou canst bear thy life apart from Cleopatra's smile; then in some far land must thou dwell till these things are forgotten. And now my task is done, so fare thee well! At times I will come to visit thee and see that thou needest nothing.'

So she went, and I was nursed thenceforward, and that skilfully, by the physician and two women-slaves; and as my wound healed so my strength came back to me, slowly at first, then most swiftly. In four days from that time I left my couch, and in three more I could walk an hour in the palace gardens; another week and I could read and think, though I went no more to Court. And at length one afternoon Charmion came and bade me make ready, for the fleet would sail in two days, first for the coast of Syria, and thence to the gulf of Issus and Cilicia.

Thereon, with all formality, and in writing, I craved leave of Cleopatra that I might be left, urging that my health was so feeble that I could not travel. But a message was sent to me in answer that I must come.

And so, on the appointed day, I was carried in a litter down to the boat, and together with that very soldier who had cut me down, the Captain Brennus, and others of his troop (who, indeed, were sent to guard me), we rowed aboard a vessel where she lay at anchor with the rest of the great fleet. For Cleopatra was voyaging as though to war in much pomp, and escorted by a fleet of ships, among which her galley, built like a house and lined throughout with cedar and silken hangings, was the most beautiful and costly that the world has ever seen. But I went not on this vessel, and therefore it chanced that I did not see Cleopatra or Charmion till we landed at the mouth of the river Cydnus.

The signal being made, the fleet set sail; and, the wind being fair, we came to Joppa on the evening of the second day. Thence we sailed slowly with contrary winds up the coast of Syria, making Cæsarea, and Ptolemais, and Tyrus, and Berytus, and past Lebanon's white brow crowned with his crest of cedars, on to Heraclea and across the gulf of Issus to the mouth of Cydnus. And ever as we journeyed, the strong breath of the sea brought back my health, till at length, save for a line of white upon my head where the sword had fallen, I was almost as I had been. And one night, as we drew near Cydnus, while Brennus and I sat alone together on the deck, his eye fell upon the white mark his sword had made, and he swore a great oath by his heathen Gods. 'An thou hadst died, lad,' he said, 'methinks I could never again have held up my head! Ah! that was a coward stroke, and I am shamed to think that it was I who struck it, and thou on the ground and with thy back to me! Knowest thou that when thou didst lie between life and death, I came every day to ask tidings of thee? and I swore by Taranis that if thou didst die I'd turn my back upon that soft palace life and then away for the bonny North.'

'Nay, trouble not, Brennus,' I answered; 'it was thy duty.'

'Mayhap! but there are duties that a brave man should not do—nay, not at the bidding of any Queen who ever ruled in Egypt! Thy blow had dazed me or I had not struck. What is it, lad?—art in trouble with this Queen of ours? Why art thou dragged a prisoner upon this pleasure party? Knowest thou that we are strictly charged that if thou dost escape our lives shall pay the price?'

'Ay, in sore trouble, friend,' I answered; 'ask me no more.'

'Then, being of the age thou art, there's a woman in it—that I swear—and, perchance, though I am rough and foolish, I might make a guess. Look thou, lad, what sayest thou? I am weary of the service of Cleopatra and this hot land of deserts and of luxury, that sap a man's strength and drain his pocket; and so are others whom I know of. What sayest thou: let's take one of these unwieldy vessels and away to the North? I'll lead thee to a better land than Egypt—a land of lake and mountain, and great forests of sweet-scented pine; ay, and find thee a girl fit to mate with—my own niece—a girl strong and tall, with wide blue eyes and long fair hair, and arms that could crack thy ribs were she of a mind to hug thee! Come, what sayest thou? Put away the past, and away for the bonny North, and be a son to me.'

For a moment I thought, and then sadly shook my head; for though I was sorely tempted to be gone, I knew that my fate lay in Egypt, and I might not fly my fate.

'It may not be, Brennus,' I answered. 'Fain would I that it might be, but I am bound by a chain of destiny which I cannot break, and in the land of Egypt I must live and die.'

'As thou wilt, lad,' said the old warrior. 'I should have
dearly loved to marry thee among my people, and make a
son of thee. At the least, remember that while I am here
thou hast Brennus for a friend. And one thing more; beware
of that beauteous Queen of thine, for, by Taranis, perhaps
an hour may come when she will hold that thou knowest too
much, and then ——' and he drew his hand across his throat.
'And now good-night; a cup of wine, then to sleep, for to-
morrow the foolery ——'

[*Here several lengths of the second roll of papyrus are so
broken as to be undecipherable. They seem to have been
descriptive of Cleopatra's voyage up the Cydnus to the city of
Tarsus.*]

And—[*the writing continues*]—to those who could take
joy in such things, the sight must, indeed, have been a
gallant one. For the stern of our galley was covered with
sheets of beaten gold, the sails were of the scarlet of Tyre,
and the oars of silver touched the water to a measure of music.
And there, in the centre of the vessel, beneath an awning
ablaze with gold embroidery, lay Cleopatra, attired as the
Roman Venus (and surely Venus was not more fair!), in
thin robes of whitest silk, bound in beneath her breast with
a golden girdle delicately graven over with scenes of love.
All about her were little rosy boys, chosen for their beauty,
and clad in naught save downy wings strapped upon their
shoulders, and on their backs Cupid's bow and quiver, who
fanned her with fans of plumes. Upon the vessel's decks,
handling the cordage, that was of silken web, and softly
singing to the sound of harps and the beat of oars, were
no rough sailors, but women lovely to behold, some robed
as Graces and some as Nereids—that is, scarce robed at all
except in their scented hair. And behind the couch, with drawn

sword, stood Brennus, in splendid armour and winged helm of gold; and by him others—I among them—in garments richly worked, and knew that I was indeed a slave! On the high poop also burned censers filled with costliest incense, of which the fragrant steam hung in little clouds about our wake.

Thus, as in a dream of luxury, followed by many ships, we glided on toward the wooded slopes of Taurus, at whose foot lay that ancient city Tarshish. And ever as we came the people gathered on the banks and ran before us, shouting: ' Venus is risen from the sea! Venus hath come to visit Bacchus!' We drew near to the city, and all its people—everyone who could walk or be carried—crowded down in thousands to the docks, and with them came the whole army of Antony, so that at length the Triumvir was left alone upon the judgment seat.

Dellius, the false-tongued, came also, fawning and bowing, and in the name of Antony gave the ' Queen of Beauty ' greeting, bidding her to a feast that Antony had made ready. But she made high answer, and said, ' Forsooth, it is Antony who should wait on us; not we on Antony. Bid the noble Antony to our poor table this night—else we dine alone.'

Dellius went, bowing to the ground; the feast was made ready; and then at last I set eyes on Antony. He came clad in purple robes, a great man and beautiful to see, set in the stout prime of life, with bright eyes of blue, and curling hair, and features cut sharply as a Grecian gem. For he was great of form and royal of mien, and with an open countenance on which his thoughts were so clearly written that all might read them; only the weakness of the mouth belied the power of the brow. He came attended by his generals, and when he reached the couch where Cleopatra lay he stood astonished, gazing on her with wide-opened eyes. She, too, gazed on him earnestly; I saw the red blood run up beneath her skin, and a great pang of jealousy seized upon my heart. And Charmion, who saw all beneath her downcast eyes, saw this also and smiled. But Cleopatra spoke no word, only she stretched out her white hand for him to kiss ; and he, saying no word, took her hand and kissed it.

'Behold, noble Antony!' she said at last in her voice of music, ' thou hast called me, and I am come.'

'Venus has come,' he answered in his deep notes, and still holding his eyes fast fixed upon her face. ' I called a woman—a Goddess hath risen from the deep!'

'To find a God to greet her on the land,' she laughed with ready wit. 'Well, a truce to compliments, for being on the earth even Venus is ahungered. Noble Antony, thy hand.'

The trumpets blared, and through the bowing crowd Cleopatra, followed by her train, passed hand in hand with Antony to the feast.

[Here there is another break in the papyrus.]

CHAPTER XV.

OF THE FEAST OF CLEOPATRA; OF THE MELTING OF
THE PEARL; OF THE SAYING OF HARMACHIS; AND
OF CLEOPATRA'S VOW OF LOVE.

ON the third night the feast was once more prepared in the hall of the great house that had been set aside to the use of Cleopatra, and on this night its splendour was greater even than on the nights before. For the twelve couches that were set about the table were embossed with gold, and those of Cleopatra and Antony were of gold set with jewels. The dishes also were all of gold set with jewels, the walls were hung with purple cloths sewn with gold, and on the floor, covered with a net of gold, fresh roses were strewn ankle-deep, that as the slaves trod them sent up their perfume. Once again I was bidden to stand, with Charmion and Iras and Merira, behind the couch of Cleopatra, and, like a slave, from time to time call out the hours as they flew. And there being no help, I went wild at heart; but this I swore—it should be for the last time, since I could not bear that shame. For though I would not yet believe what Charmion told me—that Cleopatra was about to become the Love of Antony—yet I could no more endure this ignominy and torture. For from Cleopatra now I had no words save such as a Queen speaks to her slave, and methinks it gave her dark heart pleasure to torment me.

Thus it came to pass that I, the Pharaoh, crowned of Khem, stood among eunuchs and waiting-women behind the couch of Egypt's Queen while the feast went merrily and the wine-cup passed. And ever Antony sat, his eyes fixed upon the face of Cleopatra, who from time to time let her deep glance lose itself in his. and then for a little while their talk died away. For he told her tales of war and of deeds that he had done—ay, and love-jests such as are not meet for the ears of women. But she took offence at nothing; rather, falling into his humour, she would cap his stories with others of a finer wit, but not less shameless.

At length, the rich meal being finished, Antony gazed at the splendour around him.

'Tell me, then, most lovely Egypt,' he said; 'are the sands of Nile compact of gold, that thou canst, night by night, thus squander the ransom of a King upon a single feast? Whence comes this untold wealth?'

I bethought me of the tomb of the Divine Menkau-ra, whose holy treasure was thus wickedly wasted, and looked up so that Cleopatra's eye caught mine; but, reading my thoughts, she frowned heavily.

'Why, noble Antony,' she said, 'surely it is nothing! In Egypt we have our secrets, and know whence to conjure riches at our need. Say, what is the value of this golden service, and of the meats and drinks that have been set before us?'

He cast his eyes about, and hazarded a guess.

'Maybe a thousand sestertia.'[1]

---

[1] About eight thousand pounds of English money.—ED.

'Thou hast understated it by half, noble Antony! But such as it is I give it thee and those with thee as a free token of my friendship. And more will I show thee now : I myself will eat and drink ten thousand sestertia at a draught.'

'That cannot be, fair Egypt!'

She laughed, and bade a slave bring her white vinegar in a glass. When it was brought she set it before her and laughed again, while Antony, rising from his couch, drew near and set himself at her side, and all the company leant forward to see what she would do. And this she did. She took from her ear one of those great pearls which last of all had been drawn from the body of the Divine Pharaoh ; and before any could guess her purpose she let it fall into the vinegar. Then came silence, the silence of wonder, and slowly the peerless pearl melted in the strong acid. When it was melted she lifted the glass and shook it, then drank the vinegar, to the last drop.

'More vinegar, slave!' she cried ; 'my meal is but half finished!' and she drew forth the second pearl.

'By Bacchus, no! that shalt thou not!' cried Antony, snatching at her hands ; 'I have seen enough :' and at that moment, moved to it by I know not what, I called aloud :

'The hour falls, O Queen!—*the hour of the coming of the curse of Menkau-ra!*'

An ashy whiteness grew upon Cleopatra's face, and she turned upon me furiously, while all the company gazed wondering, not knowing what the words might mean.

'Thou ill-omened slave!' she cried. 'Speak thus once more and thou shalt be scourged with rods!—ay, scourged like an evildoer—that I promise thee, Harmachis!'

'What means the knave of an astrologer?' asked Antony. 'Speak, sirrah! and make clear thy meaning, for those who deal in curses must warrant their wares.'

'I am a servant of the Gods, noble Antony. That which

the Gods put in my mind that must I say ; nor can I read their meaning,' I answered humbly.

' Oh, oh ! thou servest the Gods, dost thou, thou many-coloured mystery?' This he said having reference to my splendid robes. ' Well, I serve the Goddesses, which is a softer cult. And there's this between us : that though what they put in my mind I say, neither can I read their meaning,' and he glanced at Cleopatra as one who questions.

' Let the knave be,' she said impatiently; ' to-morrow we'll be rid of him. Sirrah, begone!'

I bowed and went ; and, as I went, I heard Antony say : ' Well, he may be a knave—for that all men are—but this for thy astrologer : he hath a royal air and the eye of a King—ay, and wit in it.'

Without the door I paused, not knowing what to do, for I was bewildered with misery. And, as I stood, some one touched me on the hand. I glanced up—it was Charmion, who in the confusion of the rising of the guests, had slipped away and followed me.

For in trouble Charmion was ever at my side.

' Follow me,' she whispered ; ' thou art in danger.'

I turned and followed her. Why should I not ?

' Whither go we ? ' I asked at length.

' To my chamber,' she said. ' Fear not; we ladies of Cleopatra's Court have small good fame to lose : if anyone by chance should see us, they'll think that it is a love-tryst, and such are all the fashion.'

I followed, and, presently, skirting the crowd, we came unseen to a little side entrance that led to a stair, up which we passed. The stair ended in a passage ; we turned down it till we found a door on the left hand. Charmion entered silently, and I followed her into a dark chamber. Being in, she barred the door and, kindling tinder to a flame, lit a

hanging lamp. As the light grew strong I gazed around.
The chamber was not large, and had but one casement, closely
shuttered. For the rest, it was simply furnished, having white
walls, some chests for garments, an ancient chair, what I
took to be a tiring table, on which were combs, perfumes, and
all the frippery that pertains to woman, and a white bed with
a broidered coverlid, over which was hung a gnat-gauze.

'Be seated, Harmachis,' she said, pointing to the chair.
I took the chair, and Charmion, throwing back the gnat-gauze,
sat herself upon the bed before me.

'Knowest thou what I heard Cleopatra say as thou didst
leave the banqueting-hall?' she asked presently.

'Nay, I know not.'

'She gazed after thee, and, as I went over to her to do
some service, she murmured to herself: "By Serapis, I will
make an end! I will wait no longer: to-morrow he shall be
strangled!"'

'So!' I said, 'it may be; though, after all that has
been, I can scarce believe that she will murder me.'

'Why canst thou not believe it, thou most foolish of
men? Dost forget how nigh thou wast to death there in the
Alabaster Hall? Who saved thee then from the knives of the
eunuchs? Was it Cleopatra? Or was it I and Brennus?
Stay, I will tell thee. Thou canst not yet believe it, because,
in thy folly, thou dost not think it possible that the woman
who has but lately been as a wife to thee can now, in so short
a time, doom thee to be basely done to death. Nay, answer
not—I know all; and I tell thee this: thou hast not measured
the depth of Cleopatra's perfidy, nor canst thou dream the
blackness of her wicked heart. She had surely slain thee in
Alexandria had she not feared that thy slaughter being noised
abroad might bring trouble on her. Therefore has she brought
thee here to kill thee secretly. For what more canst thou

give her? She has thy heart's love, and is wearied of thy strength and beauty. She has robbed thee of thy royal birthright and brought thee, a King, to stand amidst the waiting-women behind her at her feasts; she has won from thee the great secret of the holy treasure!'

'Ah, thou knowest that?'

'Yes, I know all; and to-night thou seest how the wealth stored against the need of Khem is being squandered to fill up the wanton luxury of Khem's Macedonian Queen! Thou seest how she has kept her oath to wed thee honourably. Harmachis—at length thine eyes are open to the truth!'

'Ay, I see too well; and yet she swore she loved me, and I, poor fool, I believed her!'

'She swore she loved thee!' answered Charmion, lifting her dark eyes: 'now I will show thee how she loves thee. Knowest thou what was this house? It was a priest's college; and, as thou wottest, Harmachis, priests have their ways. This little room aforetime was the room of the Head Priest, and the chamber that is beyond and below was the gathering-place of the other priests. The old slave who keeps the house told me all this, and also she revealed what I shall show thee. Now, Harmachis, be silent as the dead, and follow me!"

She blew out the lamp, and by the little light that crept through the shuttered casement led me by the hand to the far corner of the room. Here she pressed upon the wall, and a door opened in its thickness. We entered, and she closed the spring. Now we were in a little chamber, some five cubits in length by four in breadth; for a faint light struggled into the closet, and also the sound of voices, I knew not whence. Loosing my hand, she crept to the end of the place, and looked steadfastly at the wall; then crept back, and, whispering 'Silence!' led me forward with her. Then I saw that

there were eyeholes in the wall, which pierced it, and were
hidden on the farther side by carved work in stone. I looked
through the hole that was in front of me, and I saw this : six
cubits below was the level of the floor of another chamber, lit
with fragrant lamps, and most richly furnished. It was the
sleeping-place of Cleopatra, and there, within ten cubits of
where we stood, sat Cleopatra on a gilded couch ; and by her
side sat Antony.

'Tell me,' Cleopatra murmured—for this place was so
built that every word spoken in the room below came to
the ears of the listener above—'tell me, noble Antony, wast
pleased with my poor festival ? '

'Ay,' he answered in his deep soldier's voice, ' ay, Egypt,
I have made feasts, and been bidden to feasts, but never saw
I aught like thine ; and I tell thee this, though I am rough of
tongue and unskilled in pretty sayings such as women love,
thou wast the richest sight of all that splendid board. The
red wine was not so red as thy beauteous cheek, the roses smelt
not so sweet as the odour of thy hair, and no sapphire there
with its changing light was so lovely as thy eyes of ocean
blue.'

'What ! Praise from Antony ! Sweet words from the
lips of him whose writings are so harsh ! Why, it is praise
indeed ! '

'Ay,' he went on, 'it was a royal feast, though I grieve
that thou didst waste that great pearl ; and what meant that
hour-calling astrologer of thine, with his ill-omened talk of
the curse of Menkau-ra ? '

A shadow fled across her glowing face. 'I know not ; he
was lately wounded in a brawl, and methinks the blow has
crazed him.'

'He seemed not crazed, and there was that about his
voice which rings in my ears like some oracle of fate. So

T

wildly, too, he looked upon thee, Egypt, with those piercing
eyes of his, like one who loved and yet hated through the
love.'

'He is a strange man, I tell thee, noble Antony, and a
learned.   Myself, at times, I almost fear him, for he is deeply
versed in the ancient arts of Egypt.   Knowest thou that the
man is of royal blood, and once he plotted to slay me ?   But I
won him over, and slew him not, for he had the key to secrets
that I fain would learn ; and, indeed, I loved his wisdom, and
to listen to his deep talk of all hidden things.'

'By Bacchus, I grow jealous of the knave !   And now,
Egypt ? '

'And now I have sucked his knowledge dry, and have no
more cause to fear him.   Didst thou not see that I have made
him stand these three nights a slave amid my slaves, and
call aloud the hours as they fled in festival.   No captive King
marching in thy Roman triumphs can have suffered pangs so
keen as that proud Egyptian Prince when he stood shamed
behind my couch.'

Here Charmion laid her hand on mine and pressed it, as
though in tenderness.

'Well, he shall trouble us no more with his words of evil
omen,' Cleopatra went on slowly ; ' to-morrow morn he dies—
dies swiftly and in secret, leaving no trace of what his fate
has been.   On this is my mind fixed ; of a truth. noble
Antony, it is fixed.   Even as I speak the fear of this man
grows and gathers in my breast.   Half am I minded to give
the word even now, for I breathe not freely till he be dead,'
and she made as though to rise.

'Let it be till morning,' he said, catching her by the
hand ; ' the soldiers drink, and the deed will be ill done.   'Tis
pity, too.   I love not to think of men slaughtered in their
sleep.'

'In the morning, perchance, the hawk may have flown,' she answered, pondering. 'He hath keen ears, this Harmachis, and can summon things to aid him that are not of the earth. Perchance, even now he hears me in the spirit: for, of a truth, I seem to feel his presence breathing round me. I could tell thee—but no, let him be! Noble Antony, be my tiring-woman and loose me this crown of gold, it chafes my brow. Be gentle, hurt me not—so.'

He lifted the uræus crown from her brows, and she shook loose her heavy weight of hair that fell about her like a garment.

'Take back thy crown, royal Egypt,' he said, speaking low, 'take it from my hand; I will not rob thee of it, but rather set it more firmly on that beauteous brow.'

'What means my Lord?' she asked, smiling and looking into his eyes.

'What mean I? Why then, this: thou camest hither at my bidding to make answer of the charges laid against thee as to matters politic. And knowest thou, Egypt, that hadst thou been other than thou art thou hadst not gone back to queen it on the Nile; for of this I am sure, the charges against thee are true in fact. But, being what thou art—and look thou! never did Nature serve a woman better!—I forgive thee all. For the sake of thy grace and beauty I forgive thee that which had not been forgiven to virtue, or to patriotism, or to the dignity of age! See now how good a thing is woman's wit and loveliness, that can make kings forget their duty and cozen even blindfolded Justice to peep ere she lifts her sword! Take back thy crown, O Egypt! It is now my care that, though it be heavy, it shall not chafe thee.'

'These are royal words, most noble Antony,' she made answer; 'gracious and generous words, such as befit the Conqueror of the world! And touching my misdeeds in the

T 2

past—if misdeeds there have been—I say this, and this alone
—then I knew not Antony. For, knowing Antony, who could
sin against him? What woman could lift a sword against one
who must be to all women as a God—one who, seen and
known, draws after him the whole allegiance of the heart, as
the sun draws flowers? And what more can I say and not
cross the bounds of woman's modesty? Why, only this—set
that crown upòn my brow, great Antony, and I will take it as
a gift from thee, by the giving made doubly dear, and to thy
uses I will guard it.

'There, now I am thy vassal Queen, and through me all
old Egypt that I rule does homage to Antony the Triumvir,
who shall be Antony the Emperor of Rome and Khem's
Imperial Lord!'

And, having set the crown upon her locks, he stood
gazing on her, grown passionate in the warm breath of her
living beauty, till at length he caught her by both hands and
drawing her to him kissed her thrice, saying :

'Cleopatra, I love thee, Sweet—I love thee as I never
loved before.' She drew back from his embrace, smiling
softly ; and as she did so the golden circlet of the sacred
snakes fell, being but loosely set upon her brow, and rolled
away into the darkness beyond the ring of light.

I saw the omen, and even in the bitter anguish of my heart
knew its evil import. But these twain took no note.

'Thou lovest me? she said, most sweetly ; 'how know I
that thou lovest me? Perchance it is Fulvia whom thou
lovest—Fulvia, thy wedded wife?'

'Nay, it is not Fulvia, 'tis thou, Cleopatra, and thou alone.
Many women have looked favourably upon me from my boy-
hood up, but to never a one have I known such desire as to
thee, O thou Wonder of the World, like unto whom no
woman ever was! Canst thou love me Cleopatra, and to me

be true, not for my place and power, not for that which I can
give or can withhold, not for the stern music of my legions'
tramp, or for the light that flows from my bright Star of
Fortune ; but for myself, for the sake of Antony, the rough
captain, grown old in camps ? Ay, for the sake of Antony
the reveller, the frail, the unfixed of purpose, but who yet
never did desert a friend, or rob a poor man, or take an
enemy unawares ? Say, canst thou love me, Egypt ? Oh ! if
thou wilt, why, I am more happy than though I sat to-night
in the Capitol at Rome crowned absolute Monarch of the
World ! '

And, ever as he spoke, she gazed on him with wonderful
eyes, and in them shone a light of truth and honesty such as
was strange to me.

'Thou speakest plainly,' she said, 'and thy words are
sweet to mine ears—they would be sweet, even were things
otherwise than they are, for what woman would not love to
see the world's master at her feet ? But things being as they
are, why, Antony, what can be so sweet as thy sweet words ?
The harbour of his rest to the storm-tossed mariner—surely
that is sweet ! The dream of Heaven's bliss which cheers the
poor ascetic priest on his path of sacrifice—surely that is
sweet ! The sight of Dawn, the rosy-fingered, coming in his
promise to glad the watching Earth -surely that is sweet !
But, ah ! not one of these, nor all dear delightful things that
are, can match the honey-sweetness of thy words to me, O
Antony ! For thou knowest not—never canst thou know—
how drear my life hath been, and empty, since thus it is
ordained that in love only can woman lose her solitude ! And
I have *never* loved—never might I love—till this happy night!
Ay, take me in thy arms, and let us swear a great vow of
love—an oath that may not be broken while life is in us !
Behold ! Antony ! now and for ever I do vow most strict

fidelity unto thee!   Now and for ever I am thine, and thine alone!'

Then Charmion took me by the hand and drew me thence.

'Hast seen enough?' she asked, when we were once more within the chamber and the lamp was lit.

'Yea,' I answered; 'my eyes are opened.'

CHAPTER XVI.

OF THE PLAN OF CHARMION ; OF THE CONFESSION OF
CHARMION ; AND OF THE ANSWER OF HARMACHIS.

 some while I sat with bowed head,
and the last bitterness of shame
sank into my soul. This, then,
was the end. For this I had
betrayed my oaths; for this I had
told the secret of the pyramid; for
this I had lost my Crown, my
Honour, and, perchance, my hope
of Heaven! Could there be another
man in the wide world so steeped
in sorrow as I was that night?
Surely not one! Where should I
turn? What could I do? And
even through the tempest of my torn heart the bitter voice
of jealousy called aloud. For I loved this woman, to whom
I had given all; and she at this moment—she was——Ah!
I could not bear to think of it; and in my utter agony, my
heart burst in a river of tears such as are terrible to weep!

Then Charmion drew near me, and I saw that she, too,
was weeping.

'Weep not, Harmachis!' she sobbed, kneeling at my
side. 'I cannot endure to see thee weep. Oh! why wouldst

thou not be warned ? Then hadst thou been great and happy, and not as now. Listen, Harmachis! Thou didst hear what that false and tigerish woman said—to-morrow she hands thee over to the murderers ! '

' It is well,' I gasped.

' Nay : it is not well. Harmachis, give her not this last triumph over thee. Thou hast lost all save life : but while life remains, hope remains also, and with hope the chance of vengeance.'

' Ah ! ' I said, starting from my seat. ' I had not thought of that. Ay—the chance of vengeance ! It would be sweet to be avenged ! '

' It would be sweet, Harmachis, and yet this—Vengeance is an arrow that in falling oft pierces him who shot it. My-self—I know it,' and she sighed. ' But a truce to talk and grief. There will be time for us twain to grieve, if not to talk, in all the heavy coming years. Thou must fly—before the coming of the light must thou fly. Here is a plan. To-morrow, ere the dawn, a galley that but yesterday came from Alexandria, bearing fruit and stores, sails thither again, and its captain is known to me, but to thee he is not known. Now, I will find thee the garb of a Syrian merchant, and cloak thee, as I know how, and furnish thee with a letter to the captain of the galley. He shall give thee passage to Alexandria; for to him thou wilt seem but as a merchant going on the business of thy trade. Brennus is officer of the guard to-night, and Brennus is a friend to me and thee. Per-haps he will guess somewhat; or, perhaps, he will not guess; at the least, the Syrian merchant shall safely pass the lines. What sayest thou ? '

' It is well,' I answered wearily; ' little do I reck the issue.'

' Rest thou, then, here, Harmachis, while I make these

matters ready; and, Harmachis, grieve not overmuch; there are others who should grieve more heavily than thou.' And she went, leaving me alone with my agony which rent me like a torture-bed. Had it not been for that fierce desire of vengeance which from time to time flashed across my tormented mind as the lightning over a midnight sea, methinks my reason had left me in that dark hour. At length I heard her footstep at the door, and she entered, breathing heavily, for she bore a sack of clothing in her arms.

'It is well,' she said; 'here is the garb with spare linen, and writing-tablets, and all things needful. I have seen Brennus also, and told him that a Syrian merchant would pass the guard an hour before the dawn. And though he made pretence of sleep, I think he understood, for he answered, yawning, that if they but had the pass-word, " Antony," fifty Syrian merchants might go through about their lawful business. And here is the letter to the captain—thou canst not mistake the galley, for she is moored along to the right—a small galley, painted black, as thou dost enter on the great quay, and, moreover, the sailors make ready for sailing. Now I will wait here without, while thou dost put off the livery of thy service and array thyself.'

When she was gone I tore off my gorgeous garments and spat upon them and trod them on the ground. Then I put on the modest robe of a merchant, and bound the tablets round me, on my feet the sandals of untanned hide, and at my waist the knife. When it was done Charmion entered once again and looked on me.

'Too much art thou still the royal Harmachis,' she said; 'see, it must be changed.'

Then she took scissors from her tiring-table, and, bidding me be seated, she cut off my locks, clipping the hair close to the head. Next she found stains of such sort as women use to make dark the eyes, and mixed them cunningly, rubbing the stuff on my face and hands and on the white mark in my hair where the sword of Brennus had bitten to the bone.

'Now thou art changed—somewhat for the worse, Harmachis,' she said, with a dreary laugh, 'scarce myself should I know thee. Stay, there is one more thing,' and, going to a chest of garments, she drew thence a heavy bag of gold.

'Take thou this,' she said; 'thou wilt have need of money.'

'I cannot take thy gold, Charmion.'

'Yes, take it. It was Sepa who gave it to me for the furtherance of our cause, and therefore it is fitting that thou shouldst spend it. Moreover, if I want money, doubtless Antony, who is henceforth my master, will give me more; he is much beholden to me, and this he knows well. There, waste not the precious time in haggling o'er the pelf—not yet art thou all a merchant, Harmachis;' and, without more words, she thrust the pieces into the leather bag that hung across my shoulders. Then she made fast the sack containing the spare garments, and, so womanly thoughtful was she, placed in it an alabaster jar of pigment, with which I might stain my countenance afresh, and, taking the broidered robes of my office that I had cast off, hid them in the secret passage. And so at last all was made ready.

'Is it time that I should go?' I asked.

'Not yet a while. Be patient, Harmachis, for but one little hour more must thou endure my presence, and then, perchance, farewell for ever.'

I made a gesture signifying that this was no time for sharp words.

'Forgive me my quick tongue,' she said; 'but from a salt spring bitter waters well. Be seated, Harmachis; I have heavier words to speak to thee before thou goest.'

'Say on,' I answered; 'words, however heavy, can move me no more.'

She stood before me with folded hands, and the lamp-light shone upon her beauteous face. I noticed idly how great was its pallor and how wide and dark were the rings about the deep black eyes. Twice she lifted her white face and strove to speak, twice her voice failed her; and when at last it came it was in a hoarse whisper.

'I cannot let thee go,' she said—' I cannot let thee go unwitting of the truth.

'*Harmachis, 'twas I who did betray thee !* '

I sprang to my feet, an oath upon my lips; but she caught me by the hand.

'Oh, be seated,' she said—' be seated and hear me; then, when thou hast heard, do to me as thou wilt. Listen. From that evil moment when, in the presence of thy uncle Sepa, for the second time I set eyes upon thy face, I loved thee—how much, thou canst little guess. Think upon thine own love for Cleopatra, and double it, and double it again, and perchance thou mayst come near to my love's mighty sum. I loved thee, day by day I loved thee more, till in thee and for thee alone I seemed to live. But thou wast cold—thou wast worse than cold! thou didst deal with me not as a breathing woman, but rather as the instrument to an end—as a tool with which to grave thy fortunes. And then I saw —yes, long before thou knewest it thyself—thy heart's tide was setting strong towards that ruinous shore whereon to-day thy life is broken. And at last that night came, that dreadful night when, hid within the chamber, I saw thee cast my kerchief to the winds, and with sweet words cherish my royal Rival's gift. Then—oh, thou knowest—in my pain I betrayed the secret that thou wouldst not see, and thou didst make a mock of me, Harmachis! Oh! the shame of it—

thou in thy foolishness didst make a mock of me! I went thence, and within me were rising all the torments which can tear a woman's heart, for now I was sure that thou didst love Cleopatra! Ay, and so mad was I, even that night I was minded to betray thee : but I thought—not yet, not yet; to-morrow he may soften. Then came the morrow, and all was ready for the bursting of the great plot that should make thee Pharaoh. And I too came—thou dost remember—and again thou didst put me away when I spake to thee in parables, as something of little worth—as a thing too small to claim a moment's weighty thought. And, knowing that this was because—though thou knewest it not—thou didst love Cleopatra, whom now thou must straightway slay, I grew mad, and a wicked Spirit entered into me, possessing me utterly, so that I was myself no longer, nor could control myself. And because thou hadst scorned me, I did this, to my everlasting shame and sorrow!—I passed into Cleopatra's presence and betrayed thee and those with thee, and our holy cause, saying that I had found a writing which thou hadst let fall and read all this therein.'

I gasped and sat silent; and gazing sadly at me she went on :

' When she understood how great was the plot, and how deep its roots, Cleopatra was much troubled; and, at first, she would have fled to Sais or taken ship and run for Cyprus, but I showed her that the ways were barred. Then she said she would cause thee to be slain, there, in the chamber, and I left her so believing; for, at that hour, I was glad that thou shouldst be slain—ay, even if I wept out my heart upon thy grave, Har-machis. But what said I just now?—Vengeance is an arrow that oft falls on him who looses it. So it was with me; for between my going and thy coming Cleopatra hatched a deeper plan. She feared that to slay thee would only be to light a fiercer fire of revolt ; but she saw that to bind thee to her, and, having left men awhile in doubt, to show thee faithless, would strike the imminent danger at its roots and wither it. This plot once formed, being great, she dared its doubtful issue, and—need I go on ? Thou knowest, Harmachis, how she won ; and thus the shaft of vengeance that I loosed fell upon my own head. For on the morrow I knew that I had sinned for naught, that the burden of my betrayal had been laid on the wretched Paulus, and that I had but ruined the cause to which I was sworn and given the man I loved to the arms of wanton Egypt.'

She bowed her head awhile, and then, as I spoke not, once more went on :

' Let all my sin be told, Harmachis, and then let justice come. See now, this thing happened. Half did Cleopatra learn to love thee, and deep in her heart she bethought her of taking thee to wedded husband. For the sake of this half love of hers she spared the lives of those in the plot whom she had meshed, bethinking her that if she wedded thee she might use them and thee to draw the heart of Egypt, which loves not her nor any Ptolemy. And then, once again she entrapped thee, and in thy folly thou didst betray to her the secret of the hidden wealth of Egypt, which to-day she squanders to delight the luxurious Antony ; and, of a truth, at that time she purposed to make good her oath and marry thee. But on the very morn when Dellius came for answer she sent for me, and, telling me all—for my wit, above any, she holds at price—demanded of me my judgment whether she should defy Antony and wed thee, or whether she should put the thought away and come to Antony. And I—now mark thou all my sin—I, in my bitter jealousy, rather than I would see her thy wedded wife and thou her loving lord, counselled her most strictly that she should come to Antony, well knowing—for I had had speech with Dellius—that if she came, this weak Antony would fall like a ripe fruit at her feet, as, indeed, he has fallen. And but now I have shown thee the issue of the scheme. Antony loves Cleopatra and Cleopatra loves Antony, and thou art robbed, and matters have gone well for me, who of all women on the earth to-night am the wretchedest by far. For when I saw how thy heart broke but now, my heart seemed to break with thine, and I could no longer bear the burden of my evil deeds, but knew that I must tell them and take my punishment.

'And now, Harmachis, I have no more to say; save that I thank thee for thy courtesy in hearkening, and this one thing I add. Driven by my great love I have sinned against thee unto death! I have ruined thee, I have ruined Khem, and myself also have I ruined! Let death reward me! Slay thou me, Harmachis—I will gladly die upon thy sword; ay, and kiss its blade! Slay thou me and go; for if thou slayest me not, myself I will surely slay!' And she threw herself upon her knees, lifting her fair breast toward me, that I might smite her with my dagger. And, in my bitter fury, I was minded to strike; for, above all, I thought how, when I was fallen, this woman, who herself was my cause of shame, had scourged me with her whip of scorn. But it is hard to slay a fair woman; and, even as I lifted my hand to strike, I remembered that she had now twice saved my life.

'Woman! thou shameless woman!' I said, 'arise! I slay thee not! Who am I, that I should judge thy crime. that, with mine own, doth overtop all earthly judgment?'

'Slay me, Harmachis!' she moaned; 'slay me, or I slay myself! My burden is too great for me to bear! Be not so deadly calm! Curse me, and slay!'

'What was it that thou didst say to me just now, Charmion —that as I had sown so I must reap? It is not lawful that

thou shouldst slay thyself ; it is not lawful that I, thine equal
in sin, should slay thee because through thee I sinned. As
thou hast sown, Charmion, so must *thou* also reap. Base
woman ! whose cruel jealousy has brought all these woes
on me and Egypt, live—live on, and from year to year pluck
the bitter fruit of crime ! Haunted be thy sleep by visions of
thy outraged Gods, whose vengeance awaits thee and me in
their dim Amenti ! Haunted be thy days by memories of that
man whom thy fierce love brought to shame and ruin, and
by the sight of Khem a prey to the insatiate Cleopatra and a
slave to Roman Antony.'

'Oh, speak not thus, Harmachis ! Thy words are sharper
than any sword ; and more surely, if more slowly, shall
they slay ! Listen, Harmachis,' and she grasped my robe :
'when thou wast great, and all power lay within thy grasp,
thou didst reject me. Wilt reject me now that Cleopatra
hath cast thee from her—now that thou art poor and shamed
and with no pillow to thy head ? Still am I fair, and still I
worship thee. Let me fly with thee, and make atonement
by my lifelong love. Or, if this be too great a thing to ask,
let me be but as thy sister and thy servant—thy very slave,
so that I may still look upon thy face, and share thy trouble
and minister to thee. O Harmachis, let me but come and I
will brave all things and endure all things, and nothing but
Death himself shall stay me from thy side. For I do believe
that the love that sank me to so low a depth, dragging thee
with me, can yet lift me to an equal height, and thee with
me ! '

'Wouldst tempt me to fresh sin, woman ? And dost thou
think, Charmion, that in some hovel where I must hide, I
could bear, day by day, to look upon thy fair face, and seeing,
remember that those lips betrayed me ? Not thus easily
shalt thou atone ! This I know even now : many and heavy

shall be thy lonely days of penance! Perchance that hour
of vengeance yet may come, and perchance thou shalt live
to play thy part in it. Thou must still abide in the Court
of Cleopatra; and, while thou art there, if I yet live, I will
from time to time find means to give thee tidings. Perhaps
a day may dawn when once more I shall need thy service.
Now, swear that, in this event, thou wilt not fail me a second
time.'

'I swear, Harmachis!—I swear! May everlasting torments, too hideous to be dreamed—more hideous even, by
far, than those that wring me now—be my portion if I fail
thee in one jot or tittle—ay, though I wait a lifetime for thy
word!'

'It is well; see that thou keep the oath—not twice may
we betray. I go to work out my fate; abide thou to work
out thine. Perchance our divers threads will once more
mingle ere the web be spun. Charmion, who unasked didst
love me—and who, prompted by that gentle love of thine,
didst betray and ruin me—fare thee well!'

She gazed wildly upon my face—she stretched out her arms
as though to clasp me; then, in the agony of her despair,
she cast herself at length and grovelled upon the ground.

I took up the sack of clothing and the staff and gained the
door, and, as I passed it, I threw one last glance upon her.
There she lay, with arms outstretched—more white than
her white robes—her dark hair streaming down her, and her
fair brows hidden in the dust.

And thus I left her, nor did I again set my eyes upon her
till nine long years had come and gone.

[Here ends the second and largest roll of papyrus.]

BOOK III.

The Vengeance of Harmachis

CHAPTER L.

MADE my way down the stair in safety, and presently stood in the courtyard of the great house. It was but an hour from dawn, and none were stirring. The last reveller had drunk his fill, the dancing-girls had ceased their dancing, and silence lay upon the city. I drew near the gate, and was challenged by an officer who stood on guard, wrapped in a heavy cloak.

'Who passes?' said the voice of Brennus.

'A merchant, may it please you, Sir, who, having brought gifts from Alexandria to a lady of the Queen's household, and, having been entertained of the lady, now departs to his galley,' I answered in a feigned voice.

'Umph!' he growled. 'The ladies of the Queen's household keep their guests late. Well; it is a time of festival.

The pass-word, Sir Shopkeeper? Without the pass-word you must needs return and crave the lady's further hospitality.'

' " *Antony*," Sir; and a right good word, too. Ah! I've wandered far, and never saw I so goodly a man or so great a general. And, mark you, Sir! I've travelled far, and seen many generals.'

' Ay; " *Antony* " 's the word! And Antony is a good general in his way—when it is a sober way, and when he cannot find a skirt to follow. I've served with Antony—and against him, too; and know his points. Well, well; he's got an armful now! '

And all this while that he was holding me in talk, the sentry had been pacing to and fro before the gate. But now he moved a little way to the right, leaving the entrance clear.

' Fare thee well, Harmachis, and begone! ' whispered Brennus, leaning forward and speaking quickly. ' Linger not. But at times bethink thee of Brennus who risked his neck to save thine. Farewell, lad, I would that we were sailing North together,' and he turned his back upon me and began to hum a tune.

' Farewell, Brennus, thou honest man,' I answered, and was gone. And, as I heard long afterwards, when on the morrow the hue and cry was raised because the murderers could not find me, though they sought me everywhere to slay me, Brennus did me a service. For he swore that as he kept his watch alone an hour after midnight he saw me come and stand upon the parapet of the roof, that then I stretched out my robes and they became wings on which I floated up to Heaven, leaving him astonished. And all those about the Court lent ear to this history, believing in it, because of the great fame of my magic; and they wondered much what the marvel might portend. The tale also travelled into Egypt, and did much to save my good name among those whom I had betrayed;

for the more ignorant among them believed that I acted not
of my will, but of the will of the dread Gods, who of their own
purpose wafted me to Heaven. And thus to this day the saying
runs that ' *When Harmachis comes again Egypt shall be free.*'
But alas, Harmachis comes no more ! Only Cleopatra, though
she was much afraid, doubted her of the tale, and sent an
armed vessel to search for the Syrian merchant, but not to
find him, as shall be told.

When I reached the galley of which Charmion had spoken,
I found her about to sail, and gave the writing to the captain,
who conned it, looking on me curiously, but said nothing.

So I went aboard, and immediately we dropped swiftly
down the river with the current. And having come to the
mouth of the river unchallenged, though we passed many
vessels, we put out to sea with a strong favouring wind that
before night freshened to a great gale. Then the sailor
men, being much afraid, would have put about and 'run for
the mouth of Cydnus again, but could not because of the
wildness of the sea. All that night it blew furiously, and
by dawn our mast was carried away, and we rolled helplessly
in the trough of the great waves. But I sat wrapped in a
cloak, little heeding ; and because I showed no fear the sailors
cried out that I was a wizard, and sought to cast me into
the sea, but the captain would not. At dawn the wind
slackened, but ere noon it once more blew in terrible fury,
and at the fourth hour from noon we came in sight of the rocky
coast of that cape in the island of Cyprus which is called
Dinaretum, where is a mountain named Olympus, and thither-
wards we drifted swiftly. Then, when the sailors saw the
terrible rocks, and how the great waves that smote on them
spouted up in foam, once more they grew much afraid, and
cried out in their fear. For, seeing that I still sat unmoved,

they swore that I certainly was a wizard, and came to cast me forth as a sacrifice to the Gods of the sea. And this time the captain was over-ruled, and said nothing. Therefore, when they came to me I rose and defied them, saying, ' Cast me forth, if ye will ; but if ye cast me forth ye shall perish.'

For in my heart I cared little, having no more any love of life, but rather a desire to die, though I greatly feared to pass into the presence of my Holy Mother Isis. But my weariness and sorrow at the bitterness of my lot overcame even this heavy fear ; so that when, being mad as brute beasts, they seized me and, lifting me, hurled me into the raging waters, I did but utter one prayer to Isis and made ready for death. But it was fated that I should not die ; for, when I rose to the surface of the water, I saw a spar of wood floating near me, to which I swam and clung. And a great wave came and swept me, riding, as it were, upon the spar, as when a boy I had learned to do in the waters of the Nile, past the bulwarks of the galley where the fierce-faced sailors clustered to see me drown. And when they saw me come mounted on the wave, cursing them as I came, and saw, too, that the colour of my face had changed—for the salt water had washed away the pigment, they shrieked with fear and threw themselves down upon the deck. And within a very little while, as I rode toward the rocky coast, a great wave poured into the vessel, that rolled broadside on, and pressed her down into the deep, whence she rose no more.

So she sank with all her crew. And in that same storm also sank the galley which Cleopatra had sent to search for the Syrian merchant. Thus all traces of me were lost, and of a surety she believed that I was dead.

But I rode on toward the shore. The wind shrieked and the salt waves lashed my face as, alone with the tempest, I rushed upon my way, while the sea-birds screamed about my head. I felt no fear, but rather a wild uplifting of the heart; and in the stress of my imminent peril the love of life seemed to waken again. And so I plunged and drifted, now tossed high toward the lowering clouds, now cast into the deep valleys of the sea, till at length the rocky headland loomed before me, and I saw the breakers smite upon the stubborn rocks, and through the screaming of the wind heard the sullen thunder of their fall and the groan of stones sucked seaward from the beach. On! high-throned upon the mane of a mighty billow—fifty cubits beneath me the level of the hissing waters; above me the inky sky! It was done! The spar was torn from me, and, dragged downwards by the weight of the bag of gold and the clinging of my garments, I sank struggling furiously.

Now I was under—the green light for a moment streamed through the waters, and then came darkness, and on the darkness pictures of the past. Picture after picture—all the long scene of life was written here. Then in my ears I only heard the song of the nightingale, the murmur of the summer sea, and the music of Cleopatra's laugh of victory, following me softly and yet more soft as I sank away to sleep.

Once more my life came back, and with it a sense of deadly sickness and of aching pain. I opened my eyes and saw kind faces bending over me, and knew that I was in the room of a builded house.

'How came I hither?' I asked faintly.

'Of a truth, Poseidon brought thee, Stranger,' answered a rough voice in barbarous Greek; 'we found thee cast high upon the beach like a dead dolphin and brought thee to our house, for we are fisher-folk. And here, methinks, thou must lie a while, for thy left leg is broken by the force of the waves.'

I strove to move my foot and could not. It was true, the bone was broken below the knee.

'Who art thou, and how art thou named?' asked the rough-bearded sailor.

'I am an Egyptian traveller whose ship has sunk in the fury of the gale, and I am named Olympus,' I answered, for these people called a mountain that we had sighted Olympus, and therefore I took the name at hazard. And as Olympus I was henceforth known.

Here with these rough fisher-folk I abode for the half of a year, paying them a little out of the sum of gold that had come safely ashore upon me. For it was long before my bones grew together again, and then I was left somewhat of a cripple; for I, who had been so tall and straight and strong, now limped—one limb being shorter than the other. And after I recovered from my hurt, I still lived there, and toiled with them at the trade of fishing; for I knew not whither I should go or what I should do, and, for a while, I was fain to become a peasant fisherman, and so wear my weary life away. And these people entreated me kindly, though, as others, they feared me much, holding me to be a wizard brought hither by the sea. For my sorrows had stamped so strange an aspect on my face that men gazing at me grew fearful of what lay beneath its calm.

There, then, I abode, till at length, one night as I lay and strove to sleep, great restlessness came upon me, and a mighty desire once more to see the face of Sihor. But whether this desire was of the Gods or born of my own heart, not knowing, I cannot tell. So strong was it, at the least, that before it was dawn I rose from my bed of straw and clothed myself in my fisher garb, and, because I had no wish to answer questions, thus I took farewell of my humble hosts. First I placed some pieces of gold on the well-cleaned table of wood, and then taking a pot of flour I strewed it in the form of letters, writing :

'*This gift from Olympus, the Egyptian, who returns into the sea.*'

Then I went, and on the third day I came to the great city of Salamis, that is also on the sea. Here I abode in the fishermen's quarters till a vessel was about to sail for Alexandria, and to the captain of this vessel, a man of Paphos, I hired myself as a sailor. We sailed with a favouring wind, and on the fifth day I came to Alexandria, that hateful city, and saw the light glancing on its golden domes.

Here I might not abide. So again I hired myself out as a sailor, giving my labour in return for passage, and we passed up the Nile. And I learned from the talk of men that Cleopatra had come back to Alexandria, drawing Antony with her and that they lived together with royal state in the palace on the Lochias. Indeed, the boatmen already had a song thereon, which they sang as they laboured at the oar. Also I heard how the galley that was sent to search for the vessel which carried the Syrian merchant had foundered with all her crew, and the tale that the Queen's astronomer, Harmachis, had flown to Heaven from the roof of the house at Tarsus. And the sailors wondered because I sat and laboured and would not sing their ribald song of the loves of Cleopatra. For they, too, began to fear me, and mutter concerning me among themselves. Then I knew that I was a man accursed and set apart—a man whom none might love.

On the sixth day we drew nigh to Abouthis, where I left the craft, and the sailors were right glad to see me go. And, with a breaking heart, I walked through the fertile fields, seeing faces that I knew well. But in my rough disguise and limping gait none knew me. At length, as the sun sank, I came near to the great outer pylon of the temple; and here I

crouched down in the ruins of a house, not knowing why
I had come or what I was about to do. Like a lost ox I had
strayed from far, back to the fields of my birth, and for what?
If my father, Amenemhat, still lived, surely he would turn his
face from me. I dared not go into the presence of my father.
I sat hidden there among the broken rafters, and idly watched
the pylon gates, to see if, perchance, a face I knew should issue
from them. But none came forth or entered in, though the
great gates stood wide; and then I saw that herbs were growing
between the stones, where no herbs had grown for ages. What
could this be? Was the temple deserted? Nay; how could
the worship of the eternal Gods have ceased, that for thousands
of years had, day by day, been offered in the holy place?
Was, then, my father dead? It well might be. And yet,
why this silence? Where were the priests: where the worshippers?

I could bear the doubt no more, but as the sun sank red I
crept like a hunted jackal through the open gates, and on till
I reached the first great Hall of Pillars. Here I paused and
gazed around me—not a sight, not a sound, in the dim and
holy place! I went on with a beating heart to the second
great hall, the hall of six-and-thirty pillars where I had been
crowned Lord of all the Lands: still not a sight or a sound!
Thence, half fearful of my own footfall, so terribly did it echo
in the silence of the deserted Holies, I passed down the
passage of the names of the Pharaohs towards my father's
chamber. The curtain still swung over the doorway; but
what would there be within?—also emptiness? I lifted it,
and noiselessly passed in, and there in his carven chair at
the table on which his long white beard flowed down, sat my
father, Amenemhat, clad in his priestly robes. At first I
thought that he was dead, he sat so still; but at length he
turned his head, and I saw that his eyes were white and

sightless. He was blind, and his face was thin as the face of a dead man, and woeful with age and grief.

I stood still and felt the blind eyes wandering over me. I could not speak to him—I dared not speak to him; I would go and hide myself afresh.

I had already turned and grasped the curtain, when my father spoke in a deep, slow voice:

'Come hither, thou who wast my son and art a traitor. Come hither, thou Harmachis, on whom Khem builded up her hope. Not in vain, then, have I drawn thee from far away! Not in vain have I held my life in me till I heard thy footfall creeping down these empty Holies, like the footfall of a thief!'

'Oh! my father,' I gasped, astonished. 'Thou art blind: how knowest thou me?'

'How do I know thee?—and askest thou that who hast learned of our lore? Enough, I know thee and I brought thee hither. Would, Harmachis, that I knew thee not! Would that I had been blasted of the Invisible ere I drew thee down from the womb of Nout, to be my curse and shame, and the last woe of Khem!'

'Oh, speak not thus!' I moaned; 'is not my burden already more than I can bear? Am I not myself betrayed and utterly outcast? Be pitiful, my father!'

'Be pitiful!—be pitiful to thee who hast shown so great pity? It was thy pity which gave up noble Sepa to die beneath the hands of the tormentors!'

'Oh, not that—not that!' I cried.

'Ay, traitor, that!—to die in agony, with his last poor breath proclaiming thee, his murderer, honest and innocent! Be pitiful to thee, who gavest all the flower of Khem as the price of a wanton's arms!—thinkest thou that, labouring in the darksome desert mines, those noble ones in thought are pitiful to thee, Harmachis? Be pitiful to thee, by whom this

Holy Temple of Abouthis hath been ravaged, its lands seized, its priests scattered, and I alone, old and withered, left to count out its ruin—to thee, who hast poured the treasures of *Her* into thy leman's lap, who hast forsworn Thyself, thy Country, thy Birthright, and thy Gods! Yea, thus am I pitiful: Accursed be thou, fruit of my loins!—Shame be thy portion, Agony thy end, and Hell receive thee at the last! Where art thou? Yea, I grew blind with weeping when I heard the truth—sure, they strove to hide it from me. Let me find thee that I may spit upon thee, thou Renegade! thou Apostate! thou Outcast!'——and he rose from his seat and staggered like a living Wrath toward me, smiting the air with his wand. And as he came with outstretched arms, awful to see, suddenly his end found him, and with a cry he sank down upon the ground, the red blood streaming from his lips. I ran to him and lifted him; and as he died, he babbled:

'He was my son, a bright-eyed lovely boy, and full of promise as the Spring; and now—and now——oh, would that he were dead!'

Then came a pause and the breath rattled in his throat.

'Harmachis,' he gasped, 'art there?'

'Yea, father.'

'Harmachis, atone!—atone! Vengeance can still be wreaked—forgiveness may still be won. There's gold; I've hidden it—Atoua—she can tell thee—ah, this pain! Farewell!'

And he struggled faintly in my arms and was dead.

Thus, then, did I and my holy father, the Prince Amenemhat, meet together for the last time in the flesh, and for the last time part.

CHAPTER II.

OF THE LAST MISERY OF HARMACHIS; OF THE CALLING DOWN
OF THE HOLY ISIS BY THE WORD OF FEAR; OF THE PRO-
MISE OF ISIS; OF THE COMING OF ATOUA, AND OF THE
WORDS OF ATOUA.

CROUCHED upon the floor gazing at the dead body of my father, who had lived to curse me, the utterly accursed, while the darkness crept and gathered round us, till at length the dead and I were alone in the black silence. Oh, how tell the misery of that hour! Imagination cannot dream it, nor words paint it forth. Once more in my wretchedness I bethought me of death. A knife was at my girdle, with which I might cut the thread of sorrow and set my spirit free. Free? ay, free to fly and face the last vengeance of the Holy Gods! Alas! and alas! I did not dare to die. Better the earth with all its woes than the quick approach of those unimagined terrors that, hovering in dim Amenti, wait the advent of the fallen.

I grovelled on the ground and wept tears of agony for the lost unchanging past—wept till I could weep no more;

x

but no answer came from the silence—no answer but the echoes of my grief. Not a ray of hope ! My soul wandered in a darkness more utter than that which was about me—I was forsaken of the Gods and cast out of men. Terror took hold upon me crouching in that lonely place hard by the majesty of the awful Dead. I rose to fly. How could I fly in this gloom ?—how find my path down the passages and amid the columns ? And where should I fly who had no place of refuge ? Once more I crouched down, and the great fear grew on me till the cold sweat ran from my brow and my soul was faint within me. Then, in my last despair, I prayed aloud to Isis, to whom I had not dared to pray for many days.

'O Isis ! Holy Mother !' I cried; 'put away Thy wrath, and of Thine infinite pity, O Thou all-pitiful, hearken to the voice of the anguish of him who was Thy son and servant, but who by sin hath fallen from the vision of Thy love. O throned Glory, who, being in all things, hast of all things understanding and of all griefs knowledge, cast the weight of Thy mercy against the scale of my evil-doing, and make the balance equal. Look down upon my woe, and measure it ; count up the sum of my repentance, and take Thou note of the flood of sorrow that sweeps my soul away. O Thou Holy, whom it was given to me to look upon face to face, by that dread hour of commune I summon Thee ; I summon Thee by the mystic word. Come, then, in mercy, to save me ; or, in anger, to make an end of that which can no more be borne.'

And, rising from my knees, I stretched out my arms and dared to cry aloud the Word of Fear, to use which unworthily is death.

Swiftly the answer came. For in the silence I heard the sound of the shaken sistra heralding the coming of the Glory. Then, at the far end of the chamber, grew the semblance of the horned moon, gleaming faintly in the darkness, and betwixt

the golden horns rested a small dark cloud, in and out of which the fiery serpent climbed.

My knees waxed loose in the presence of the Glory, and I sank down before it.

Then spake the small, sweet Voice within the cloud:

'Harmachis, who wast my servant and my son, I have heard thy prayer, and the summons that thou hast dared to utter, which on the lips of one with whom I have communed, hath power to draw Me from the Uttermost. No more, Harmachis, may we be one in the bond of Love Divine, for thou hast put Me away of thine own act. Therefore, after this long silence I come, Harmachis, clothed in terrors, and, perchance, ready for vengeance, for not lightly can Isis be drawn from the halls of Her Divinity.'

'Smite, Goddess!' I answered. 'Smite, and give me over to those who wreak Thy vengeance; for I can no longer bear the burden of my woe!'

'And if thou canst not bear thy burden here, upon this upper earth,' came the soft reply, 'how then shalt thou bear the greater burden that shall be laid upon thee there, coming defiled and yet unpurified into my dim realm of Death, that is Life and Change unending? Nay, Harmachis, I smite not, for not all am I wroth that thou hast dared to utter the awful Word which calls Me down to thee. Hearken, Harmachis; I praise not, and I reproach not, for I am the Minister of Reward and Punishment and the Executrix of Decrees; and if I give, I give in silence; and if I smite, in silence I do smite. Therefore, I will add naught to thy burden by the weight of heavy words, though through thee it has come to pass that soon shall Isis, the Mother-Mystery, be but a memory in Egypt. Thou hast sinned, and heavy shall be thy punishment, as I did warn thee, both in the flesh and in my kingdom of Amenti. But I told thee that there is a road of repentance, and surely thy feet are set thereon, and therein must thou walk with a humble heart, eating of the bread of bitterness, till such time as thy doom be measured.'

' Have I, then, no hope, O Holy ? '

' That which is done, Harmachis, is done, nor can its issues be altered. Khem shall no more be free till all its temples are as the desert dust; strange Peoples shall, from age to age, hold her hostage and in bonds; new Religions shall arise and wither within the shadow of her pyramids, for to every World, Race, and Age the countenances of the Gods are changed. This is the tree that shall spring from thy seed of sin, Harmachis, and from the sin of those who tempted thee ! '

' Alas ! I am undone ! ' I cried.

' Yea, thou art undone; and yet shall this be given to thee : thy Destroyer thou shalt destroy—for so, in the purpose of my justice, it is ordained. When the sign comes to thee, arise, go to Cleopatra, and in such manner as I shall put into thy heart do Heaven's vengeance on her ! And now for thyself one word, for thou hast put Me from thee, Harmachis, and no more shall I come face to face with thee till, cycles hence, the last fruit of thy sin hath ceased to be upon this earth ! Yet, through the vastness of the unnumbered years, remember thou this: that Love Divine is Love Eternal, which cannot be extinguished, though it be everlastingly estranged. Repent, my son; repent and do well while there is yet time, that at the dim end of ages thou mayst once more be gathered unto Me. Still, Harmachis, though thou seest Me not; still, when the very name by which thou knowest Me has become a meaningless mystery to those who shall be after thee ; still I, whose hours are eternal—I, who have watched Universes wither, wane, and, beneath the breath of Time, melt into nothingness; again to gather, and, re-born, thread the maze of space—still, I say, I shall companion thee. Wherever thou goest, in whatever form of life thou livest, there I shall be! Art thou wafted to the farthest star, art thou buried in Amenti's lowest deep—in lives, in deaths, in sleeps, in wakings, in remembrances, in oblivions, in all the fevers of the outer Life, in all the changes of the Spirit—still, if thou wilt but atone and forget Me no more, I shall be with thee, waiting thine hour of redemption. For this is the nature of Love Divine, wherewith it loves that which partakes of its divinity and by the holy tie hath once been bound to it. Judge then, Harmachis: was it well to put this from thee to win the dust of earthly woman? And, now, dare not again to utter the Word of Power till these things are done! Harmachis, for this season, fare thee well!'

As the last note of the sweet Voice died away, the fiery snake climbed into the heart of the cloud. Now the cloud rolled from the horns of light, and was gathered into the blackness. The vision of the crescent moon grew dim and vanished. Then, as the Goddess passed, once more came the faint and dreadful music of the shaken sistra, and all was still.

I hid my face in my robe, and even then, though my outstretched hand could touch the chill corpse of that father who had died cursing me, I felt hope come back into my heart, knowing that I was not altogether lost nor utterly rejected of Her whom I had forsaken, but whom I yet loved. And then weariness overpowered me, and I slept.

I woke, the faint lights of dawn were creeping from the opening in the roof. Ghastly they lay upon the shadowy sculptured walls and ghastly upon the dead face and white beard of my father, the gathered to Osiris. I started

up, remembering all things, and wondering in my heart what
I should do, and as I rose I heard a faint footfall creeping
down the passage of the names of the Pharaohs.

'*La ! La ! La !*' mumbled a voice that I knew for the
voice of the old wife, Atoua. 'Why, 'tis dark as the House
of the Dead ! The Holy Ones who built this Temple loved
not the blessed sun, however much they worshipped him.
Now, where's the curtain ? '

Presently it was drawn, and Atoua entered, a stick in one
hand and a basket in the other. Her face was somewhat
more wrinkled, and her scanty locks were somewhat
whiter than aforetime, but for the rest she was as she had
ever been. She stood and peered around with her sharp
black eyes, for as yet she could see nothing because of the
shadows.

'Now where is he ? ' she muttered. 'Osiris—glory to His
name—send that he has not wandered in the night, and he
blind ! Alack ! that I could not return before the dark.
Alack ! and alack ! what times have we fallen on, when the
Holy High Priest and the Governor, by descent, of Abouthis,
is left with one aged crone to minister to his infirmity ! O
Harmachis, my poor boy, thou hast laid trouble at our doors !
Why, what's this ? Surely he sleeps not, there upon the
ground ?—'twill be his death ! Prince ! Holy Father ! Amenemhat ! awake, arise ! ' and she hobbled towards the corpse.
' Why, how is it ! By Him who sleeps, he's dead ! untended
and alone—*dead ! dead !*' and she sent her long wail of grief
ringing up the sculptured walls.

'Hush ! woman, be still ! ' I said, gliding from the
shadows.

' Oh, what art thou ? ' she cried, casting down her basket.
' Wicked man, hast thou murdered this Holy One, the only
Holy One in Egypt ? Surely the curse will fall on thee, for

though the Gods do seem to have forsaken us now in our hour of trial, yet is their arm long, and certainly they will be avenged on him who hath slain their anointed ! '

' Look on me, Atoua,' I cried.

' Look ! ay, I look—thou wicked wanderer who hast dared this cruel deed ! Harmachis is a traitor and lost far away, and Amenemhat his holy father is murdered, and now I'm all alone without kith or kin. I gave them for him. I gave them for Harmachis, the traitor ! Come, slay me also, thou wicked one ! '

I took a step toward her, and she, thinking that I was about to smite her, cried out in fear :

' Nay, good Sir, spare me ! Eighty and six, by the Holy Ones, eighty and six, come next flood of Nile, and yet I would not die, though Osiris is merciful to the old who served him ! Come no nearer—help ! help !

' Thou fool, be silent,' I said ; ' knowest thou me not ? '

' Know thee ? Can I know every wandering boatman to whom Sebek grants to earn a livelihood till Typhon claims his own ? And yet—why, 'tis strange—that changed countenance !—that scar !—that stumbling gait ! It is thou, Harmachis !—'tis thou, O my boy ! Art come back to glad mine old eyes ? I hoped thee dead ! Let me kiss thee ?— nay, I forget. Harmachis is a traitor, ay, and a murderer ! Here lies the holy Amenemhat, murdered by the traitor, Harmachis ! Get thee gone ! I'll have none of traitors and of parricides ! Get thee to thy wanton !—it is not thou whom I did nurse.'

' Peace ! woman ; peace ! I slew not my father—he died, alas !—he died even in my arms ! '

' Ay, surely, and cursing thee, Harmachis ! Thou hast given death to him who gave thee life ! *La ! la !* I am old, and I've seen many a trouble ; but this is the heaviest of them all ! I never liked the looks of mummies; but I would I were one this hour ! Get thee gone, I pray thee ! '

' Old nurse, reproach me not ! Have I not enough to bear?'

' Ah ! yes, yes !—I did forget ! Well; and what is thy sin ? A woman was thy bane, as women have been to those before thee, and shall be to those after thee. And what a woman ! *La ! la !* I saw her, a beauty such as never was— an arrow pointed by the evil Gods for destruction ! And thou, a young man bred as a priest—an ill training—a very ill training ! 'Twas no fair match. Who can wonder that she mastered thee ? Come, Harmachis; let me kiss thee ! It is not for a woman to be hard upon a man because he loved our sex too much. Why, that is but nature ; and Nature knows her business, else she had made us otherwise. But here is an evil case. Knowest thou that this Macedonian Queen of thine hath seized the temple lands and revenues, and driven away the priests—all, save the holy Amenemhat, who lies here, and whom she left, I know not why ; ay, and caused the worship of the Gods to cease within these walls. Well, he's gone !— he's gone ! and indeed he is better with Osiris, for his life was a sore burden to him. And hark thou, Harmachis: he hath not left thee empty-handed ; for, so soon as the plot failed, he gathered all his wealth, and it is large, and hid it—where, I can show thee—and it is thine by right of descent.'

' Talk not to me of wealth, Atoua. Where shall I go and how shall I hide my shame ? '

' Ah ! true, true ; here mayst thou not abide, for if they found thee, surely they would put thee to the dreadful death —ay, to the death by the waxen cloth. Nay, I will hide thee, and, when the funeral rites of the holy Amenemhat have been performed, we will fly hence, and cover us from the eyes of men till these sorrows are forgotten. *La ! la !* it is a sad world, and full of trouble as the Nile mud is of beetles. Come, Harmachis, come.'

CHAPTER III.

OF THE LIFE OF HIM WHO WAS NAMED THE LEARNED OLYMPUS,
IN THE TOMB OF THE HARPERS THAT IS BY TÁPÉ ; OF HIS
COUNSEL TO CLEOPATRA ; OF THE MESSAGE OF CHARMION ;
AND OF THE PASSING OF OLYMPUS DOWN TO ALEXANDRIA.

THESE things then came to pass. For eighty days I was hidden of the old wife, Atoua, while the body of the Prince, my father, was made ready for burial by those skilled in the arts of embalming. And when at last all things were done in order, I crept from my hiding-place and made offerings to the spirit of my father, and placing lotus-flowers on his breast went thence sorrowing And on the following day, from where I lay hid, I saw the Priests of the Temple of Osiris and of the holy Shrine of Isis come forth, and in slow procession bear his painted coffin to the sacred lake and lay it beneath the funeral tent in the consecrated boat. I saw them celebrate the symbol of the trial of the dead, and name him above all men just, and then bear him thence to lay him by his wife, my mother, in the deep tomb that he had hewn in the rock near to the resting-place of the

most Holy Osiris, where, notwithstanding my sins, I, too,
hope to sleep ere long. And when all these things were done
and the deep tomb sealed, the wealth of my father having
been removed from the hidden treasury and placed in safety,
I fled, disguised, with the old wife, Atoua, up the Nile till we
came to Tápé,[1] and here in this great city I lay a while, till a
place could be found where I should hide myself.

And such a place I found. For to the north of the great
city are brown and rugged hills, and desert valleys blasted of
the sun, and in this place of desolation the Divine Pharaohs,
my forefathers, hollowed out their tombs in the solid rock, the
most part of which are lost to this day, so cunningly have
they been hidden. But some are open, for the accursed
Persians and other thieves broke into them in search of treasure. And one night—for by night only did I leave my hiding-
place—just as the dawn was breaking on the mountain tops,
I wandered alone in this sad valley of death, like to which
there is no other, and presently came to the mouth of a tomb
hidden amid great rocks, which afterwards I knew for the place
of the burying of the Divine Rameses, the third of that name,
now long gathered to Osiris. And by the faint light of the
dawn creeping through the entrance I saw that it was spacious
and that within were chambers.

On the following night, therefore, I returned, bearing
lights, with Atoua, my nurse, who ever ministered faithfully
to me as when I was little and without discretion. And we
searched the mighty tomb and came to the great Hall of the
Sarcophagus of granite, in which the Divine Rameses sleeps,
and saw the mystic paintings on the walls: the symbol of
the Snake unending, the symbol of Ra resting upon the
Scarabæus, the symbol of Ra resting upon Nout, the symbol
of the Headless men, and many others, whereof, being

---

[1] Thebes.—ED.

initiated, well I read the mysteries. And opening from the long descending passage I found chambers in which were paintings beautiful to behold, and of all manner of things. For beneath each chamber is entombed the master of the craft of which the paintings tell, he who was the chief of the servants of that craft in the house of this Divine Rameses. And on the walls of the last chamber—on the left-hand side, looking toward the Hall of the Sarcophagus—are paintings exceeding beautiful, and two blind harpers playing upon their bent harps before the God Mou ; and beneath the flooring these harpers, who harp no more, are soft at sleep. Here, then, in this gloomy place, even in the tomb of the Harpers and the company of the dead, I took up my abode ; and here for eight long years I worked out my penance and made atonement for my sin. But Atoua, because she loved to be near the light, abode in the chamber of Boats—that is, the first chamber on the right-hand side of the gallery looking toward the Hall of the Sarcophagus.

And this was the manner of my life. On every second day the old wife, Atoua, went forth and brought water from the city and such food as is necessary to keep the life from failing, and also tapers made from fat. And one hour at the time of sunrise and one hour at the time of sunset did I go forth also to wander in the valley for my health's sake and to save my sight from failing in the great darkness of the tomb. But the other hours of the day and night, except when I climbed the mountain to watch the course of the stars, I spent in prayer and meditation and sleep, till the cloud of sin lifted from my heart and once more I drew near to the Gods, though with Isis, my heavenly Mother, I might speak no more. And I grew exceeding wise also, pondering on all those mysteries to which I held the key. For abstinence and prayer and sorrowful solitude wore away the grossness of my flesh, and with the eyes of the Spirit I learned to look deep into the heart of things till the joy of Wisdom fell like dew upon my soul.

Soon the rumour was wafted about the city that a certain holy man named Olympus abode in solitude in the tombs of the awful Valley of the Dead ; and hither came people bearing sick that I might cure them. And I gave my mind to the study of simples, in which Atoua instructed me ; and by lore and the weight of thought I gained great skill in medicine, and healed many sick. And thus ever, as time went on, my fame was noised abroad ; for it was said that I was also a magician and that in the tombs I had commune with the Spirits of the Dead. And this, indeed, I did—though jt is not lawful for me to speak of these matters. Thus, then, it came to pass that no more need Atoua go forth to seek food and water, for the people brought it—more than was needful, for I would receive no fee. Now at first, tearing lest some in the hermit Olympus might know the lost Harmachis, I would only meet those who came in the darkness of the tomb. But afterwards, when I learned how it was held through all the land that Harmachis was certainly no more, I came forth and sat in the mouth of the tomb, and ministered to the sick, and at times calculated nativities for the great. And thus my fame grew continually, till at length folk journeyed even from Memphis and Alexandria to visit me ; and from them I learned how Antony had left Cleopatra for a while, and, Fulvia being dead, had married Octavia, the sister of Cæsar. Many other things I learned also.

And in the second year I did this : I despatched the old wife, Atoua, disguised as a seller of simples, to Alexandria, bidding her seek out Charmion, and, if yet she found her faithful, reveal to her the secret of my way of life. So she went, and in the fifth month from her sailing returned, bearing Charmion's greetings and a token. And she told me that she

had found means to see Charmion, and, in talk, had let fall
the name of Harmachis, speaking of me as one dead ; at which
Charmion, unable to control her grief, wept aloud. Then,
reading her heart—for the old wife was very clever, and held
the key of knowledge—she told her that Harmachis yet lived,
and sent her greetings. Thereon Charmion wept yet more
with joy, and kissed the old wife, and made her gifts, bidding
her tell me that she ever kept her vow, and waited for my
coming and the hour of vengeance. So, having learned many
secrets, Atoua returned again to Tápé.

And in the following year messengers came to me from
Cleopatra, bearing a sealed roll and great gifts. I opened the
roll, and read this in it :

‘ Cleopatra to Olympus, the learned Egyptian who dwells
in the Valley of Death by Tápé—

‘ The fame of thy renown, O learned Olympus, hath reached
our ears. Tell thou, then, this to us, and if thou tellest aright
greater honour and wealth shalt thou have than any in Egypt :
How shall we win back the love of noble Antony, who is be-
witched of cunning Octavia and tarries long from us ? ’

Now, in this I saw the hand of Charmion, who had made
my renown known to Cleopatra.

All that night I took counsel with my wisdom, and on the
morrow wrote my answer as it was put into my heart to the
destruction of Cleopatra and of Antony. And thus I wrote :

‘ Olympus the Egyptian to Cleopatra the Queen—

‘ Go forth into Syria with one who shall be sent to lead
thee ; thus shalt thou win Antony to thy arms again, and
with him gifts more great than thou canst dream.’

And with this letter I dismissed the messengers, bidding
them share the presents sent by Cleopatra among their
company.

So they went wondering.

But Cleopatra, seizing on the advice to which her passion prompted her, departed straightway with Fonteius Capito into Syria, and there the thing came about as I had foretold, for Antony was subdued of her and gave her the greater part of Cilicia, the ocean shore of Arabia Nabathæa, the balm-bearing provinces of Judæa, the province of Phœnicia, the province of Cœle-Syria, the rich isle of Cyprus, and all the library of Pergamus. And to the twin children that, with the son Ptolemy, Cleopatra had borne to Antony, he impiously gave the names of ' Kings, the Children of Kings '—of Alexander Helios, as the Greeks name the sun, and of Cleopatra Selene, the moon, the long-winged.

These things then came to pass.

Now on her return to Alexandria Cleopatra sent me great gifts, of which I would have none, and prayed me, the learned Olympus, to come to her at Alexandria; but it was not yet time, and I would not. But thereafter she and Antony sent many times to me for counsel, and I ever counselled them to their ruin, nor did my prophecies fail.

Thus the long years rolled away, and I, the hermit Olympus, the dweller in a tomb, the eater of bread and the drinker of water, by strength of the wisdom that was given me of the avenging Power, became once more great in Khem. For I grew ever wiser as I trampled the desires of the flesh beneath my feet and turned my eyes to heaven.

At length eight full years were accomplished. The war with the Parthians had come and gone, and Artavasdes, King of Armenia, had been led in triumph through the streets of Alexandria. Cleopatra had visited Samos and Athens; and, by her counselling, the noble Octavia had been driven, like some discarded concubine. from the house of Antony at Rome. And now, at the last, the measure of the folly of Antony was full even to the brim. For this Master of the World had no longer the good gift of reason; he was lost in Cleopatra as I had been lost. Therefore, in the event, Octavianus declared war against him.

And as I slept upon a certain day in the chamber of the Harpers, in the tomb of Pharaoh that is by Tápé, there came to me a vision of my father, the aged Amenemhat, and he stood over me, leaning on his staff, and spoke, saying:

'Look forth, my son.'

Then I looked forth, and with the eyes of my Spirit saw the sea, and two great fleets grappling in war hard by a rocky coast. And the emblems of one were those of Octavian, and of the other those of Cleopatra and Antony. The ships of Antony and Cleopatra bore down upon the ships of Cæsar, and drove them on, for victory inclined to Antony.

I looked again. There sat Cleopatra in a gold-decked galley watching the fight with eager eyes. Then I cast my Spirit on her so that she seemed to hear the voice of dead Harmachis crying in her ear.

'*Fly, Cleopatra,*' it seemed to say, '*fly or perish!*

She looked up wildly, and again she heard my Spirit's cry. Now a mighty fear took hold of her. She called aloud to the sailors to hoist the sails and make signal to her fleet to put about. This they did wondering but little loath, and fled in haste from the battle.

Then a great roar went up from friend and foe.

'Cleopatra is fled! Cleopatra is fled!' And I saw wreck and red ruin fall upon the fleet of Antony and awoke from my trance.

The days passed, and again a vision of my father came to me and spoke, saying:

'Arise, my son!—the hour of vengeance is at hand! Thy plots have not failed; thy prayers have been heard. By the bidding of the Gods, as she sat in her galley at the fight of Actium, the heart of Cleopatra was filled with fears, so that, deeming she heard thy voice bidding her fly or perish, she fled with all her fleet. Now the strength of Antony is broken on the sea. Go forth, and as it shall be put into thy mind, so do thou.'

In the morning I awoke, wondering, and went to the mouth of the tomb, and there, coming up the valley, I saw the messengers of Cleopatra, and with them a Roman guard.

'What will ye with me now?' I asked, sternly.

'This is the message of the Queen and of great Antony,' answered the Captain, bowing low before me, for I was much feared of all men. 'The Queen commands thy presence at Alexandria. Many times has she sent, and thou wouldst not come; now she bids thee to come, and that swiftly, for she has need of thy counsel.'

'And if I say Nay, soldier, what then?'

'These are my orders, most holy Olympus; that I bring thee by force.'

I laughed aloud. 'By force, thou fool! Use not such talk to me, lest I smite thee where thou art. Know, then, that I can kill as well as cure!'

'Pardon, I beseech thee!' he answered, shrinking. 'I say but those things that I am bid.'

'Well, I know it, Captain. Fear not; I come.'

So on that very day I departed, together with the aged Atoua. Ay, I went as secretly as I had come; and the tomb of the Divine Rameses knew me no more. And with me I took all the treasure of my father, Amenemhat, for I was not minded to go to Alexandria empty-handed and as a suppliant, but rather as a man of much wealth and condition. Now, as I went, I learned that Antony, following Cleopatra, had, indeed, fled from Actium, and knew that the end drew nigh.

For this and many other things I had foreseen in the darkness of the tomb of Tápé, and planned to bring about.

Thus, then, I came to Alexandria, and entered into a house which had been made ready for me at the palace gates.

And that very night Charmion came to me—Charmion whom I had not seen for nine long years.

CHAPTER IV.

OF THE MEETING OF CHARMION WITH THE LEARNED OLYMPUS; OF HER SPEECH WITH HIM; OF THE COMING OF OLYMPUS INTO THE PRESENCE OF CLEOPATRA; AND OF THE COMMANDS OF CLEOPATRA.

LAD in my plain dark robe, I sat in the guest-chamber of the house that had been made ready for me. I sat in a carven lion-footed chair, and looked upon the swinging lamps of scented oil, the pictured tapestries, the rich Syrian rugs—and, amidst all this luxury, bethought me of that tomb of the Harpers which is at Tápé, and of the nine long years of dark loneliness and preparation. I sat; and crouched upon a rug, near to the door, lay the aged Atoua. Her hair was white as snow, and shrivelled with age was the wrinkled countenance of the woman who, when all deserted me, had yet clung to me, in her great love forgetting my great sins. Nine years! nine long years! and now, once again, I set my foot in Alexandria! Once again in the appointed circle of things I came forth from the solitude of preparation to be a fate to Cleopatra; and this second time I came not forth to fail.

And yet how changed the circumstance! I was out of the story: my part now was but the part of the sword in the hands of Justice; I might no more hope to make Egypt free and great and sit upon my lawful throne. Khem was lost, and lost was I, Harmachis. In the rush and turmoil of events, the great plot of which I had been the pivot was covered up and forgotten; scarce a memory of it remained. The curtain of dark night was closing in upon the history of my ancient Race; its very Gods were tottering to their fall; I could already, in the spirit, hear the shriek of the Roman eagles as they flapped their wings above the furthest banks of Sihor.

Presently I roused myself and bade Atoua go seek a mirror and bring it to me, that I might look therein.

And I saw this: a face shrunken and pallid, on which no smile came; great eyes grown wan with gazing into darkness looking out beneath the shaven head, emptily, as the hollow eye-pits of a skull; a wizened halting form wasted by abstinence, sorrow, and prayer; a long wild beard of iron grey; thin blue-veined hands that ever trembled like a leaf; bowed shoulders and lessened limbs. Time and grief had done their work indeed; scarce could I think myself the same as when, the royal Harmachis—in all the splendour of my strength and youthful beauty—I first had looked upon the woman's loveliness that did destroy me. And yet within me burned the same fire as of yore; yet I was not changed, for time and grief have no power to alter the immortal spirit of man. Seasons may come and go; Hope, like a bird, may fly away; Passion may break its wings against the iron bars of Fate; Illusions may crumble as the cloudy towers of sunset flame; Faith, as running water, may slip from beneath our feet; Solitude may stretch itself around us like the measureless desert sand; Old Age may creep as the gathering night over our bowed heads grown hoary in their shame—yea, bound to

Fortune's wheel, we may taste of every turn of chance—now
rule as Kings, now serve as Slaves ; now love, now hate ; now
prosper, and now perish.   But still, through all, we are the
same ; for this is the marvel of Identity.

And as I sat and thought these things in bitterness of heart,
there came a knocking at the door.

'Open, Atoua ! ' I said.

She rose and did my bidding ; and a woman entered, clad
in Grecian robes.   It was Charmion, still beautiful as of old,
but sad faced now and very sweet to see, with a patient fire
slumbering in her downcast eyes.

She entered unattended ; and, speaking no word, the old
wife pointed to where I sat, and went.

'Old man,' she said, addressing me, ' lead me to the learned
Olympus.   I come upon the Queen's business.'

I rose, and, lifting my head, looked upon her.

She gazed, and gave a little cry.

'Surely,' she whispered, glancing round, ' surely thou art
not that ——' And she paused.

'That Harmachis whom once thy foolish heart did love,
O Charmion ?   Yes, I am he and what thou seest, most fair
lady.   Yet is Harmachis dead whom thou didst love ; but
Olympus, the skilled Egyptian, waits upon thy words ! '

'Cease ! ' she said, ' and of the past but one word, and
then—why, let it lie.   Not well, with all thy wisdom, canst thou
know a true woman's heart, if thou dost believe, Harmachis,
that it can change with the changes of the outer form, for then
assuredly could no love follow its beloved to that last place of
change—the Grave.   Know thou, learned Physician, I am of
that sort who, loving once, love always, and being not beloved
again, go virgin to the death.'

She ceased and, having naught to say, I bowed my head in

answer. Yet though I said nothing and though this woman's passionate folly had been the cause of all our ruin, to speak truth, in secret I was thankful to her who, wooed of all and living in this shameless Court, had still through the long years poured out her unreturned love upon an outcast, and who, when that poor broken slave of Fortune came back in such unlovely guise, held him yet dear at heart. For what man is there who does not prize that gift most rare and beautiful, that one perfect thing which no gold can buy—a woman's unfeigned love?

'I thank thee that thou dost not answer,' she said; 'for the bitter words which thou didst pour upon me in those days that long are dead, and far away in Tarsus, have not lost their poisonous sting, and in my heart is no more place for the arrows of thy scorn, new venomed through thy solitary years. So let it be. Behold! I put it from me, that wild passion of my soul,' and she looked up and stretched out her hands as though to press some unseen presence back, 'I put it from me—though forget it I may not! There, 'tis done, Harmachis; no more shall my love trouble thee. Enough for me that once more my eyes behold thee, before sleep seals thee from their sight. Dost remember how, when I would have died by thy dear hand, thou wouldst not slay, but didst bid me live to pluck the bitter fruit of crime, and be accursed by visions of the evil I had wrought and memories of thee whom I have ruined?'

'Ay, Charmion, I remember well.'

'Surely the cup of punishment has been filled. Oh! couldst thou see into the record of my heart, and read in it the suffering that I have borne—borne with a smiling face—thy justice would be satisfied indeed!'

'And yet, if report be true, Charmion, thou art the first of all the Court, and therein the most powerful and beloved. Does not Octavianus give it out that he makes war, not on

Antony, nor even on his mistress, Cleopatra, but on Charmion and Iras ? '

' Yes, Harmachis, and think what it has been to me thus, because of my oath to thee, to be forced to eat the bread and do the tasks of one whom so bitterly I hate !—one who robbed me of thee, and who, through the workings of my jealousy, brought me to be that which I am, brought thee to shame, and all Egypt to its ruin ! Can jewels and riches and the flattery of princes and nobles bring happiness to such a one as I, who am more wretched than the meanest scullion wench ? Oh, I have often wept till I was blind ; and then, when the hour came, I must arise and tire me, and, with a smile, go do the bidding of the Queen and that heavy Antony. May the Gods grant me to see them dead—ay, the twain of them !—then myself I shall be content to die ! Thy lot has been hard, Harmachis ; but at least thou hast been free, and many is the time that I have envied thee the quiet of thy haunted cave.'

' I do perceive, O Charmion, that thou art mindful of thy oaths ; and it is well, for the hour of vengeance is at hand.'

' I am mindful, and in all things I have worked for thee in secret—for thee, and for the utter ruin of Cleopatra and the Roman. I have fanned his passion and her jealousy, I have egged her on to wickedness and him to folly, and of all have I caused report to be brought to Cæsar. Listen ! thus stands the matter. Thou knowest how went the fight at Actium. Thither went Cleopatra with her fleet, sorely against the will of Antony. But, as thou sentest me word, I entreated him for the Queen, vowing to him, with tears, that, did he leave her, she would die of grief ; and he, poor slave, believed me. And so she went, and in the thick of the fight, for what cause I know not, though perchance thou knowest, Harmachis, she made signal to her squadron, and, putting about fled from the battle, sailing for Peloponnesus. And now, mark the end! When Antony saw that she was gone, he, in his madness, took a galley, and deserting all, followed hard after her, leaving his fleet to be shattered and sunk, and his great army in Greece, of twenty legions and twelve thousand horse, without a leader. And all this no man would believe, that Antony, the smitten of the Gods, had fallen so deep in shame. Therefore for a while the army tarried, and but now to-night comes news brought by Canidius, the General, that, worn with doubt and being at length sure that Antony had deserted them, the whole of his great force has yielded to Cæsar.'

'And where, then, is Antony?'

'He has built him a habitation on a little isle in the Great Harbour and named it Timonium; because, forsooth, like Timon, he cries out at the ingratitude of mankind that has forsaken him. And there he lies smitten by a fever of the mind, and thither thou must go at dawn, so wills the Queen, to cure him of his ills and draw him to her arms; for he will not see her, nor knows he yet the full measure of his woe. But first my bidding is to lead thee instantly to Cleopatra, who would ask thy counsel.'

'I come,' I answered, rising. 'Lead thou on.'

And so we passed the palace gates and along the Alabaster Hall, and presently once again I stood before the door of Cleopatra's chamber, and once again Charmion left me to warn her of my coming.

Presently she came back and beckoned to me. 'Make strong thy heart,' she whispered, 'and see that thou dost not betray thyself, for still are the eyes of Cleopatra keen. Enter!'

'Keen, indeed, must they be to find Harmachis in the learned Olympus! Had I not willed it, thyself thou hadst not known me, Charmion,' I made answer.

Then I entered that remembered place and listened once more to the plash of the fountain, the song of the nightingale, and the murmur of the summer sea. With bowed head and halting gait I came, till at length I stood before the couch of Cleopatra—that same golden couch on which she had sat the night she overcame me. Then I gathered my strength, and looked up. There before me was Cleopatra, glorious as of old, but, oh! how changed since that night when I saw Antony clasp her in his arms at Tarsus! Her beauty still clothed her like a garment; the eyes were yet deep and unfathomable as the blue sea, the face still splendid in its great loveliness. And yet all was changed. Time, that could not touch her charms, had stamped upon her presence such a look of weary grief as may not be written. Passion, beating ever in that fierce heart of hers, had written his record on her brow, and in her eyes shone the sad lights of sorrow.

I bowed low before this most royal woman, who once had been my love and my destruction, and yet knew me not.

She looked up wearily, and spoke in her slow, well remembered voice:

'So thou art come at length, Physician. How callest thou thyself?—Olympus? 'Tis a name of promise, for surely now that the Gods of Egypt have deserted us, we do need aid from Olympus. Well, thou hast a learned air, for learning goes not with beauty. Strange, too, there is that about thee which recalls what I know not. Say, Olympus, have we met before?'

'Never, O Queen, have my eyes fallen on thee in the body,' I answered in a feigned voice. 'Never till this hour, when I come forth from my solitude to do thy bidding and cure thee of thy ills.'

'Strange! and even in the voice——Pshaw! 'tis some memory that I cannot catch. In the body, thou sayest? then, perchance, I knew thee in a dream?'

'Ay, O Queen ; we have met in dreams.'

'Thou art a strange man, who talkest thus, but, if what I hear be true, one well learned; and, indeed, I mind me of thy counsel when thou didst bid me join my Lord Antony in Syria, and how things befell according to thy word. Skilled must thou be in the casting of nativities and in the law of auguries, of which these Alexandrian fools have little knowledge. Once I knew such another man, one Harmachis,' and she sighed : ' but he is long dead—as I would I were also !—and at times I sorrow for him.'

She paused, while I sank my head upon my breast and stood silent.

'Interpret me this, Olympus. In the battle at that accursed Actium, just as the fight raged thickest and Victory began to smile upon us, a great terror seized my heart, and thick darkness seemed to fall before my eyes, while in my ears a voice, ay, the voice of that long dead Harmachis, cried " *Fly ! fly, or perish !* " and I fled. But from my heart the terror leapt to the heart of Antony, and he followed after me, and thus was the battle lost. Say, then, what God brought this evil thing about ? '

' Nay, O Queen,' I answered, ' it was no God—for wherein hast thou angered the Gods of Egypt ? Hast thou robbed the temples of their Faith ? Hast thou betrayed the trust of Egypt ? Having done none of these things, how, then, can the Gods of Egypt be wroth with thee ? Fear not, it was nothing but some natural vapour of the mind that overcame thy gentle soul, made sick with the sight and sound of slaughter ; and as for the noble Antony, where thou didst go needs must that he should follow.'

And as I spoke, Cleopatra turned white and trembled, glancing at me the while to find my meaning. But I well knew that the thing was of the avenging Gods, working through me, their instrument.

'Learned Olympus,' she said, not answering my words; 'my Lord Antony is sick and crazed with grief. Like some poor hunted slave he hides himself in yonder sea-girt Tower and shuns mankind—yes, he shuns even me, who, for his sake, endure so many woes. Now, this is my bidding to thee. To-morrow, at the coming of the light, do thou, led by Charmion, my waiting-lady, take boat and row thee to the Tower and there crave entry, saying that ye bring tidings from the army. Then he will cause you to be let in, and thou, Charmion, must break this heavy news that Canidius bears; for Canidius him-self I dare not send. And when his grief is past, do thou, Olympus, soothe his fevered frame with thy draughts of value, and his soul with honeyed words, and draw him back to me, and all will yet be well. Do thou this, and thou shalt have gifts more than thou canst count, for I am yet a Queen and yet can pay back those who serve my will.'

'Fear not, O Queen,' I answered, 'this thing shall be done, and I ask no reward, who have come hither to do thy bidding to the end.'

So I bowed and went and, summoning Atoua, made ready a certain potion.

CHAPTER V.

OF THE DRAWING FORTH OF ANTONY FROM THE TIMONIUM BACK TO CLEOPATRA; OF THE FEAST MADE BY CLEOPATRA; AND OF THE MANNER OF THE DEATH OF EUDOSIUS THE STEWARD.

it was yet dawn Charmion came again, and we walked to the private harbour of the palace. There, taking boat, we rowed to the island mount on which stands the Timonium, a vaulted tower, strong, small, and round. And, having landed, we twain came to the door and knocked, till at length a grating was thrown open in the door, and an aged eunuch, looking forth, roughly asked our business.

' Our business is with the Lord Antony,' said Charmion.

' Then it is no business, for Antony, my master, sees neither man nor woman.'

' Yet will he see us, for we bring tidings. Go tell him that the Lady Charmion brings tidings from the army.'

The man went, and presently returned.

' The Lord Antony would know if the tidings be good or ill, for, if ill, then will he none of it, for with evil tidings he has been overfed of late.'

'Why—why, it is both good and ill. Open, slave, I will make answer to thy master!' and she slipped a purse of gold through the bars.

'Well, well,' he grumbled, as he took the purse, 'the times are hard, and likely to be harder; for when the lion's down who will feed the jackal? Give thy news thyself, and if it do but draw the noble Antony out of this hall of Groans, I care not what it be. Now the palace door is open, and there's the road to the banqueting-chamber.'

We passed on, to find ourselves in a narrow passage, and, leaving the eunuch to bar the door, advanced till we came to a curtain. Through this entrance we went, and found ourselves in a vaulted chamber, ill-lighted from the roof. On the further side of this rude chamber was a bed of rugs, and on them crouched the figure of a man, his face hidden in the folds of his toga.

'Most noble Antony,' said Charmion drawing near, 'unwrap thy face and hearken to me, for I bring thee tidings.'

Then he lifted up his head. His face was marred by sorrow; his tangled hair, grizzled with years, hung about his hollow eyes, and white on his chin was the stubble of an unshaven beard. His robe was squalid, and his aspect more wretched than that of the poorest beggar at the temple gates. To this, then, had the love of Cleopatra brought the glorious and renowned Antony, aforetime Master of half the World!

'What will ye with me, Lady,' he asked, 'who would perish here alone? And who is this man who comes to gaze on fallen and forsaken Antony?'

'This is Olympus, noble Antony, that wise physician, the skilled in auguries, of whom thou hast heard much, and whom Cleopatra, ever mindful of thy welfare, though but little thou dost think of hers, has sent to minister to thee.'

'And, can thy physician minister to a grief such as my

grief? Can his drugs give me back my galleys, my honour, and my peace? Nay! Away with thy physician! What are thy tidings?—quick!—out with it! Hath Canidius, perchance, conquered Cæsar? Tell me but that, and thou shalt have a province for thy guerdon—ay! and if Octavianus be dead, twenty thousand sestertia to fill its treasury. Speak—nay—speak not! I fear the opening of thy lips as never I feared an earthly thing. Surely the wheel of fortune has gone round and Canidius has conquered? Is it not so? Nay—out with it! I can no more!'

'O noble Antony,' she said, 'steel thy heart to hear that which I needs must tell thee! Canidius is in Alexandria. He has fled fast and far, and this is his report. For seven whole days did the legions wait the coming of Antony, to lead them to victory, as aforetime, putting aside the offers of the envoys of Cæsar. But Antony came not. And then it was rumoured that Antony had fled to Tænarus, drawn thither by Cleopatra. The man who first brought that tale to the camp the legionaries cried shame on—ay, and beat him to the death! But ever it grew, until at length there was no more room to doubt; and then, O Antony, thy officers slipped one by one away to Cæsar, and where the officers go there the men follow. Nor is this all the story; for thy allies—Bocchus of Africa, Tarcondimotus of Cilicia, Mithridates of Commagene, Adallas of Thrace, Philadelphus of Paphlagonia, Archelaus of Cappadocia, Herod of Judæa, Amyntas of Galatia, Polemon of Pontus, and Malchus of Arabia—all, all have fled or bid their generals fly back to whence they came; and already their ambassadors crave cold Cæsar's clemency.'

'Hast done thy croaking, thou raven in a peacock's dress, or is there more to come?' asked the smitten man, lifting his white and trembling face from the shelter of his hands. 'Tell me more; say that Egypt's dead in all her beauty; say that

Octavianus lowers at the Canopic gate; and that, headed by dead Cicero, all the ghosts of Hell do audibly shriek out the fall of Antony! Yea, gather up every woe that can o'erwhelm those who once were great, and loose them on the hoary head of him whom—in thy gentleness—thou art still pleased to name "the noble Antony"!'

'Nay, my Lord, I have done.'

'Ay, and so have I done—done, quite done! It is altogether finished, and thus I seal the end,' and snatching a sword from the couch, he would, indeed, have slain himself had I not sprung forward and grasped his hand. For it was not my purpose that he should die as yet; since had he died at that hour Cleopatra had made her peace with Cæsar, who rather wished the death of Antony than the ruin of Egypt.

'Art mad, Antony? Art, indeed, a coward?' cried Charmion, 'that thou wouldst thus escape thy woes, and leave thy partner to face the sorrow out alone?'

'Why not, woman? Why not? She would not be long alone. There's Cæsar to keep her company. Octavianus loves a fair woman in his cold way, and still is Cleopatra fair. Come now, thou Olympus! thou hast held my hand from dealing death upon myself, advise me of thy wisdom. Shall I, then, submit myself to Cæsar, and, I, Triumvir, twice Consul, and aforetime absolute Monarch of all the East, endure to follow in his triumph along those Roman ways where I myself have passed in triumph?'

'Nay, Sire,' I answered. 'If thou dost yield, then art thou doomed. All last night I questioned of the Fates concerning thee, and I saw this: when thy star draws near to Cæsar's it pales and is swallowed up; but when it passes from his radiance, then bright and big it shines, equal in glory to his own. All is not lost, and while some part remains, everything may be regained. Egypt can yet be held, armies can still be raised. Cæsar has withdrawn himself; he is not yet at the gates of Alexandria, and perchance may be appeased. Thy mind in its fever has fired thy body; thou art sick and canst not judge aright. See, here, I have a potion that shall make thee whole, for I am well skilled in the art of medicine,' and I held out the phial.

'A potion, thou sayest man!' he cried. 'More like it is a poison, and thou a murderer, sent by false Egypt, who would fain be rid of me now that I may no more be of service to her. The head of Antony is the peace offering she would send to Cæsar—she for whom I have lost all! Give me thy draught. By Bacchus! I will drink it, though it be the very elixir of Death!'

'Nay, noble Antony; it is no poison, and I am no murderer. See, I will taste it, if thou wilt,' and I held forth the subtle drink that has power to fire the veins of men.

'Give it me, Physician. Desperate men are brave men. There!—— Why, what is this? Yours is a magic draught! My sorrows seem to roll away like thunder-clouds before the southern gale, and the spring of Hope blooms fresh upon the desert of my heart. Once more I am Antony, and once again I see my legions' spears asparkle in the sun, and hear the thunderous shout of welcome as Antony—beloved Antony— rides in pomp of war along his deep-formed lines! There's hope! there's hope! I may yet see the cold brows of Cæsar— that Cæsar who never errs except from policy—robbed of their victor bays and crowned with shameful dust!'

'Ay,' cried Charmion, 'there still is hope, if thou wilt but play the man! O my Lord! come back with us; come back to the loving arms of Cleopatra! All night she lies upon her golden bed, and fills the hollow darkness with her groans for "Antony!" who, enamoured now of Grief, forgets his duty and his love!'

'I come! I come! Shame upon me, that I dared to doubt
her! Slave, bring water, and a purple robe: not thus can I
be seen of Cleopatra. Even now I come.'

In this fashion, then, did we draw Antony back to Cleopatra, that the ruin of the twain might be made sure.

We led him up the Alabaster Hall and into Cleopatra's
chamber, where she lay, her cloudy hair about her face and
breast, and tears flowing from her deep eyes.
'O Egypt!' he cried, 'behold me at thy feet!'
She sprang from the couch. 'And art thou here, my love?'
she murmured; 'then once again are all things well. Come
near, and in these arms forget thy sorrows and turn my grief
to joy. Oh, Antony, while love is left to us, still have we all!'
And she fell upon his breast and kissed him wildly.

That same day, Charmion came to me and bade me prepare a poison of the most deadly power. And this at first I
would not do, fearing that Cleopatra would therewith make an
end of Antony before the time. But Charmion showed me
that this was not so, and told me also for what purpose
was the poison. Therefore I summoned Atoua, the skilled in
simples, and all that afternoon we laboured at the deadly
work. And when it was done, Charmion came once more,
bearing with her a chaplet of fresh roses, that she bade me
steep in the poison.
This then I did.
That night at the great feast of Cleopatra, I sat near
Antony, who was at her side, and wore the poisoned wreath.
Now as the feast went on, the wine flowed fast, till Antony
and the Queen grew merry. And she told him of her plans,
and of how even now her galleys were being drawn by the

canal that leads from Bubastis on the Pelusiac branch of the Nile, to Clysma at the head of the Bay of Heroopolis. For it was her design, should Cæsar prove stubborn, to fly with Antony and her treasure down the Arabian Gulf, where Cæsar had no fleet, and seek some new home in India, whither her foes might not follow. But, indeed, this plan came to nothing, for the Arabs of Petra burnt the galleys, incited thereto by a message sent by the Jews of Alexandria, who hated Cleopatra and were hated of her. For I caused the Jews to be warned of what was being done.

Now, when she had made an end of telling him, the Queen called on him to drink a cup with her, to the success of this new scheme, bidding him, as she did so, steep his wreath of roses in the wine, and make the draught more sweet. This, then, he did, and, it being done, she pledged him. But when he was about to pledge her back, she caught his hand, crying ' *Hold !* ' whereat he paused, wondering.

Now, among the servants of Cleopatra was one Eudosius, a steward ; and this Eudosius, seeing that the fortunes of Cleopatra were at an end, had laid a plan to fly that very night to Cæsar, as many of his betters had done, taking with him all the treasure in the palace that he could steal. But this design being discovered to Cleopatra, she determined to be avenged upon Eudosius.

' Eudosius,' she cried, for the man stood near ; ' come hither, thou faithful servant ! Seest thou this man, most noble Antony ; through all our troubles he has clung to us and been of comfort to us. Now, therefore, he shall be rewarded according to his deserts and the measure of his faithfulness, and that from thine own hand. Give him thy golden cup of wine, and let him drink a pledge to our success ; the cup shall be his guerdon.'

And still wondering. Antony gave it to the man, who,

stricken in his guilty mind, took it, and stood trembling. But he drank not.

'Drink! thou slave; drink!' cried Cleopatra, half rising from her seat and flashing a fierce look on his white face. 'By Serapis! so surely as I yet shall sit in the Capitol at Rome, if thou dost thus flout the Lord Antony, I'll have thee scourged to the bones, and the red wine poured upon thy open wounds to heal them! *Ah!* at length thou drinkest! Why, what is it, good Eudosius? art sick? Surely, then, this wine must be as the water of jealousy of those Jews, that has power to slay the false and strengthen the honest only. Go, some of you, search this man's room; methinks he is a traitor!'

Meanwhile the man stood, his hands to his head. Presently he began to tremble, and then fell, shrieking, to the ground. Anon he was on his feet again, clutching at his bosom, as though to tear out the fire in his heart. He staggered, with livid, twisted face and foaming lips, to where Cleopatra lay watching him with a slow and cruel smile.

'Ah, traitor! thou hast it now!' she said. 'Prithee, is death sweet?'

'Thou wanton!' yelled the dying man, 'thou hast poisoned me! Thus mayst thou also perish!' and with one shriek he flung himself upon her. She saw his purpose, and swift and supple as a tiger sprang to one side, so that he did but grasp her royal cloak, tearing it from its emerald clasp. Down he fell upon the ground, rolling over and over in the purple chiton, till presently he lay still and dead, his tormented face and frozen eyes peering ghastly from its folds.

'Ah!' said the Queen, with a hard laugh, 'the slave died wondrous hard, and fain would have drawn me with him. See, he has borrowed my garment for a pall! Take him away and bury him in his livery.'

'What means Cleopatra?' said Antony, as the guards dragged the corpse away; 'the man drank of my cup. What is the purpose of this most sorry jest?'

'It serves a double end, noble Antony! This very night that man would have fled to Octavianus, bearing of our treasure with him. Well, I have lent him wings, for the dead fly fast! Also this: thou didst fear that I should poison thee, my Lord; nay, I know it. See now, Antony, how easy it were that I should slay thee if I had the will. That wreath of roses which thou didst steep within the cup is dewed with deadly bane. Had I, then, a mind to make an end of thee, I had not stayed thy hand. O Antony, henceforth trust me! Sooner would I slay myself than harm one hair of thy beloved head! See, here come my messengers! Speak, what did ye find?'

'Royal Egypt, we found this. All things in the chamber of Eudosius are made ready for flight, and in his baggage is much treasure.'

'Thou hearest?' she said, smiling darkly. 'Think ye, my loyal servants all, that Cleopatra is one with whom it is well to play the traitor? Be warned by this Roman's fate!'

Then a great silence of fear fell upon the company, and Antony sat also silent.

CHAPTER VI.

OF THE WORKINGS OF THE LEARNED OLYMPUS AT MEMPHIS;
OF THE POISONINGS OF CLEOPATRA; OF THE SPEECH OF
ANTONY TO HIS CAPTAINS; AND OF THE PASSING OF
ISIS FROM THE LAND OF KHEM.

I, Harmachis, must make speed with my task, setting down that which is permitted as shortly as may be, and leaving much untold. For of this I am warned, that Doom draws on and my days are wellnigh sped. After the drawing forth of Antony from the Timonium came that time of heavy quiet which heralds the rising of the desert wind. Antony and Cleopatra once again gave themselves up to luxury, and night by night feasted in splendour at the palace. They sent ambassadors to Cæsar; but Cæsar would have none of them; and, this hope being gone, they turned their minds to the defence of Alexandria. Men were gathered, ships were built, and a great force was made ready against the coming of Cæsar.

And now, aided by Charmion, I began my last work of hate and vengeance. I wormed myself deep into the secrets of the palace, counselling all things for evil. I bade Cleopatra keep

Antony gay, lest he should brood upon his sorrows : and thus she sapped his strength and energy with luxury and wine. I gave him of my draughts—draughts that sank his soul in dreams of happiness and power, leaving him to wake to a heavier misery. Soon, without my healing medicine he could not sleep, and thus, being ever at his side, I bound his weakened will to mine, till at last he would do little if I said not 'It is well.' Cleopatra, also grown very superstitious, leaned much upon me ; for I prophesied falsely to her in secret.

Moreover, I wove other webs. My fame was great through-out Egypt, for during the long years that I had dwelt in Tápé it had spread through all the land. Therefore many men of note came to me, both for their health's sake and because it was known that I had the ear of Antony and the Queen ; and, in these days of doubt and trouble, they were fain to learn the truth. All these men I worked upon with doubtful words, sapping their loyalty ; and I caused many to fall away, and yet none could bear an evil report of what I had said. Also, Cleopatra sent me to Memphis, there to move the Priests and Governors that they should gather men in Upper Egypt for the defence of Alexandria. And I went and spoke to the priests with such a double meaning and with so much wisdom that they knew me to be one of the initiated in the deeper mysteries. But how I, Olympus the physician, came thus to be initiated none might say. And afterwards they sought me secretly, and I gave them the holy sign of brotherhood ; and thereunder bade them not to ask who I might be, but send no aid to Cleopatra. Rather, I said, must they make peace with Cæsar, for by Cæsar's grace only could the worship of the Gods endure in Khem. So, having taken counsel of the Holy Apis, they promised in public to give help to Cleopatra, but in secret sent an embassy to Cæsar.

Thus, then, it came to pass that Egypt gave but little aid to its hated Macedonian Queen. Thence from Memphis I came once more to Alexandria, and, having made favourable report, continued my secret work. And, indeed, the Alexandrians could not easily be stirred, for, as they say in the market-place, 'The ass looks at its burden and is blind to its master.' Cleopatra had oppressed them so long that the Roman was like a welcome friend.

Thus the time passed on, and every night found Cleopatra with fewer friends than that which had gone before, for in evil days friends fly like swallows before the frost. Yet she would not give up Antony, whom she loved; though to my knowledge Cæsar, by his freedman, Thyreus, made promise to her of her dominions for herself and for her children if she would but slay Antony, or even betray him bound. But to this her woman's heart—for still she had a heart—would not consent, and, moreover, we counselled her against it, for of necessity we must hold him to her, lest, Antony escaping or being slain, Cleopatra might ride out the storm and yet be Queen of Egypt. And this grieved me, because Antony, though weak, was still a brave man, and a great; and, more-over, in my own heart I read the lesson of his woes. For were we not akin in wretchedness? Had not the same woman robbed us of Empire, Friends, and Honour? But pity has no place in politics, nor could it turn my feet from the path of vengeance it was ordained that I should tread. Cæsar drew nigh; Pelusium fell; the end was at hand. It was Charmion who brought the tidings to the Queen and Antony, as they slept in the heat of the day, and I came with her.

'Awake!' she cried. 'Awake! This is no time for sleep! Seleucus hath surrendered Pelusium to Cæsar, who marches straight on Alexandria!'

With a great oath, Antony sprang up and clutched Cleopatra by the arm.

'Thou hast betrayed me—by the Gods I swear it! Now thou shalt pay the price!' And snatching up his sword he drew it.

'Stay thy hand, Antony!' she cried. 'It is false—I know naught of this!' And she sprang upon him, and clung about his neck, weeping. 'I know naught, my Lord. Take thou the wife of Seleucus and his little children, whom I hold in guard, and avenge thyself. O Antony, Antony! why dost thou doubt me?'

Then Antony threw down his sword upon the marble, and, casting himself upon the couch, hid his face, and groaned in bitterness of spirit.

But Charmion smiled, for it was she who had sent secretly to Seleucus, her friend, counselling him to surrender forthwith, saying that no fight would be made at Alexandria. And that very night Cleopatra took all her great store of pearls and emeralds—those that remained of the treasure of Menkau-ra—all her wealth of gold, ebony, ivory, and cinnamon, treasure without price, and placed it in the mausoleum of granite which, after our Egyptian fashion, she had built upon the hill that is by the Temple of the Holy Isis. These riches she piled up upon a bed of flax, that, when she fired it, all might perish in the flame and escape the greed of money-loving Octavianus. And she slept henceforth in this tomb, away from Antony; but in the daytime she still saw him at the palace.

But a little while after, when Cæsar with all his great force had already crossed the Canopic mouth of the Nile and was hard on Alexandria, I came to the palace, whither Cleopatra had summoned me. There I found her in the Alabaster Hall, royally clad, a wild light in her eyes, and, with her, Iras

and Charmion, and before her guards; and stretched here
and there upon the marble, bodies of dead men, among whom
lay one yet dying.

'Greeting, thou Olympus!' she cried. 'Here is a sight
to glad a physician's heart—men dead and men sick unto
death!'

'What doest thou, O Queen?' I said affrighted.

'What do I? I wreak justice on these criminals and
traitors; and, Olympus, I learn the ways of death. I have
caused six different poisons to be given to these slaves, and with
an attentive eye have watched their working. That man,'
and she pointed to a Nubian, 'he went mad, and raved of his
native deserts and his mother. He thought himself a child
again, poor fool! and bade her hold him close to her breast
and save him from the darkness which drew near. And that
Greek, he shrieked and, shrieking, died. And this, he wept
and prayed for pity, and in the end, like a coward, breathed
his last. Now, note the Egyptian yonder, he who still lives
and groans; first he took the draught—the deadliest draught
of all, they swore—and yet the slave so dearly loves his life
he will not leave it! See, he yet strives to throw the poison
from him; twice have I given him the cup and yet he is
athirst. What a drunkard have we here! Man, man,
knowest thou not that in death only can peace be found?
Struggle no more, but enter into rest.' And even as she
spoke, the man, with a great cry, gave up the spirit.

'There!' she cried, 'at length the farce is played—away
with those slaves whom I have forced through the difficult
gates of Joy!' and she clapped her hands. But when they
had borne the bodies thence she drew me to her, and spoke
thus:

'Olympus, for all thy prophecies, the end is at hand.
Cæsar must conquer, and I and my Lord Antony be lost.

Now, therefore, the play being wellnigh done, I must make
ready to leave this stage of earth in such fashion as becomes
a Queen. For this cause, then, I do make trial of these poisons,
seeing that in my person I must soon endure those agonies of
death that to-day I give to others. These drugs please me
not ; some wrench out the soul with cruel pains, and some too
slowly work their end. But thou art skilled in the medicines
of death. Now, do thou prepare me such a draught as shall,
pangless, steal my life away.'

And as I listened the sense of triumph filled my bitter
heart, for I knew now that by my own hand should this
ruined woman die and the justice of the Gods be done.

' Spoken like a Queen, O Cleopatra ! ' I said. ' Death shall
cure thy ills, and I will brew such a wine as shall draw him
down a sudden friend and sink thee in a sea of slumber
whence, upon this earth, thou shalt never wake again. Oh !
fear not Death : Death is thy hope ; and, surely, thou shalt
pass sinless and pure of heart into the dreadful presence of
the Gods ! '

She trembled. ' And if the heart be not altogether pure,
tell me—thou dark man—what then ? Nay, I fear not the
Gods ! for if the Gods of Hell be men, there I shall Queen it
also. At the least, having once been royal, royal I shall
ever be.'

And, as she spoke, suddenly from the palace gates came a
great clamour, and the noise of joyful shouting.

' Why, what is this ? ' she said, springing from her couch.

' Antony ! Antony ! ' rose the cry ; ' Antony hath conquered ! '

She turned swiftly and ran, her long hair streaming on
the wind. I followed her, more slowly, down the great
hall, across the courtyards, to the palace gates. And here
she met Antony, riding through them, radiant with smiles

and clad in his Roman armour. When he saw her he leapt to the ground, and, all armed as he was, clasped her to his breast.

' What is it ? ' she cried ; ' is Cæsar fallen ? '

' Nay, not altogether fallen, Egypt : but we have beat his horsemen back to their trenches, and, like the beginning, so shall be the end, for, as they say here, " Where the head goes, the tail will follow." Moreover, Cæsar has my challenge, and if he will but meet me hand to hand, the world shall soon see which is the better man, Antony or Octavian.' And even as he spoke and the people cheered there came the cry of ' A messenger from Cæsar ! '

The herald entered, and, bowing low, gave a writing to Antony, bowed again, and went. Cleopatra snatched it from his hand, broke the silk and read aloud :

' Cæsar to Antony, greeting.

' This answer to thy challenge : Can Antony find no better way of death than beneath the sword of Cæsar ? Farewell ! '

And thereafter they cheered no more.

The darkness came, and before it was midnight, having feasted with those friends who to-night wept over his woes and to-morrow should betray him, Antony went forth to the gathering of the captains of the land-forces and of the fleet, attended by many, among whom was I.

When all were come together, he spoke to them, standing bareheaded in their midst, beneath the radiance of the moon. And thus he most nobly spoke :

' Friends and companions in arms ! who yet cling to me, and whom many a time I have led to victory, hearken to me now, who to-morrow may lie in the dumb dust, disempired and dishonoured. This is our design : no longer will we

hang on poised wings above the flood of war, but will
straightway plunge, perchance thence to snatch the victor's
diadem, or, failing, there to drown. Be now but true to me,
and to your honour's sake, and you may still sit, the most
proud of men, at my right hand in the Capitol of Rome.
Fail me now, and the cause of Antony is lost and lost are ye.
To-morrow's battle must be hazardous indeed, but we have
stood many a time and faced a fiercer peril, and ere the sun
had sunk, once more have driven armies like desert sands before our gale of valour and counted the spoil of hostile kings.
What have we to fear ? Though allies be fled, still is our
array as strong as Cæsar's ! And show we but as high a
heart, why, I swear to you, upon my princely word, to-morrow
night I shall deck yonder Canopic gate with the heads of
Octavian and his captains !

'Ay, cheer, and cheer again ! I love that martial music
which swells, not as from the indifferent lips of clarions, now
'neath the breath of Antony and now of Cæsar, but rather
out of the single hearts of men who love me. Yet—and now I
will speak low, as we do speak o'er the bier of some beloved
dead—yet, if Fortune should rise against me and if, borne
down by the weight of arms, Antony, the soldier, dies a
soldier's death, leaving you to mourn him who ever was
your friend, this is my will, that, after our rough fashion
of the camp, I here declare to you. You know where all my
treasure lies. Take it, most dear friends ; and, in the memory
of Antony, make just division. Then go to Cæsar and speak
thus : " Antony, the dead, to Cæsar, the living, sends greeting ;
and, in the name of ancient fellowship and of many a peril
dared, craves this boon : the safety of those who clung to him
and that which he hath given them."

'Nay, let not my tears—for I must weep—overflow your
eyes ! Why, it is not manly ; 'tis most womanish ! All men

A A

must die, and death were welcome were it not so lone. Should I fall, I leave my children to your tender care—if, perchance, it may avail to save them from the fate of helplessness. Soldiers, enough ! to-morrow at the dawn we spring on Cæsar's throat, both by land and sea. Swear that ye will cling to me, even to the last issue ! '

' We swear ! ' they cried. ' Noble Antony, we swear ! '

' It is well ! Once more my star glows bright ; to-morrow, set in the highest heaven, it yet may shine the lamp of Cæsar down ! Till then, farewell ! '

He turned to go. As he went they caught his hand and kissed it ; and so deeply were they moved that many wept like children ; nor could Antony master his grief, for, in the moonlight, I saw tears roll down his furrowed cheeks and fall upon that mighty breast.

And, seeing all this, I was much troubled. For I well knew that if these men held firm to Antony all might yet go well for Cleopatra ; and though I bore no ill-will against Antony, yet he must fall, and in that fall drag down the woman who, like some poisonous plant, had twined herself about his giant strength till it choked and mouldered in her embrace.

Therefore, when Antony went I went not, but stood back in the shadow watching the faces of the lords and captains as they spoke together.

' Then it is agreed ! ' said he who should lead the fleet. ' And this we swear to, one and all, that we will cling to noble Antony to the last extremity of fortune ! '

' Ay ! ay ! ' they answered.

' Ay ! ay ! ' I said, speaking from the shadow ; ' cling, and *die !* '

They turned fiercely and seized me.

' Who is he ? ' quoth one.

' ''Tis that dark-faced dog, Olympus!' cried another. 'Olympus, the magician!'

'Olympus, the traitor!' growled another; 'put an end to him and his magic!' and he drew his sword.

'Ay! slay him; he would betray the Lord Antony, whom he is paid to doctor.'

'Hold a while!' I said in a slow and solemn voice, 'and beware how ye try to murder the servant of the Gods. I am no traitor. For myself, I abide the event here in Alexandria, but to you I say, Flee, flee to Cæsar! I serve Antony and the Queen—I serve them truly; but above all I serve the Holy Gods; and what they make known to me, that, Lords, I do know. And I know this: that Antony is doomed, and Cleopatra is doomed, for Cæsar conquers. Therefore, because I honour you, noble gentlemen, and think with pity on your wives, left widowed, and your little fatherless children, that shall, if ye hold to Antony, be sold as slaves—therefore, I say, cling to Antony if ye will and die; or flee to Cæsar and be saved! And this I say because it is so ordained of the Gods.'

'The Gods!' they growled; 'what Gods? Slit the traitor's throat, and stop his ill-omened talk!'

'Let him show us a sign from his Gods or let him die: I do mistrust this man,' said another.

'Stand back, ye fools!' I cried. 'Stand back—free mine arms—and I will show you a sign;' and there was that in my face which frighted them, for they freed me and stood back. Then I lifted up my hands and putting out all my strength of soul searched the depths of space till my Spirit communed with the Spirit of my Mother Isis. Only the Word of Power I uttered not, as I had been bidden. And the holy mystery of the Goddess answered to my Spirit's cry, falling in awful silence upon the face of earth. Deeper and deeper grew the terrible silence; even the dogs ceased to howl, and

A A 2

in the city men stood still afeared. Then, from far away, there came the ghostly music of the sistra. Faint it was at first, but ever as it came it grew more loud, till the air shivered with the unearthly sound of terror. I said naught, but pointed with my hand toward the sky. And behold! bosomed upon the air, floated a vast veiled Shape that, heralded by the swelling music of the sistra, drew slowly near, till its shadow lay upon us. It came, it passed, it went toward the camp of Cæsar, till at length the music died away, and the awful Shape was swallowed in the night.

'It is Bacchus!' cried one. 'Bacchus, who leaves lost Antony!' and, as he spoke, there rose a groan of terror from all the camp.

But I knew that it was not Bacchus, the false God, but the Divine Isis who deserted Khem, and, passing over the edge of the world, sought her home in space, to be no more known of men. For though her worship is still upheld, though still she is here and in all Earths, Isis manifests herself no more in Egypt. I hid my face and prayed, but when I lifted it from my robe, lo! all had fled and I was alone.

CHAPTER VII.

OF THE SURRENDER OF THE TROOPS AND FLEET OF ANTONY
BEFORE THE CANOPIC GATE ; OF THE END OF ANTONY,
AND OF THE BREWING OF THE DRAUGHT OF DEATH.

the morrow, at dawn, Antony came forth and gave command that his fleet should advance against the fleet of Cæsar, and that his cavalry should open the land-battle with the cavalry of Cæsar. Accordingly, the fleet advanced in a triple line, and the fleet of Cæsar came out to meet it. But when they met, the galleys of Antony lifted their oars in greeting, and passed over to the galleys of Cæsar ; and they sailed away together. And the cavalry of Antony rode forth beyond the Hippodrome to charge the cavalry of Cæsar; but when they met, they lowered their swords and passed over to the camp of Cæsar, deserting Antony. Then Antony grew mad with rage and terrible to see. He shouted to his legions to stand firm and await attack ; and for a little while they stood. One man, how-ever—that same officer who would have slain me on the yesternight—strove to fly; but Antony seized him with his own hand, threw him to the earth, and, springing from his horse, drew his sword to slay him. He held his sword on high, while the man, covering his face, awaited death. But Antony dropped his sword and bade him rise.

'Go!' he said. 'Go to Cæsar, and prosper! I did love thee once. Why, then, among so many traitors, should I single thee out for death?'

The man rose and looked upon him sorrowfully. Then, shame overwhelming him, with a great cry he tore open his shirt of mail, plunged his sword into his own heart and fell down dead. Antony stood and gazed at him, but he said never a word. Meanwhile the ranks of Cæsar's legions drew near, and so soon as they crossed spears the legions of Antony turned and fled. Then the soldiers of Cæsar stood still mocking them; but scarce a man was slain, for they pursued not.

'Fly, Lord Antony! fly!' cried Eros, his servant, who alone with me stayed by him. 'Fly ere thou art dragged a prisoner to Cæsar!'

So he turned and fled, groaning heavily. I went with him, and as we rode through the Canopic gate, where many folk stood wondering, Antony spoke to me:

'Go, thou, Olympus; go to the Queen and say: "Antony sends greeting to Cleopatra, who hath betrayed him! To Cleopatra he sends greeting and farewell!"'

And so I went to the tomb, but Antony fled on to the palace. When I came to the tomb I knocked upon the door, and Charmion looked forth from the window.

'Open,' I cried, and she opened.

'What news, Harmachis?' she whispered.

'Charmion,' I said, 'the end is at hand. Antony is fled!

'It is well,' she answered; 'I am aweary.'

And there on her golden bed sat Cleopatra.

'Speak, man!' she cried.

'Antony has fled, his forces are fled, Cæsar draws near. To Cleopatra the great Antony sends greeting and farewell. Greeting to Cleopatra who hath betrayed him, and farewell.'

'It is a lie!' she screamed; 'I betrayed him not! Thou, Olympus, go swiftly to Antony and answer thus: " To Antony, Cleopatra, who hath not betrayed him, sends greeting and farewell. Cleopatra is no more."'

And so I went, following out my purpose. In the Alabaster Hall I found Antony pacing to and fro, tossing his hands toward the heaven, and with him Eros, for of all his servants Eros alone remained by this fallen man.

'Lord Antony,' I said, 'Egypt bids thee farewell. Egypt is dead by her own hand.'

'Dead! dead!' he whispered, 'and is Egypt dead? and is that form of glory now food for worms? Oh, what a woman was this! E'en now my heart goes out towards her. And shall she outdo me at the last, I who have been so great; shall I become so small that a woman can overtop my courage and pass where I fear to follow? Eros, thou hast loved me from a boy—mindest thou how I found thee starving in the desert, and made thee rich, giving thee place and wealth? Come, now, pay me back. Draw that sword thou wearest and make an end of the woes of Antony.'

'Oh, Sire,' cried the Greek, 'I cannot! How can I take away the life of godlike Antony?'

'Answer me not, Eros; but in the last extreme of fate this I charge thee. Do thou my bidding, or begone and leave me quite alone! No more will I see thy face, thou unfaithful servant!'

Then Eros drew his sword and Antony knelt down before him and bared his breast, turning his eyes to heaven. But Eros, crying 'I cannot! oh, I cannot!' plunged the sword to his own heart, and fell dead.

Antony rose and gazed upon him. 'Why, Eros, that was nobly done,' he said. 'Thou art greater than I, yet I have learned thy lesson!' and he knelt down and kissed him.

Then, rising of a sudden, he drew the sword from the heart of Eros, plunged it into his bowels, and fell, groaning, on the couch.

'O thou, Olympus,' he cried, 'this pain is more than I can bear! Make an end of me, Olympus!'

But pity stirred me, and I could not do this thing.

Therefore I drew the sword from his vitals, staunched the flow of blood, and, calling to those who came crowding in to see Antony die, I bade them summon Atoua from my house at the palace gates. Presently she came, bringing with her simples and life-giving draughts. These I gave to Antony, and bade Atoua go with such speed as her old limbs might to Cleopatra, in the tomb, and tell her of the state of Antony.

So she went, and after a while returned, saying that the Queen yet lived and summoned Antony to die in her arms. And with her came Diomedes. When Antony heard, his ebbing strength came back, for he was fain to look upon Cleopatra's face again. So I called to the slaves—who peeped and peered through curtains and from behind pillars to see this great man die—and together, with much toil, we bore him thence till we came to the foot of the Mausoleum.

But Cleopatra, being afraid of treachery, would no more throw wide the door; so she let down a rope from the window and we made it fast beneath the arms of Antony. Then did Cleopatra, who the while wept most bitterly, together with Charmion and Iras the Greek, pull on the rope with all their strength, while we lifted from below till the dying Antony swung in the air, groaning heavily, and the blood dropped from his gaping wound. Twice he nearly fell to earth: but Cleopatra, striving with the strength of love and of despair, held him till at length she drew him through the window-place, while all who saw the dreadful sight wept bitterly, and beat their breasts—all save myself and Charmion.

When he was in, once more the rope was let down, and, with some aid from Charmion, I climbed into the tomb, drawing up the rope after me. There I found Antony, laid upon the golden bed of Cleopatra; and she, her breast bare, her face stained with tears, and her hair streaming wildly about him, knelt at his side and kissed him, wiping the blood from his wounds with her robes and hair. And let all my shame be written: as I stood and watched her the old love awoke once more within me, and mad jealousy raged in my heart because—though I could destroy these twain—I could not destroy their love.

'O Antony! my Sweet, my Husband, and my God!' she moaned. 'Cruel Antony, hast thou the heart to die and leave me to my lonely shame? I will follow thee swiftly to the grave. Antony, awake! awake!'

He lifted up his head and called for wine, which I gave him, mixing therein a draught that might allay his pain, for it was great. And when he had drunk he bade Cleopatra lie down on the bed beside him, and put her arms about him; and this she did. Then was Antony once more a man; for, forgetting his own misery and pain, he counselled her as to her own safety: but to this talk she would not listen.

'The hour is short,' she said; 'let us speak of this great love of ours that hath been so long and may yet endure beyond the coasts of Death. Mindest thou that night when first thou didst put thine arms about me and call me "Love"? Oh! happy, happy night! Having known that night it is well to have lived—even to this bitter end!'

'Ay, Egypt, I mind it well and dwell upon its memory, though from that hour fortune has fled from me—lost in my depth of love for thee, thou Beautiful. I mind it!' he gasped; 'then didst thou drink the pearl in wanton play, and then did that astrologer of thine call out his hour—"The hour of the coming of the curse of Menkau-ra." Through all the after-days those words have haunted me, and now at the last they ring in my ears.'

'He is long dead, my love,' she whispered.

'If he be dead, then I am near him. What meant he?'

'He is dead, the accursed man!—no more of him! Oh! turn and kiss me, for thy face grows white. The end is near!'

He kissed her on the lips, and for a little while so they stayed, to the moment of death, babbling their passion in each other's ears, like lovers newly wed. Even to my jealous heart, it was a strange and awful thing to see.

Presently, I saw the Change of Death gather on his face. His head fell back.

'Farewell, Egypt; farewell!—I die!'

Cleopatra lifted herself upon her hands, gazed wildly on his ashen face, and then, with a great cry, she sank back swooning.

But Antony yet lived, though the power of speech had left him. Then I drew near and, kneeling, made pretence to minister to him. And as I ministered I whispered in his ear:

'Antony,' I whispered, 'Cleopatra was my love before she passed from me to thee. I am Harmachis, that astrologer who stood behind thy couch at Tarsus; and I have been the chief minister of thy ruin.

'*Die, Antony!—the curse of Menkau-ra hath fallen!*'

He raised himself, and stared upon my face. He could not

speak, but, gibbering, he pointed at me. Then with a groan his spirit fled.

Thus did I accomplish my revenge upon Roman Antony, the World-loser.

Thereafter, we recovered Cleopatra from her swoon, for not yet was I minded that she should die. And taking the body of Antony, Cæsar permitting, I and Atoua caused it to be most skilfully embalmed after our Egyptian fashion, covering the face with a mask of gold fashioned like to the features of Antony. Also I wrote upon his breast his name and titles, and painted his name and the name of his father within his inner coffin, and drew the form of the Holy Nout folding her wings about him.

Then with great pomp Cleopatra laid him in that sepulchre which had been made ready, and in a sarcophagus of alabaster. Now, this sarcophagus was fashioned so large that place was left in it for a second coffin, for Cleopatra would lie by Antony at the last.

These things then happened. And but a little while after I learned tidings from one Cornelius Dolabella, a noble Roman who waited upon Cæsar, and, moved by the beauty that swayed the souls of all who looked upon her, had pity for the woes of Cleopatra. He bade me warn her—for, as her physician, it was allowed me to pass in and out of the tomb where she dwelt—that in three days she would be sent away to Rome, together with her children, save Cæsarion, whom Octavian had already slain, that she might walk in the triumph of Cæsar. Accordingly I went in, and found her sitting, as now she always sat, plunged in a half stupor, and before her that blood-stained robe with which she had staunched the wounds of Antony. For on this she would continually feast her eyes.

'See how faint they grow, Olympus,' she said, lifting her
sad face and pointing to the rusty stains, 'and he so lately
dead! Why, Gratitude could not fade more fast. What is
now thy news? Evil tidings is writ large in those dark eyes
of thine, which ever bring back to me something that still
slips my mind.'

'The news is ill, O Queen,' I answered. 'I have this
from the lips of Dolabella, who has it straight from Cæsar's
secretary. On the third day from now Cæsar will send thee
and the Princes Ptolemy and Alexander and the Princess Cleopatra to Rome, there to feast the eyes of the Roman mob, and
be led in triumph to that Capitol where thou didst swear to
set thy throne.'

'Never, never!' she cried, springing to her feet. 'Never
will I walk in chains in Cæsar's triumph! What must I do?
Charmion, tell me what I can do!'

And Charmion, rising, stood before her, looking at her
through the long lashes of her downcast eyes.

'Lady, thou canst die,' she said quietly.

'Ay, of a truth I had forgotten; I can die. Olympus,
hast thou the drug?'

'Nay; but if the Queen wills it, by to-morrow morn it
shall be brewed—a drug so swift and strong that not the
Gods themselves can hold him who drinks it back from sleep.'

'Let it be made ready, thou Master of Death!'

I bowed, and withdrew myself; and all that night I and
old Atoua laboured at the distilling of the deadly draught. At
length it was done, and Atoua poured it into a crystal phial,
and held it to the light of the fire; for it was white as the
purest water.

'*La! la!*' she sang, in her shrill voice; 'a drink for
a Queen! When fifty drops of that water of my brewing have
passed those red lips of hers, thou wilt indeed be avenged of

Cleopatra, O Harmachis ! Ah, that I could be there to see thy Ruin ruined ! *La ! la !* it would be sweet to see ! '

'Vengeance is an arrow that ofttimes falls upon the archer's head,' I answered, bethinking me of Charmion's saying.

CHAPTER VIII.

OF THE LAST SUPPER OF CLEOPATRA; OF THE SONG OF
CHARMION; OF THE DRINKING OF THE DRAUGHT OF
DEATH; OF THE REVEALING OF HARMACHIS; OF THE
SUMMONING OF THE SPIRITS BY HARMACHIS; AND OF THE
DEATH OF CLEOPATRA.

 the morrow Cleopatra, having
sought leave of Cæsar, visited the
tomb of Antony, crying that the
Gods of Egypt had deserted her.
And when she had kissed the coffin
and covered it with lotus-flowers
she came back, bathed, anointed
herself, put on her most splendid
robes, and, together with Iras,
Charmion, and myself, she supped.
Now as she supped her spirit flared
up wildly, even as the sky lights
up at sunset; and once more she laughed and sparkled as in
bygone years, telling us tales of feasts which she and Antony
had eaten of. Never, indeed, did I see her look more beauteous than on that last fatal night of vengeance. And thus
her mind drew on to that supper at Tarsus when she drank
the pearl.

    'Strange,' she said; 'strange that at the last the mind of

Antony should have turned back to that night among all the nights and to the saying of Harmachis. Charmion, thou dost remember Harmachis the Egyptian?'

'Surely, O Queen,' she answered slowly.

'And who, then, was Harmachis?' I asked; for I would learn if she sorrowed o'er my memory.

'I will tell thee. It is a strange tale, and now that all is done it may well be told. This Harmachis was of the ancient race of the Pharaohs, and, having, indeed, been crowned in secret at Abydus, was sent hither to Alexandria to carry out a great plot that had been formed against the rule of us royal Lagidæ. He came and gained entry to the palace as my astrologer, for he was very learned in all magic—much as thou art, Olympus—and a man beautiful to see. Now this was his plot—that he should slay me and be named Pharaoh. In truth it was a strong one, for he had many friends in Egypt, and I had few. And on that very night when he should carry out his purpose, yea, at the very hour, came Charmion yonder, and told the plot to me; saying that she had chanced upon its clue. But, in after days—though I have said little thereon to thee, Charmion—I misdoubted me much of that tale of thine; for, by the Gods! to this hour I believe that thou didst love Harmachis, and because he scorned thee thou didst betray him; and for that cause also hast all thy days remained a maid, which is a thing unnatural. Come, Charmion, tell us; for naught it matters now at the end.'

Charmion shivered and made answer: 'It is true, O Queen; I also was of the plot, and because Harmachis scorned me I betrayed him; and because of my great love for him I have remained unwed.' And she glanced up at me and caught my eyes, then let the modest lashes veil her own.

'So! I thought it. Strange are the ways of women! But little cause, methinks, had that Harmachis to thank thee

for thy love. What sayest thou, Olympus ?   Ah, and so thou
also wast a traitor, Charmion ?   How dangerous are the paths
which Monarchs tread !   Well, I forgive thee, for thou hast
served me faithfully since that hour.

'But to my tale. Harmachis I dared not slay, lest his
great party should rise in fury and cast me from the throne.
And now mark the issue. Though he must murder me, in
secret this Harmachis loved me, and something thereof I
guessed. I had striven a little to draw him to me, for the
sake of his beauty and his wit ; and for the love of man Cleopatra never strove in vain. Therefore when, with the dagger
in his robe, he came to slay me, I matched my charms against
his will, and need I tell you, being man and women, how I
won ? Oh, never can I forget the look in the eyes of that
fallen prince, that forsworn priest, that discrowned Pharaoh,
when, lost in the poppied draught, I saw him sink into a
shameful sleep whence he might no more wake with honour !
And, thereafter—till, in the end, I wearied of him, and his
sad learned mind, for his guilty soul forbade him to be gay—
a little I came to care for him, though not to love. But he
—he who loved me—clung to me as a drunkard to the cup
which ruins him. Deeming that I should wed him, he
betrayed to me the secret of the hidden wealth of the pyramid
of *Her*—for at the time I much needed treasure—and together
we dared the terrors of the tomb and drew it forth, even from
dead Pharaoh's breast. See, this emerald was a part thereof ! '
—and she pointed to the great scarabæus that she had drawn
from the holy heart of Menkau-ra.

'And because of what was written in the tomb, and of that
Thing which we saw in the tomb—ah, pest upon it ! why does
its memory haunt me now ?—and also because of policy, for I
would fain have won the love of the Egyptians, I was minded
to marry this Harmachis and declare his place and lineage to

the world—ay, and by his aid hold Egypt from the Roman.
For Dellius had then come to call me to Antony, and after
much thought I determined to send him back with sharp
words. But on that very morning, as I tired me for the
Court, came Charmion yonder, and I told her this, for I
would see how the matter fell upon her mind. Now mark,
Olympus, the power of jealousy, that little wedge which yet
has strength to rend the tree of Empire, that secret sword
which can carve the fate of Kings! This she could in
nowise bear—deny it, Charmion, if thou canst, for now it
is clear to me!—that the man she loved should be given
to me as husband—me, whom *he* loved! And therefore,
with more skill and wit than I can tell, she reasoned with me,
showing that I should by no means do this thing, but journey
to Antony; and for that, Charmion, I thank thee, now that
all is come and gone. And by a very little, her words weighed
down my scale of judgment against Harmachis, and I went to
Antony. Thus it is through the jealous spleen of yonder
fair Charmion and the passion of a man on which I played
as on a lyre, that all these things have come to pass. For
this cause Octavian sits a King in Alexandria; for this
cause is Antony discrowned and dead; and for this cause I,
too, must die to-night! Ah! Charmion! Charmion! thou hast
much to answer, for thou hast changed the story of the world;
and yet, even now—I would not have it otherwise!'

She paused awhile, covering her eyes with her hand;
and, looking, I saw great tears upon the cheek of Charmion.

'And of this Harmachis,' I asked; 'where is he now, O
Queen?'

'Where is he? In Amenti, forsooth—making his peace
with Isis, perchance. At Tarsus I saw Antony, and loved him;
and from that moment I loathed the sight of the Egyptian,
and swore to make an end of him; for a lover done with

should be a lover dead. And, being jealous, he spoke some words of evil omen, even at that Feast of the Pearl; and on the same night I would have slain him, but before the deed was done, he was gone.'

'And whither was he gone?'

'Nay; that know not I. Brennus—he who led my guard, and last year sailed North to join his own people—Brennus swore he saw him float to the skies; but in this matter I misdoubted me of Brennus, for methinks he loved the man. Nay, he sank off Cyprus, and was drowned; perchance Charmion can tell us how?'

'I can tell thee nothing, O Queen; Harmachis is lost.'

'And well lost, Charmion, for he was an evil man to play with—ay, although I bettered him I say it! Well he served my purpose; but I loved him not, and even now I fear him; for it seemed to me that I heard his voice summoning me to fly, through the din of the fight at Actium. Thanks be to the Gods, as thou sayest, he is lost, and can no more be found.'

But I, listening, put forth my strength, and, by the arts I have, cast the shadow of my Spirit upon the Spirit of Cleopatra so that she felt the presence of the lost Harmachis.

'Nay, what is it?' she said. 'By Serapis! I grow afraid! It seems to me that I feel Harmachis here! His memory overwhelms me like a flood of waters, and he these ten years dead! Oh! at such a time it is unholy!'

'Nay, O Queen,' I answered, 'if he be dead then is he everywhere, and well at such a time—the time of thy own death—may his Spirit draw near to welcome thine at its going.'

'Speak not thus, Olympus. I would see Harmachis no more; the count between us is too heavy, and in another world than this more evenly, perchance should we be matched. Ah, the terror passes ! I was but unnerved. Well the fool's story hath served to wile away that heaviest of our hours, the hour which ends in death. Sing to me, Charmion, sing, for thy voice is very sweet, and I would soothe my soul to sleep. The memory of that Harmachis has wrung me strangely ! Sing, then, the last song that I shall hear from those tuneful lips of thine, the last of so many songs.'

'It is a sad hour for song, O Queen ! ' said Charmion ; but, nevertheless, she took her harp and sang. And thus she sang, very soft and low, the dirge of the sweet-tongued Syrian Meleager :

> *Tears for my lady dead,*
> *Heliodore !*
> *Salt tears and strange to shed,*
> *Over and o'er ;*
> *Go tears and low lament*
> *Fare from her tomb,*
> *Wend where my lady went,*
> *Down through the gloom—*
> *Sighs for my lady dead,*
> *Tears do I send,*
> *Long love remembered,*
> *Mistress and friend !*
> *Sad are the songs we sing,*
> *Tears that we shed,*
> *Empty the gifts we bring—*
> *Gifts to the dead !*
> *Ah, for my flower, my Love,*
> *Hades hath taken,*
> *Ah, for the dust above,*
> *Scattered and shaken !*
> *Mother of blade and grass,*
> *Earth, in thy breast*
> *Lull her that gentlest was*
> *Gently to rest !*

The music of her voice died away, and it was so sweet and sad that Iras began to weep and the bright tears stood in Cleopatra's stormy eyes. Only I wept not; my tears were dry.

' 'Tis a heavy song of thine, Charmion,' said the Queen. ' Well, as thou saidst, it is a sad hour for song, and thy dirge is fitted to the hour. Sing it over me once again when I lie dead, Charmion. And now farewell to music, and on to the end. Olympus, take yonder parchment and write what I shall say.'

I took the parchment and the reed, and wrote thus in the Roman tongue:

' Cleopatra to Octavianus, greeting.

' This is the state of life. At length there comes an hour when, rather than endure those burdens that overwhelm us, putting off the body we would take wing into forgetfulness. Cæsar, thou hast conquered: take thou the spoils of victory. But in thy triumph Cleopatra cannot walk. When all is lost, then we must go to seek the lost. Thus in the desert of Despair the brave do harvest Resolution. Cleopatra hath been great as Antony was great, nor shall her fame be minished in the manner of her end. Slaves live to endure their wrong; but Princes, treading with a firmer step, pass through the gates of Wrong into the royal Dwellings of the Dead. This only doth Egypt ask of Cæsar—that he suffer her to lie in the tomb of Antony. Farewell!'

This I wrote, and having sealed the writing, Cleopatra bade me go find a messenger, despatch it to Cæsar, and then return. So I went, and at the door of the tomb I called a soldier who was not on duty, and, giving him money, bade him take the letter to Cæsar. Then I went back, and there in the chamber the three women stood in silence, Cleopatra clinging to the arm of Iras, and Charmion a little apart watching the twain.

'If indeed thou art minded to make an end, O Queen,' I said, 'the time is short, for presently Cæsar will send his servants in answer to thy letter,' and I drew forth the phial of white and deadly bane and set it upon the board.

She took it in her hand and gazed thereon. 'How innocent it seems!' she said; 'and yet therein lies my death. 'Tis strange.'

'Ay, Queen, and the death of ten other folk. No need to take so long a draught.'

'I fear,' she gasped—'how know I that it will slay outright? I have seen so many die by poison and scarce one has died outright. And some—ah, I cannot think on them!'

'Fear not,' I said, 'I am a master of my craft. Or, if thou dost fear, cast this poison forth and live. In Rome thou mayst still find happiness: ay, in Rome, where thou shalt walk in Cæsar's triumph, while the laughter of the hard-eyed Latin women shall chime down the music of thy golden chains.'

'Nay, I will die, Olympus. Oh, if one would but show the path.'

Then Iras loosed her hand and stepped forward. 'Give me the draught, Physician,' she said. 'I go to make ready for my Queen.'

'It is well,' I answered; 'on thy own head be it!' and I poured from the phial into a little golden goblet.

She raised it, curtsied low to Cleopatra, then, coming forward, kissed her on the brow, and Charmion she also kissed. This done, tarrying not and making no prayer, for Iras was a Greek, she drank, and, putting her hand to her head, instantly fell down and died.

'Thou seest,' I said breaking in upon the silence, 'it is swift.'

'Ay, Olympus; thine is a master drug! Come now, I thirst; fill me the bowl, lest Iras weary in waiting at the gates!'

So I poured afresh into the goblet; but this time, making

pretence to rinse the cup, I mixed a little water with the bane, for I was not minded that she should die before she knew me.

Then did the royal Cleopatra, taking the goblet in her hand, turn her lovely eyes to heaven and cry aloud :

'O ye Gods of Egypt! who have deserted me, to you no longer will I pray, for your ears are shut unto my crying and your eyes blind to my griefs! Therefore, I make entreaty of that last friend whom the Gods, departing, leave to helpless man. Sweep hither, Death, whose winnowing wings enshadow all the world, and give me ear! Draw nigh, thou King of Kings! who, with an equal hand, bringest the fortunate head to one pillow with the slave, and by thy spiritual breath dost waft the bubble of our life far from this hell of earth! Hide me where winds blow not and waters cease to roll; where wars are done and Cæsar's legions cannot march! Take me to a new dominion, and crown me Queen of Peace! Thou art my Lord, O Death, and in thy kiss I have conceived. I am in labour of a Soul: see—it stands new-born upon the edge of Time! Now—now—go, Life! Come, Sleep! Come, Antony!'

And, with one glance to heaven, she drank, and cast the goblet to the ground.

Then at last came the moment of my pent-up vengeance, and of the vengeance of Egypt's outraged Gods, and of the falling of the curse of Menkau-ra.

'What's this?' she cried; 'I grow cold, but I die not! Thou dark physician, thou hast betrayed me!'

'Peace, Cleopatra! Presently shalt thou die and know the fury of the Gods! *The curse of Menkau-ra hath fallen!* It is finished! Look upon me, woman! Look upon this marred face, this twisted form, this living mass of sorrow! *Look! look! Who* am I?'

She stared upon me wildly.

'Oh! oh!' she shrieked, throwing up her arms; 'at last I know thee! By the Gods, thou art Harmachis!—Harmachis risen from the dead!'

'Ay, Harmachis risen from the dead to drag thee down to death and agony eternal! See, thou, Cleopatra: *I* have ruined thee as thou didst ruin me! I, working in the dark, and helped of the angry Gods, have been thy secret spring of woe! I filled thy heart with fear at Actium; I held the Egyptians from thy aid; I sapped the strength of Antony; I showed the portent of the Gods unto thy captains! By my hand at length thou diest, for I am the instrument of Vengeance! Ruin I pay thee back for ruin, Treachery for treachery, Death for death! Come hither, Charmion, partner of my plots, who betrayed me, but, repenting, art the sharer of my triumph, come watch this fallen wanton die.'

Cleopatra heard, and sank back upon the golden bed, groaning 'And thou, too, Charmion!'

A moment so she sat, then her Imperial spirit burnt up glorious before she died.

She staggered from the bed, and, with arms outstretched, she cursed me.

'Oh! for one hour of life!' she cried—'one short hour, that therein I might make thee die in such a fashion as thou canst not dream, thou and that false paramour of thine, who betrayed both me and thee! And thou didst love me! Ah, *there* I have thee still! See, thou subtle, plotting priest'—and with both hands she rent back the royal robes from her bosom—' see, on this fair breast once night by night thy head was pillowed, and thou didst sleep wrapped in these same arms. Now, put away their memory *if thou canst!* I read it in thine eyes—that mayst thou not! No torture which I bear can, in its sum, draw nigh to the rage of that deep soul

of thine, rent with longings never, never to be reached!
Harmachis, thou slave of slaves, from thy triumph-depths I
snatch a deeper triumph, and conquered yet I conquer! I
spit upon thee—I defy thee—and, dying, doom thee to the
torment of thy deathless love! O Antony! I come, my
Antony!—I come to thy own dear arms! Soon I shall find
thee, and, wrapped in a love undying and divine, together
we will float through all the depths of space, and, lips to lips
and eyes to eyes, drink of desires grown more sweet with every
draught! Or if I find thee not, then I shall sink in peace
down the poppied ways of Sleep: and for me the breast of
Night, whereon I shall be softly cradled, will yet seem thy
bosom, Antony! Oh, I die!—come, Antony—and give me
peace!'

Even in my fury I had quailed beneath her scorn, for home
flew the arrows of her winged words. Alas! and alas! it was
true—the shaft of my vengeance fell upon my own head;
never had I loved her as I loved her now. My soul was rent
with jealous torture, and thus I swore she should not die.

'Peace!' I cried; 'what peace is there for thee? Oh! ye
Holy Three, hear now my prayer. Osiris, loosen Thou the
bonds of Hell and send forth those whom I shall summon!
Come Ptolemy, poisoned of thy sister Cleopatra; come Arsinoë, murdered in the sanctuary by thy sister Cleopatra;
come Sepa, tortured to death of Cleopatra; come Divine
Menkau-ra, whose body Cleopatra tore and whose curse she
braved for greed; come one, come all who have died at the
hands of Cleopatra! Rush from the breast of Nout and greet
her who murdered you! By the link of mystic union, by the
symbol of the Life, Spirits, I summon you!'

Thus I spoke the spell; while Charmion, affrighted, clung
to my robe, and the dying Cleopatra, resting on her hands,
swung slowly to and fro, gazing with vacant eyes.

Then the answer came. The casement burst asunder, and on flittering wings that great bat entered which last I had seen hanging to the eunuch's chin in the womb of the pyramid of *Her*. Thrice it circled round, once it hovered o'er dead Iras, then flew to where the dying woman stood. To her it flew, on her breast it settled, clinging to that emerald which was dragged from the dead heart of Menkau-ra. Thrice the grey Horror screamed aloud, thrice it beat its bony wings, and lo! it was gone.

Then suddenly within that chamber sprang up the Shapes of Death. There was Arsinoë, the beautiful, even as she had shrunk beneath the butcher's knife. There was young Ptolemy, his features twisted by the poisoned cup. There was the majesty of Menkau-ra, crowned with the uræus crown; there was grave Sepa, his flesh all torn by the torturer's hooks; there were those poisoned slaves; and there were others without number, shadowy and dreadful to behold! who, thronging that narrow chamber, stood silently fixing their glassy eyes upon the face of her who slew them!

'Behold! Cleopatra!' I said. '*Behold thy peace, and die!*'

'Ay!' said Charmion. 'Behold and die! thou who didst rob me of my honour, and Egypt of her King!'

She looked, she saw the awful Shapes—her Spirit, hurrying from the flesh, mayhap could hear words to which my ears were deaf. Then her face sank in with terror, her great eyes grew pale, and, shrieking, Cleopatra fell and died: passing, with that dread company, to her appointed place.

Thus, then, I, Harmachis, fed my soul with vengeance, fulfilling the justice of the Gods, and yet knew myself empty of all joy therein. For though that thing we worship doth bring us ruin, and Love being more pitiless than Death, we in turn do pay all our sorrow back; yet we must worship on, yet stretch out our arms towards our lost Desire, and pour our heart's blood upon the shrine of our discrowned God.

For Love is of the Spirit and knows not Death.

CHAPTER IX.

OF THE FAREWELL OF CHARMION; OF THE DEATH OF
CHARMION; OF THE DEATH OF THE OLD WIFE, ATOUA;
OF THE COMING OF HARMACHIS TO ABOUTHIS; OF
HIS CONFESSION IN THE HALL OF SIX-AND-THIRTY
PILLARS; AND OF THE DECLARING OF THE DOOM OF
HARMACHIS.

HARMION unclasped my arm, to which she had clung in terror.

'Thy vengeance, thou dark Harmachis,' she said, in a hoarse voice, 'is a thing hideous to behold! O lost Egypt, with all thy sins thou wast indeed a Queen!

'Come, aid me, Prince; let us stretch this poor clay upon the bed and deck it royally, so that it may give its dumb audience to the messengers of Cæsar as becomes the last of Egypt's Queens.'

I spoke no word in answer, for my heart was very heavy, and now that all was done I was weary. Together, then, we lifted up the body and laid it on the golden bed. Charmion placed the uræus crown upon the ivory brow, and combed the night-dark hair that showed never a thread of silver, and, for the last time, shut those eyes wherein had shone all the changing glories of the sea. She folded the chill hands upon the breast whence Passion's breath had fled, and straightened the bent knees beneath the broidered robe, and by the head set flowers. And there at length Cleopatra lay, more splendid now in her cold majesty of death than in her richest hour of breathing beauty !

We drew back and looked on her, and on dead Iras at her feet.

'It is done !' quoth Charmion ; 'we are avenged, and now, Harmachis, dost follow by this same road ? ' And she nodded toward the phial on the board.

'Nay, Charmion. I fly—I fly to a heavier death ! Not thus easily may I end my space of earthly penance.'

'So be it, Harmachis ! And I, Harmachis—I fly also, but with swifter wings. My game is played. I, too, have made atonement. Oh ! what a bitter fate is mine, to have brought misery on all I love, and, in the end, to die unloved ! To thee I have atoned ; to my angered Gods I have atoned ; and now I go to find a way whereby I may atone to Cleopatra in that Hell where she is, and which I must share ! For she loved me well, Harmachis ; and, now that she is dead, methinks that, after thee, I loved her best of all. So of her cup and the cup of Iras I will surely drink ! ' And she took the phial, and with a steady hand poured that which was left of the poison into the goblet.

'Bethink thee, Charmion,' I said ; 'yet mayst thou live for many years, hiding these sorrows beneath the withered days.'

'Yet I may, but I will not ! To live the prey of so many memories, the fount of an undying shame that night by night, as I lie sleepless, shall well afresh from my sorrow-stricken heart !—to live torn by a love I cannot lose !—to stand alone like some storm-twisted tree, and, sighing day by day to the

winds of heaven, gaze upon the desert of my life, while I wait
the lingering lightning's stroke—nay, that will not I, Harmachis ! I had died long since, but I lived on to serve thee ;
now no more thou needest me, and I go. Oh, fare thee well !
—for ever fare thee well ! For not again shall I look upon thy
face, and where I go thou goest not ! For thou dost not love
me who still dost love that queenly woman thou hast hounded
to the death ! Her thou shalt never win, and thee I shall
never win, and this is the bitter end of Fate ! See, Harmachis : I ask one boon before I go and for all time become
naught to thee but a memory of shame. Tell me that thou
dost forgive me so far as thine it is to forgive, and in token
thereof kiss me—with no lover's kiss, but kiss me on the
brow, and bid me pass in peace.'

And she drew near to me with arms outstretched and
pitiful trembling lips and gazed upon my face.

' Charmion,' I answered, ' we are free to act for good or evil,
and yet methinks there is a Fate above our fate, that, blowing
from some strange shore, compels our little sails of purpose,
set them as we will, and drives us to destruction. I forgive thee, Charmion, as I trust in turn to be forgiven, and by
this kiss, the first and the last, I seal our peace.' And with
my lips I touched her brow.

She spoke no more ; only for a little while she stood
gazing on me with sad eyes. Then she lifted the goblet, and
said :

' Royal Harmachis, in this deadly cup I pledge thee !
Would that I had drunk of it ere ever I looked upon thy face !
Pharaoh, who, thy sins outworn, yet shalt rule in perfect peace
o'er worlds I may not tread, who yet shalt sway a kinglier
sceptre than that I robbed thee of, for ever, fare thee
well ! '

She drank, cast down the cup, and for a moment stood

with the wide eyes of one who looks for Death.   Then He
came, and Charmion the Egyptian fell prone upon the floor,
dead.   And for a moment more I stood alone with the dead.

I crept to the side of Cleopatra, and, now that none were
left to see, I sat down on the bed and laid her head upon
my knee, as once before it had been laid in that night of
sacrilege beneath the shadow of the everlasting pyramid.
Then I kissed her chill brow and went from the House of
Death—avenged, but sorely smitten with despair!

'Physician,' said the officer of the Guard as I went
through the gates, 'what passes yonder in the Monument?
Methought I heard the sounds of death.'

'Naught passes—all hath passed,' I made reply, and
went.

And as I went in the darkness I heard the sound of voices
and the running of the feet of Cæsar's messengers.

Flying swiftly to my house I found Atoua waiting at the
gates.   She drew me into a quiet chamber and closed the
doors.

'Is it done?' she asked, and turned her wrinkled face to
mine, while the lamplight streamed white upon her snowy
hair.   'Nay, why ask?   I—I know that it is done!'

'Ay, it is done, and well done, old wife!   All are dead!
Cleopatra, Iras, Charmion—all save myself!'

The aged woman drew up her bent form and cried: 'Now
let me go in peace, for I have seen my desire upon thy foes
and the foes of Khem.   *La! la!*—not in vain have I lived on
beyond the years of man!   I have seen my desire upon thy
enemies—I have gathered the dews of Death, and thy foe hath
drunk thereof!   Fallen is the brow of Pride! the Shame of
Khem is level with the dust!   Ah, would that I might have
seen that wanton die!'

'Cease, woman! cease! The Dead are gathered to the Dead! Osiris holds them fast, and everlasting silence seals their lips! Pursue not the fallen great with insults! Up!— let us fly to Abouthis, that all may be accomplished!'

'Fly thou, Harmachis!—Harmachis, fly—but I fly not! To this end only I have lingered on the earth. Now I untie the knot of life and let my spirit free! Fare thee well, Prince, the pilgrimage is done! Harmachis, from a babe have I loved thee, and love thee yet!—but no more in this world may I share thy griefs—I am spent. Osiris, take thou my Spirit!' and her trembling knees gave way and she sank to the ground.

I ran to her side and looked upon her. She was already dead, and I was alone upon the earth without a friend to comfort me!

Then I turned and went, no man hindering me, for all was confusion in the city, and departed from Alexandria in a vessel I had made ready. On the eighth day, I landed, and, in the carrying out of my purpose, travelled on foot across the fields to the Holy Shrines of Abouthis. And here, as I knew, the worship of the Gods had been lately set up again in the Temple of the Divine Sethi: for Charmion had caused Cleopatra to repent of her decree of vengeance and to restore the lands that she had seized, though the treasure she restored not. And the temple having been purified, now, at the season of the Feast of Isis, all the High Priests of the ancient Temples of Egypt were gathered together to celebrate the coming home of the Gods into their holy place.

I gained the city. It was on the seventh day of the Feast of Isis. Even as I came the long array wended through the well-remembered streets. I joined in the multitude that followed, and with my voice swelled the chorus of the solemn

C C

chant as we passed through the pylons into the imperishable
halls. How well known were the holy words:

> *'Softly we tread, our measured footsteps falling*
> *Within the Sanctuary Sevenfold;*
> *Soft on the Dead that liveth are we calling:*
> *" Return, Osiris, from thy Kingdom cold !*
> *Return to them that worship thee of old."* '

And, then, when the sacred music ceased, as aforetime on the
setting of the majesty of Ra, the High Priest raised the statue
of the living God and held it on high before the multitude.

With a joyful shout of

> *' Osiris ! our hope, Osiris ! Osiris !'*

the people tore the black wrappings from their dress, showing
the white robes beneath, and, as one man, bowed before the
God.

Then they went to feast each at his home; but I stayed in
the court of the temple.

Presently a priest of the temple drew near, and asked me
of my business. And I answered him that I came from
Alexandria, and would be led before the council of the High
Priests, for I knew that the Holy Priests were gathered together
debating the tidings from Alexandria.

Thereon the man left, and the High Priests, hearing that
I was from Alexandria, ordered that I should be led into their
presence in the second Hall of Columns—and so I was led in.
It was already dark, and between the great pillars lights were
set, as on that night when I was crowned Pharaoh of the
Upper and the Lower Land. There, too, was the long line
of Dignitaries seated in their carven chairs, and taking counsel
together. All was the same; the same cold images of Kings
and Gods gazed with the same empty eyes from the everlasting walls. Ay, more; among those gathered there were

five of the very men who, as leaders of the great plot, had sat here to see me crowned, being the only conspirators who had escaped the vengeance of Cleopatra and the clutching hand of Time.

I took my stand on the spot where once I had been crowned and made me ready for the last act of shame with such bitterness of heart as cannot be written.

'Why, it is the physician Olympus,' said one. 'He who lived a hermit in the Tombs of Tápé, and who but lately was of the household of Cleopatra. Is it, then, true that the Queen is dead by her own hand, Physician?'

'Yea, holy Sirs, I am that physician; also Cleopatra is dead by *my* hand.'

'By thy hand? Why, how comes this?—though well is she dead, forsooth, the wicked wanton!'

'Your pardon, Sirs, and I will tell you all, for I am come hither to that end. Perchance among you there may be some—methinks I see some—who, nigh eleven years ago, were gathered in this hall to secretly crown one Harmachis, Pharaoh of Khem?'

'It is true!' they said; 'but how knowest thou these things, thou Olympus?'

'Of the rest of those seven-and-thirty nobles,' I went on, making no answer, 'are two-and-thirty missing. Some are dead, as Amenemhat is dead; some are slain, as Sepa is slain; and some, perchance, yet labour as slaves within the mines, or live afar, fearing vengeance.'

'It is so,' they said: 'alas! it is so. Harmachis the accursed betrayed the plot, and sold himself to the wanton Cleopatra!'

'It is so,' I went on, lifting up my head. 'Harmachis betrayed the plot and sold himself to Cleopatra; and, holy Sirs—*I am that Harmachis!*'

The Priests and Dignitaries gazed astonished. Some rose and spoke; some said naught.

'I am that Harmachis! I am that traitor, trebly steeped in crime!—a traitor to my Gods, a traitor to my Country, a traitor to my Oath! I come hither to say that I have done this. I have executed the Divine vengeance on her who ruined me and gave Egypt to the Roman. And now that, after years of toil and patient waiting, this is accomplished by my wisdom and the help of the angry Gods, behold I come with all my shame upon my head to declare the thing I am, and take the traitor's guerdon!'

'Mindest thou of the doom of him who hath broke the oath that may not be broke?' asked he who first had spoken, in heavy tones.

'I know it well,' I answered; 'I court that awful doom.'

'Tell us more of this matter, thou who wast Harmachis.'

So, in cold clear words, I laid bare all my shame, keeping back nothing. And ever as I spoke I saw their faces grow more hard, and knew that for me there was no mercy; nor did I ask it, nor, had I asked, could it have been granted.

When, at last, I had done, they put me aside while they took counsel. Then they drew me forth again, and the eldest among them, a man very old and venerable, the Priest of the Temple of the Divine Hatshepu at Tápé, spoke, in icy accents:

'Thou Harmachis, we have considered this matter. Thou hast sinned the threefold deadly sin. On thy head lies the burden of the woe of Khem, this day enthralled of Rome. To Isis, the Mother Mystery, thou hast offered the deadly insult, and thou hast broken thy holy oath. For all of these sins there is, as well thou knowest, but one reward, and that reward is thine. Naught can it weigh in the balance of our justice that thou hast slain her who was thy cause of stumbling; naught that thou comest to name thyself the vilest thing who ever stood within these walls. On thee also must fall the curse of Menkau-ra, thou false priest! thou forsworn patriot! thou Pharaoh shameful and discrowned! Here, where we set the Double Crown upon thy head, we doom thee to the doom! Go to thy dungeon and await the falling of its stroke! Go, remembering what thou mightest have been and what thou art, and may those Gods who through thy evil doing shall perchance ere long cease to be worshipped within these holy temples, give to thee that mercy which we deny! Lead him forth!'

So they took me and led me forth. With bowed head I went, looking not up, and yet I felt their eyes burn upon my face.

Oh! surely of all my shames this is the heaviest!

CHAPTER X.

OF THE LAST WRITING OF HARMACHIS, THE ROYAL EGYPTIAN.

HEY led me to the prison chamber that is high in the pylon tower and here I wait my doom. I know not when the sword of Fate shall fall. Week grows to week, and month to month, and still it is delayed. Still it quivers unseen above my head. I know that it will fall, but when I know not. Perchance, I shall wake in some dead hour of midnight to hear the stealthy steps of the slayers and be hurried forth. Perchance, they are now at hand. Then will come the secret cell! the horror! the nameless coffin! and at last it will be done! Oh, let it come! let it come swiftly!

All is written; I have held back nothing—my sin is sinned —my vengeance is finished. Now all things end in darkness and in ashes, and I prepare to face the terrors that are to come in other worlds than this. I go, but not without hope I go: for, though I see Her not, though no more She answers to my prayers, still I am aware of the Holy Isis, who

is with me for evermore and whom I shall yet again behold
face to face. And then at last in that far day I shall find
forgiveness; then the burden of my guilt will roll from me
and innocency come back and wrap me round, bringing me
holy Peace.

Oh! dear land of Khem, as in a dream I see thee! I see
Nation after Nation set its standard on thy shores, and its
yoke upon thy neck! I see new Religions without end calling
out their truths upon the banks of Sihor, and summoning
thy people to their worship! I see thy temples—thy holy
temples—crumbling in the dust: a wonder to the sight of
men unborn, who shall peer into thy tombs and desecrate
the great ones of thy glory! I see thy mysteries a mockery
to the unlearned, and thy wisdom wasted like waters on the
desert sands! I see the Roman Eagles stoop and perish,
their beaks yet red with the blood of men, and the long
lights dancing down the barbarian spears that follow in their
wake! And then, at last, I see Thee once more great, once
more free, and having once more a knowledge of thy Gods—
ay, thy Gods with a changed countenance, and called by other
names, but still thy Gods!

The sun sinks over Abouthis. The red rays of Ra flame
on temple roofs, upon green fields, and the wide waters of
father Sihor. So as a child I watched him sink; just so his
last kiss touched the further pylon's frowning brow; just
that same shadow lay upon the tombs. All is unchanged!
I—I only am changed—so changed, and yet the same!

Oh, Cleopatra! Cleopatra, thou Destroyer! if I might but
tear thy vision from my heart! Of all my griefs, this is the
heaviest grief—still must I love thee! Still must I hug this

serpent to my heart! Still in my ears must ring that low laugh of triumph—the murmur of the falling fountain—the song of the nightinga——

[*Here the writing on the third roll of papyrus abruptly ends. It would almost seem that the writer was at this moment broken in upon by those who came to lead him to his doom.*]

THE END.